Conte

This book sets out to record the events from that day in 1986 up to the current time showing how today's network has evolved.

It is always a balance in writing such a history as to how much detail to include. Every registration change would lead to tedious reading so a balance has been struck to just record those significant events.

In addition to events in Loughborough certain other happenings in the wider geographic area are recorded as these often had a bearing on the Loughborough scene at a later date.

Chapter 1	4
Setting the scene	
Chapter 2	6
Preparing for deregulation day 26 October 1986	
Chapter 3	8
The main players	
Chapter 4	12
Deregulation day – 26 October 1986	
Chapter 5	14
Chronology	
Chapter 6	41
Compare and contrast	
Chapter 7	43
The current scene	
Chapter 8	50

John Bennett

Loughborough's Buses | *The deregulated years*

Chapter 1
Setting the scene

Loughborough is a relatively small, University, town with a population of circa 59,000 in North Leicestershire. It has always been a border town as far as bus services are concerned. It sat on the boundary of Trent Motor Traction and Midland Red (Midland Fox from 15 January 1984). Quite often in these circumstances independent operators flourish. This was the case here. Long established independents Barton Transport, South Notts and Howletts of Quorn served the town with frequent routes. Trent was mainly confined to the Town Services but had a small share in the two joint routes to Leicester with Midland Red. Newer independent County Travel had established itself before deregulation in 1986 and Kinchbus and Paul S Winson were soon to follow.

Prior to deregulation in October 1986 the bus network was in a fairly static position. This long established, cosy, operation was about to be shattered by deregulation, the entry in to the market by new comers and the takeover of the traditional independents by larger groups and the wide scale use of minibuses. Loughborough would never be the same again.

▶
The 'Loughborough Sock Man' – a statue which can be found in the Market Place representing the town's hosiery industry.

▲ *An aerial view of Loughborough Town Centre.*

Chapter 2
Preparing for deregulation day 26 October 1986

Operators had to declare their hand six months earlier as to which routes and their timetables that they wished to operate commercially, ie without any subsidy. The County Council, in this case Leicestershire, then had time to issue tenders and contracts for routes and timetables that they deemed socially necessary but were not commercially provided for.

The Special Edition of Notices & Proceedings (N&P) issued on 31 March 1986 detailed all the routes which were to be provided commercially (table 1, page 50). In Loughborough's case there wasn't really much change and initially it looked like the long established pattern of routes and operators would continue. Trent did not register the 101 to Nottingham leaving this area north of Loughborough for the County Council to decide what would need replacing. Nor did Trent register the evening and Sunday operation on the core town routes 1 & 2. Tenders were issued for these evening & Sunday town routes and for a Wolds Village route to replace the former Trent 101.

Both Midland Fox and Trent registered their own shares of Leicester routes 625/6/7 and X67/620 maintaining the existing relationship. But Midland Fox then brought in their 'commercial network' in Charnwood early on 2 August and took control of the whole of 625-7 ending the long standing joint working arrangement with Trent and renumbered the route to 125-7. Trent however carried on running its one-bus share of the previous joint timetable. Independents Barton Transport and South Notts simply registered everything so there was no change here. Midland Fox had recently, on 25 May, withdrawn from the Charnwood Forest villages and this link between Leicester and Loughborough was being provided jointly by County Travel (Leicester) and Gibson Brothers, a Leicester CityBus subsidiary, and was registered commercially by them. This new commercial registration linked the route across Leicester to form a Loughborough to Kibworth Beauchamp route.

At this time Leicester CityBus (LCB) were looking to expand out of their traditional City area and had already purchased traditional independent Gibson Brothers at Barlestone back in August 1979. Moving on they had formed a close relationship with County Travel which was soon to feature in a number of new jointly operated services.

The County Council tenders were awarded and GK Kinch of Barrow-on-Soar, a newcomer to local bus work, was the main beneficiary. GK Kinch had hitherto been a top class coach operator. These tenders awarded were for the evening and Sunday operation on Trent daytime core Town routes 1 & 2 (numbered 11 evenings and 12 Sundays) and an all day Mon-Sat Wolds Village service numbered 10 replacing the Leicestershire part of the former Trent 101. GK Kinch also put its toe in the water by commercially registering two peak only routes, the PS1 (Poundsaver 1) between Loughborough and Leicester via the A6, 126/7 route, and LW1 & 2 between Sileby and Loughborough over the X67/6 route. From these seedlings big changes were about to start happening.

Out of the Loughborough area GK Kinch also picked up a Sunday contract for service 14, hourly from Leicester to Coalville, Ashby and 2-hourly on to Swadlincote on what was a Midland Fox core Monday to Saturday route.

Loughborough's Buses | *The deregulated years*

Chapter 3
The main players

Trent – arrived in Loughborough on 5 February 1919 as a result of the takeover of the Loughborough Road Car Co Ltd. It inherited the Road Car depot on The Rushes. By 1926 Trent had been invited by the Town Clerk to start some new services to developing parts of the town but it wanted some form of protection against other operators, whereas local independent Allen's of Mountsorrel offered an enthusiastic plan which was accepted by the Town Council. Allen's started their new town routes on 13 June 1927. The scene was thus set on the Town Services for the next 26 years and it was not until 20 September 1953 that Trent would become the main Town operator when Allen's sold the routes. Trent thus consolidated its position in the town from this date. In 1937 the depot was extended and rebuilt.

The long standing Town network using route numbers in the 123 to 136 series was completely revised on 22 May 1977 as part of the 'Company Action Plan' which was being implemented across Trent and Midland General at the time. New simpler route numbers 1 to 7 were introduced, using seven buses on the Town network. In addition there was a one bus working, joint with Midland Red on service 620 and another also joint with Midland Red on services 625-7. Service 623 to Derby and 66 to Nottingham completed the picture. As an aside the long standing joint 625-7 Leicester to Loughborough route was changed two weeks earlier on 7 May and extended to Shepshed, every twenty minutes, absorbing the former Midland Red 675 Loughborough to Shepshed route. This newly extended twenty minute frequency also covered the Blackbrook Road and Schofield Road part of former Trent Town Services 123, 125 & 130, Trent giving way here to Midland Red.

From 1 October 1978 service 66 from Loughborough to Nottingham was replaced by a new two-hourly 101 still running to Nottingham via the A60 villages but then continuing as an 'express' to Derby replacing the former X42. This was operated by Derby and Nottingham depots with minimal Loughborough depot involvement.

On 1 October 1979 service 623, Leicester, Loughborough to Derby was cut back from five journeys a day to three: 0900,1300 & 1700 Leicester to Derby and 1100, 1505 Derby to Leicester plus 1840 Derby to Loughborough.

The next change to Loughborough operations occurred on 17 August 1980 when the Town Services were completely revised. Cross Town routes 1 & 2 became 1, 2, 3 & 4 by incorporating the Empress Road area, from previous route 3, into the core town routes. And 5, 6 & 7 were changed to all run and interwork with each other from the Station. These changes saved a further bus, now six down from seven. Service 623 was cut back even further, now comprising just one off peak shopping return trip to Derby – with the Leicester end of the route being withdrawn. This was reduced further still from 29 April 1984 to Tuesdays, Fridays and Saturdays only as a 'Shopaway' route 215. (Given the twenty minute frequency between Loughborough and Derby today this does seem quite incredible!).

By 26 October 1986 the allocation of Loughborough depot was eleven. This comprised Leopard/Plaxton fleet number 139, Leyland Nationals 421, 432, 442, 443, 444, 461, 462, 471 & 533 and Leyland Atlantean/ECW 583. The Town Services were recast for the commercial network and were numbered 1-5. The Leicester service 620 was renumbered to 6. And although Midland Fox had changed 625-7 from 2 August, Trent carried on running its former share of the old route but renumbered this into the new Midland Fox 125-7 series of route numbers. Certain peak hour journeys however were extended beyond Shepshed to Belton instead of going to Coalville from this date.

Midland Red – opened their first depot in Leicester in 1922 and their service 133 reached Loughborough via Rothley and Mountsorrel on 28 February 1923. This was later renumbered to 470 and by 1928 to 626, a service number which was to last for many years. On 25 November 1935 Midland Red acquired J Squires of Sileby but this was later transferred to Trent on 2

▲ *The Trent depot on The Rushes, Loughborough, seen in happier times on 16 June 1985.*

January 1938 and formed the basis of the later joint 620 between Loughborough and Leicester via Sileby. Initially though, only Midland Red operated through as their 655/659 with Trent running between Sileby (with extensions to Seagrave) and Loughborough only as their 121/122/127. On 30 July 1955 the Allen's of Mountsorrel share of the 'main road', Loughborough to Leicester was sold to Midland Red who also acquired Kemp & Shaw from Allen's on the same date. Although now owned by Midland Red, Kemp & Shaw continued to operate its share of the 'main road' until 1 January 1959. And on 1 February 1959 Midland Red took over the last remaining independent operator on the 'main road' Loughborough to Leicester, Boyer of Rothley. Just Midland Red and Trent now remained as joint operators, using long established route numbers 625-8.

On 29 March 1974 the Birmingham & Midland Motor Omnibus Co. (t/a Midland Red) was renamed Midland Red Omnibus Co Ltd.

On 1 May 1980 the Midland Red Leicester Sandacre garage closed.

On 6 September 1981 Midland Red was split and the new Midland Red (East) Ltd took control of Leicestershire part.

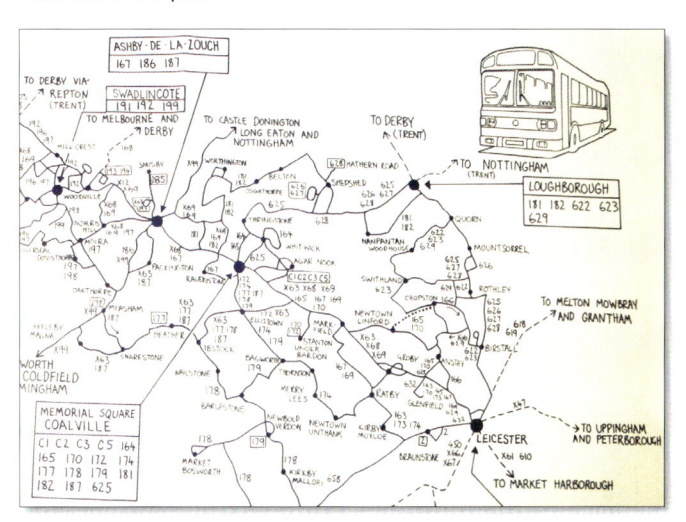

▲ *Part of the Midland Red (East) – North West Leicestershire route map dated August 1982.*

On 15 January 1984 Midland Red (East) started trading as Midland Fox with a new livery. From the same date the Midland Fox share of service 620, joint with Trent, from Loughborough to Leicester route via Sileby, was renumbered X67 and extended to Coventry. The route was also altered in that Thurmaston was no longer served and a different route through Barrow was taken. Thus the gradual breakdown of joint operation on this long standing route had begun. There were now two uncoordinated route numbers, X67 & 620 and a different route in part was being taken – the joint hourly frequency remained however.

Trent Leyland National URB 471S climbing up Snell's Nook Lane, Loughborough on route 6 to Nanpantan. This section of route was only used by service 6 between 17 August 1980 and October 1986.

On 2 June 1984 Midland Fox opened an outstation for six buses in Loughborough within the Trent depot in The Rushes. These six buses operated on the joint 625/6/7/8 route and also on Charnwood Forest routes 7b & 7c.

On 1 July 1984 Midland Fox starting picking up at all stops within Leicester – these had hitherto been protected by an Area Stop Agreement and thus unleashed competition against Leicester CityBus.

On 30 September 1985 – Midland Fox reopened their Leicester Sandacre garage for a new fleet of Fox Cub minibuses.

On 25 May 1986 Midland Fox withdrew their services 7b & 7c, renumbered from 622/623/629 on 1 July 1984, between Leicester and Loughborough via Charnwood Forest, leaving this route to CountyLink 121-4 which was now running two buses per hour on this corridor.

From 2 August 1986 Midland Fox introduced their 'commercial deregulation' timetable on the Leicester, Loughborough, Shepshed to Coalville corridor two months early. Existing services 625, 626 & 627 were renumbered 126 & 127 and a revised timetable of four buses per hour was introduced between Leicester, Loughborough and Shepshed. The Coalville service was detached and operated as a standalone 125 between Loughborough and Coalville only. This new timetable removed the joint operation with Trent. Existing 626/627, Coalville to Shepshed via Osgathorpe and Belton, remained running until 25 October when the responsibility for it passed to Leicestershire CC.

County Travel – on 1 April 1968 County Travel of Leicester acquired the long established operator A H Barkus & Son of Curzon Garage, Woodhouse Eaves. Barkus had operated a Woodhouse Eaves to Loughborough route via Quorn with up to ten departures a day. Barkus had previously acquired Prestwells also of Woodhouse Eaves in December 1954. With this acquisition County Travel now had a Woodhouse Eaves to Loughborough route. Earlier in the 1960s County Travel had also acquired John E Bass, an operator from Fleckney, and a route from Fleckney to Leicester. These two routes would be the basis of major developments to come.

▲ *Howletts of Quorn KUT 587P on layover at Loughborough Bus Station for the Sileby route. In the background is a Midland Red D9 5334, 6334 HA, on the 681 to Coalville which dates this photo to between 1975 & 1976.*

▲ *Early route branding for service 121 on County Travel PNR 319M.*

G Howlett & Son Ltd of Quorn – had traditionally operated on the Sileby to Loughborough corridor via Barrow. On 17 December 1979 the Tricentrol Group of Dunstable acquired the business and its subsidiary L Pole & Sons Ltd. Nineteen vehicles were acquired plus the premises at 94 Barrow Road, Quorn. (L Pole & Sons Ltd had been acquired by Howletts in July 1962). On 31 March 1985 the Quorn depot was closed and the operation moved to the Tourmaster depot in Loughborough on Bishop Meadow Road, home of Tricentrol Group's other subsidiary Housden Cauldwell. It subsequently traded as Tourmaster before selling out to County Travel in 1987. The frequency of the Sileby route had traditionally been hourly, fitting in between the joint Midland Red/Trent 620. But from 5 May 1986 the frequency was increased to every forty minutes using a second bus. This second bus was often an ex Nottingham City Transport Fleetline double-decker.

Leicester CityBus – on 23 August 1979 Leicester CityBus acquired Gibsons Brothers of Barlestone. This gave the City operator a country bus depot at Barlestone and whilst initially the traditional ex Gibsons routes were just operated from there it was to become a much bigger player in the Loughborough area in the years ahead. On 9 May 1982 the Leicester Citybus (Gibson) division joined with County Travel to offer a new joint service 121 from Loughborough via Woodhouse Eaves to Leicester and on to Fleckney via Wigston joining up the fragmented County Travel routes under a new joint brand name 'CountyLink'. This competed with, and offered a better service than, the traditional infrequent Midland Fox routes 622/623/629, later 7b & 7c from 1 July 1984, forcing them to withdraw when part of their 'commercial' network was introduced early in Charnwood on 25 May 1986.

Barton Transport plc – although based in Chilwell, Nottinghamshire, Barton had a traditional network of routes in North West Leicestershire. These were the 3, 10 & 310 from Nottingham to Loughborough, the 11 from Nottingham to Coalville via Shepshed and the 130, 140 from Melton Mowbray to Loughborough. From the mid 1930s a depot had been maintained at Kegworth but this closed in 1974 with operations then being from Long Eaton, Chilwell and Melton Mowbray depots. Long Eaton too closed in 1983.

10

South Notts – based in Gotham, Nottinghamshire had been around since 1926 but in 1929 extended their Nottingham to Gotham route to Loughborough whilst at the same time Barton took a 50% shareholding in the company. This key trunk route from Nottingham to Loughborough via Gotham and East Leake then continued relatively unchanged.

Paul S Winson – although primarily a Loughborough coach operator Paul S Winson has played its part in the Loughborough bus scene over the years. The business grew out of a takeover of Jack Moons Charnwood Coaches in 1983 and then acquired the former Willowbrook factory on Royal Way as its depot in April 1994. It now has around 30 vehicles specialising in private hire, coach tours, school contracts and a niche bus operation.

GK Kinch – started in business in July 1968 as a one man taxi firm. This soon expanded into mini coaches and the first full size coach was purchased in 1971. A niche for good quality coach hire was soon established and the business moved from its initial base at 235 Loughborough Road, Mountsorrel to Hayhill Industrial Estate at Barrow upon Soar. The business expanded into executive coach hire and coaches were regularly entered in the Brighton Coach Rally. Hire rates began to drop which no longer justified a profitable operation and fleet renewals so the business changed direction and looked at bus operation when the opportunity of deregulation came along.

United Counties – historically United Counties had always operated the express services to London from Nottingham, Loughborough and Leicester rather than the local companies Trent and Midland Red. In the National Express era service 455, Nottingham, Loughborough, Leicester, Northampton to London was still contracted to United Counties. Changes to this long standing service were made however by National Express from 18 September 1983 by speeding them up and offering more direct services to London using the M1 and hence the slow 'all stops' Nottingham to Northampton link was lost. From this date, as a replacement, United Counties and Midland Red East (MRE) joined forces and extended the fledgling MRE service X61, Market Harborough to Leicester to become a two-hourly Northampton to Nottingham route via Leicester and Loughborough.

▲ *Tourmaster, ex Nottingham City Transport Fleetline AAL 179A, seen in Loughborough, Bus Station on the Sileby route in 1986 shortly after the increase in frequency necessitating the use of a second bus.*

▲ *A South Notts Fleetline, this one being ex Southend Transport WJN 353J, stands in Loughborough Bus Station on the service to Nottingham.*

▲ *Typical of the Barton presence in Loughborough is this Leopard, OAL 631M, seen pulling out of Shakespeare Street, from the Bus Station in Loughborough on a short working of service 10 to Kegworth. This is post the Wellglade takeover of Barton in December 1986 because of the 1000 added to the fleet number 387 and the presence of a Wayfarer ticket machine.*

Loughborough's Buses | *The deregulated years*

11

Chapter 4
Deregulation day 26 October 1986

The new registered routes in Table 1 started operating plus those subsequently registered by contract award by competitive tender for socially necessary services for Leicestershire County Council.

GK Kinch started the following commercially operated routes:

- PS1 – Loughborough to Leicester via Mountsorrel Mon to Fri peak hours
- LW1 – Sileby to Loughborough Mon to Fri peak hours
- LW2 – Loughborough to Sileby Mon to Fri peak hours (the reverse of LW1)
- 10 – Loughborough to Nottingham via the Wolds Villages, Mon to Sat, 1 x bus
- 11 – Loughborough Town Service Mon to Sat evenings, 2 x buses
- 12 – Loughborough Town Service Sundays, 2 buses
- 14 – Leicester to Swadlincote via Coalville Sundays, 3 buses
- 15 – Barrow to Coalville Sundays. Placing journeys for service 14.

A GK Kinch newspaper advertisement for the new routes starting on D-Day, 26 October 1986.

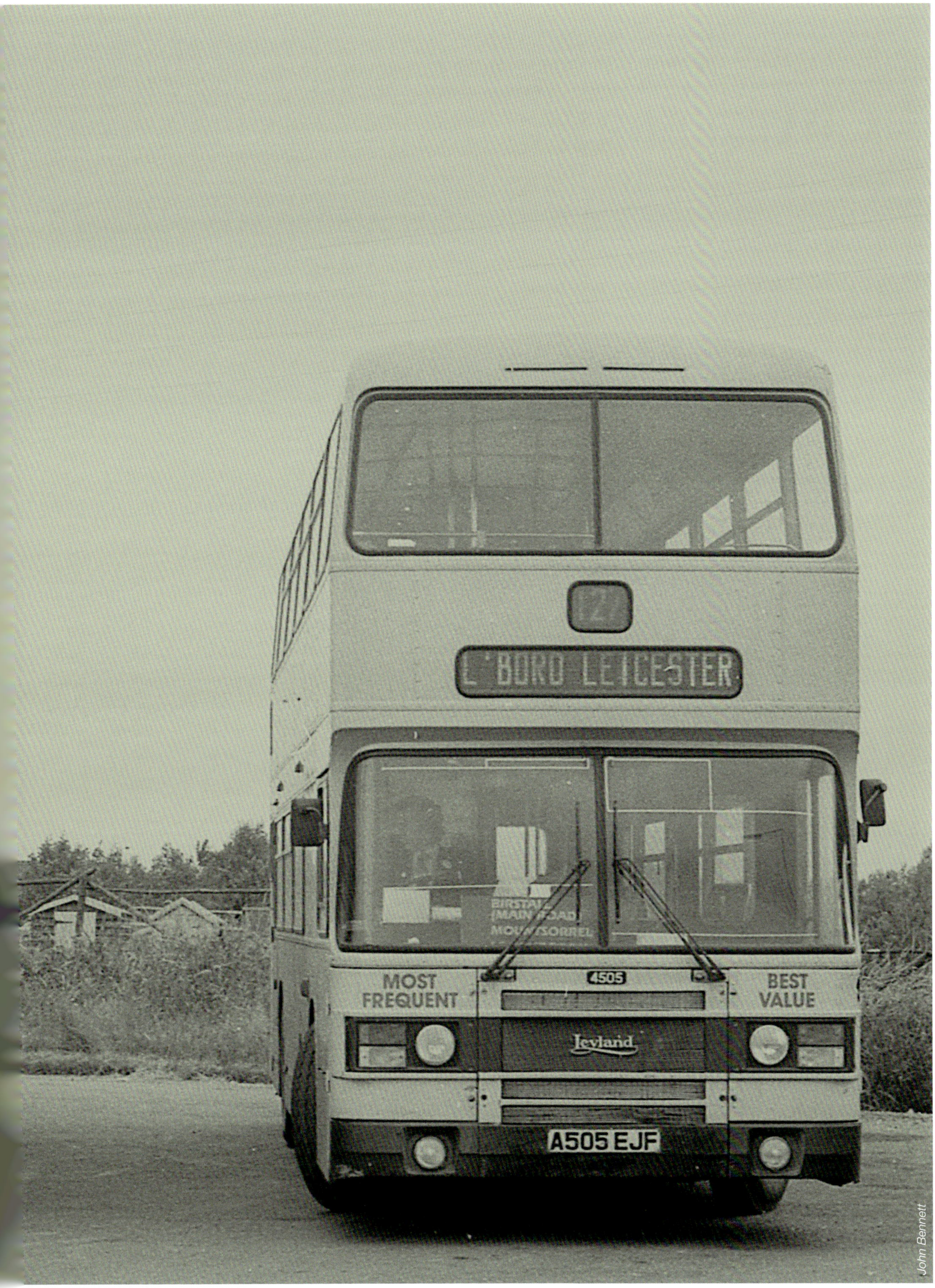

John Bennett

Chapter 5
Chronology

26 October 1986 – the detached part of Midland Fox 125, Loughborough to Coalville since 2 August, was renumbered 128 and extended to Nottingham hourly.

The Trent 125-7, Leicester, Loughborough, Shepshed to Coalville, timetable was modified to run to and from Belton in the peak hours instead of Coalville.

27 to 31 December 1986 – Trent decided not to operate Loughborough Town Services during the week between Christmas and New Year for its own commercial reasons but keen to make an impact GK Kinch stepped in and for four days, the 27, 29, 30 and 31st, operated five buses on Town routes 11, 12, 13, 14 & 15 using what buses and coaches he could muster together.

▲ *Seen picking up at a Trent bus stop in Shelthorpe between Christmas and New Year 1986 when no Trent buses were running is GK Kinch A102 HJF a DAF/Plaxton coach.*

▲ *Paul S Winson 'Centrelink 33' branded coach AJF 199A seen on Pytchley Drive, Loughborough in 1987. A Trent Leyland National can be seen disappearing in the distance.*

30 December 1986 – under the National Bus Company privatisation programme Trent was sold to its management team. The new holding company was Wellglade Limited.

27 January 1987 – the first sign of competition on Loughborough Town Services came from Paul S Winson in the shape of Centrelink 33 which provided an hourly cross town service, with driver breaks, between Shelthorpe and Thorpe Acre on Mondays to Saturdays. This only ran until 28 March however.

HIGHLIGHTS OF 1986
- *County Travel/Leicester Citybus saw off Midland Fox in Charnwood Forest*
- *Deregulation occurred on 26 October*
- *GK Kinch started some new competitive routes on a limited scale*
- *Trent was sold to its management team.*

14

Steve Smith

PUBLIC ANNOUNCEMENT

CENTRELINK TOWN SERVICE

It is with regret that we find it necessary to withdraw the Town Service as from Saturday 28th March 1987.

We would like to thank everyone who has supported the service during the last two months and sincerely hope the public may continue to enjoy the concessionary fares that were introduced by ourselves.

Centrelink Management

9 February 1987 – flushed with the early success of commercial routes PS1, LW1 & LW2 (above) GK Kinch re-registered them as PS1 to PS4 (PS = Poundsaver).

- The new PS1, Loughborough to Leicester via Quorn, Mountsorrel and Rothley, over the Midland Fox route 126/7 was increased to almost hourly Mondays to Saturdays.
- The new PS2 & PS3, a Barrow to Leicester service via Sileby and Birstall running six times a day Mondays to Saturdays.
- The new PS4, a Sileby to Loughborough service via Barrow running thirteen times a day Mondays to Fridays and even more frequently on Saturdays including up to 2330 in the evening.
- The Sunday tendered route 14, Leicester to Swadlincote and the 15 placing journeys were withdrawn from this date.
- And also from this date a new Mondays to Fridays inter peak timetable was introduced on Town Services 11 and 12 each running hourly requiring one off peak bus, marketed as 'Half Price Shoppers Specials'. This was introduced whilst the Paul S Winson Centrelink 33 was still running and was in no doubt in response.

The competition was hotting up.

23 February 1987 – the response from Midland Fox to the GK Kinch PS1 incursion on its main 126/7 route was Midland Wolf. Two Leyland Nationals were painted in a special livery and operated directly in front of the Kinch buses using route number X25.

▲ *This 'midland wolf' logo was used on two of Midland Fox's Leyland Nationals, JOX 491P & PUK 641R, from 23 February 1987 on a short lived X25 from Leicester to Loughborough to run directly in front of GK Kinch service 1. It was withdrawn on 29 August 1987.*

▲ *Midland Wolf Leyland National JOX 491P seen in Loughborough Bus Station in 1987 displaying its 'Cheap Fares' notice immediately in front of a GK Kinch double decker on route PS1.*

G. K. KINCH COACHES

IMPORTANT NEWS

FEBRUARY 23 1987

PLEASE READ CAREFULLY

DEAR TRAVELLER,

TODAY SEES THE START OF A COMPETITIVE BUS WAR BETWEEN MIDLAND FOX LTD. AND OURSELVES. AS YOU WILL RECALL OUR SERVICES STARTED EXACTLY 4 MONTHS AGO TODAY ON OCTOBER 27TH WHEN THE GOVERNMENT'S NEW TRANSPORT ACT BECAME EFFECTIVE. ON THAT DATE WE BECAME THE FIRST PEOPLE TO ACTUALLY COMMENCE A SERVICE ON THE LEICESTER TO LOUGHBOROUGH ROUTE AT SENSIBLE PRICES WHICH PEOPLE COULD AFFORD. OUR PASSENGERS HAVE INFORMED US THAT THEY WERE FED UP PAYING EXHORBITANT PRICES WITH A SERVICE THEY COULD NOT ALWAYS RELY ON WITH DRIVERS THAT WERE SOMETIMES RUDE AND OFFENSIVE FROM DIFFERENT BUS COMPANIES. AS YOU WELL KNOW WE HAVE NO PROOF OF THIS BUT THE SUCCESS WE HAVE HAD DURING THE 4 MONTHS HAS NOW LED TO A BITTER BUS WAR BETWEEN OUR TWO SELVES. MIDLAND FOX LTD. ARE PART OF THE NATIONAL BUS GROUP AND HAVE THE STRENGTH IN DEPTH TO FLOOD THIS MAIN ROUTE WITH THEIR VEHICLES. WITH EFFECT FROM TODAY THEY HAVE INTRODUCED A SERVICE NO. X25 RUNNING APPROXIMATELY 5 MINUTES IN FRONT OF OUR VEHICLES. THE VEHICLES ARE PAINTED NAVY FRONT AND BEIGE AND CARRY THE NAME, MIDLAND WOLF. WE UNDERSTAND THAT THEY HAVE A GREEN SIGN IN THE WINDOW STATING 'CHEAP FARES' AND THAT THEY CHARGE FARES EQUIVILENT TO OUR OWN.

BY PUTTING THIS NEW SERVICE OUT WE CAN CLAIM VICTORY IN PROCLAIMING THAT WE HAVE BROUGHT THE FARES DOWN FOR YOU THE CUSTOMER AND ONLY CAN WE KEEP THEM DOWN IF WE CAN RELY ON THE SUPPORT YOU HAVE GIVEN US IN THE PAST. IF YOU REMEMBER THAT OUR TIMINGS REMAIN UNALTERED AND THAT WE WILL ALWAYS TURN UP JUST BEHIND THE MIDLAND WOLF.

IF THE MIDLAND WOLF SUCCEED IN TAKING OUR PASSENGERS THEN OUR SERVICE WILL SOON CEASE. PLEASE REMEMBER THAT MIDLAND WOLF (MIDLAND FOX LTD.) CAN EASILY WITHDRAW THEIR CHEAP SERVICE ONCE WE HAVE CEASED AND ONE WOULD PRESUME THAT PRICES WILL BE BACK TO WHERE THEY ARE NOW ON THE RED AND YELLOW MIDLAND FOX VEHICLES.

PLEASE CONTINUE TO SUPPORT US

NOW IS THE CRUCIAL TIME WHEN WE NEED YOUR HELP TO FIGHT OFF THIS CHALLENGE

▲ *A GK Kinch notice to customers asking them to be loyal in the face of the Midland Wolf challenge.*

March 1987 – Housden Caldwell Coaches Ltd formally became Tourmaster (Loughborough) Ltd. The Sileby to Loughborough service still continued unchanged at its 40 minute frequency.

▲ A Tourmaster Leyland National JND998N, which started its life with Greater Manchester PTE, on the former Howletts route to Sileby seen loading in Loughborough Bus Station in 1987. It later passed with the business to County Travel and was reregistered 531 PP.

▲ Trent Leyland National PRR 442R seen in Shelthorpe, turning from Manor Road into Broadway, and heading for Thirlmere Drive on the new evening service 10 which was introduced on 29 June 1987.

30 March 1987 – 'All Change for Trent' was the slogan used to market a number of changes to the Loughborough network from this date. New services were introduced to support existing ones meaning that a confusing array of service numbers were now being used, eg 1, 2, 2A, 2X, 3, 3A, 4, 4A, 5, 5X, 6, 7, 23, 24, 34, 35 & 453. A two-page feature in the Loughborough Echo was used to provide full timetables of the above routes.

26 April 1987 – The traditional Midland Red X99 service, Birmingham to Nottingham via Tamworth, Ashby and Castle Donington was withdrawn. At the split of Midland Red in 1981 this was operated jointly by Midland Red North from Tamworth garage and Midland Red East from Coalville. Later Midland Red East withdrew leaving the whole route to Midland Red North. On 26 April 1987 there were significant cutbacks at Midland Red North and the X99 was a casualty. This prompted Midland Fox to return to the route

▲ Congestion at Loughborough Market Place! Here we see GK Kinch ex WMPTE Fleetline GOG 564N loading in the middle of the road, the trunk A6, on service 1 to Shepshed whilst in the layby is a Midland Fox DMS on service 127 also to Shepshed whilst squeezed in behind is a Trent Leyland National on a Town Service.

but this time instead of running direct to Nottingham from Ashby via the A453 and Castle Donington it was rerouted via Coalville, Shepshed and Loughborough and the A60 to Nottingham absorbing the 128. The timetable was three-hourly to Birmingham but still hourly over the Coalville to Nottingham section. From 2 October 1988 the Birmingham part of the route was withdrawn and the hourly 99 Coalville – Shepshed – Loughborough – Nottingham was born. This was set to last until 2009.

▲ Midland Fox Leopard/Plaxton BVP 785V seen loading on service 99 to Nottingham in Loughborough Bus Station. This would have arrived in from Coalville.

Loughborough's Buses | *The deregulated years*　　17

3 May 1987 – CountyLink, the joint County Travel/LCB 121-4 route was extended from Loughborough to Derby two-hourly as route number 144. Its terminal points were now Derby and Kibworth via Loughborough and Leicester. This was prompted by the withdrawal of Derbyshire CC tendered service X44 (operated jointly by Trent and East Midland) which had been providing a two-hourly link between Derby and Leicester via East Midlands Airport and the M1 since October 1986. The running time of the new 144 at 1 hour 50 minutes did not compare too favourably though with the previous X44 at 58 minutes.

▲ *County Travel Metropolitan KJD 261P, ex London Transport MD61, loading at Loughborough Bus Station on service 124 for Leicester in June 1987.*

4 May 1987 – Tourmaster deregistered its routes and County Travel re-registered. The business transferred to County Travel. Since March 1985 Tourmaster had been operating out of their depot in Loughborough on Bishop Meadow Road - this depot now passing to County Travel. This was a very strategic move which would play out later.

▲ *County Travel GOG 551N, an ex WMPTE Daimler Fleetline, on service 144 between Hathern and Long Whatton heading for Derby in July 1987.*

1 June 1987 – Trent was still running its former one bus working on services 125-7 albeit slightly amended for the Belton extension since October - and this was further extended to Osgathorpe. There was now a 0715 hrs Osgathorpe to Leicester journey and a 1630 hrs return. During the day buses still terminated in Shepshed whilst during the evening and on Sundays Coalville was still served.

6 June 1987 – Midland Fox withdrew their X67 (formerly 620) between Leicester and Loughborough via Sileby and Barrow and replaced it with a new services 136/137 running at half hourly from Leicester to Sileby continuing hourly to Heathcote Drive [136] or Barrow [137]. This followed evening withdrawals by Trent on service 6 on this hitherto, long standing, joint route from 1 June. The County Council replaced the withdrawn Trent evening journeys by a contract operated by County Travel. The 136/137 pattern of service only lasted until 12 March 1988 when they were withdrawn, apart from three am peak and two pm peak journeys which lasted a little longer until 18 July 1988. The remainder of the route was covered by new Fox Cub route 7 between Birstall, Windmill Avenue and Leicester only, running every 30 minutes.

13 July 1987 – Leicester Citybus had been suffering a loss of business to the frequent Fox Cub competition in the City and was looking at avenues to generate new business. Loughborough looked like an opportunity as Trent was still running Leyland Nationals at low frequencies on the Town Services. So a plan was devised to introduce a frequent minibus network and hopefully dislodge Trent back to its heartland in Derbyshire and Nottinghamshire. The brand name 'Trippit' was chosen and a brand new fleet of eleven green and yellow Optare City Pacer minibuses were acquired for the new operation which started, in a fanfare of publicity, on this date.

Comprehensive cover of the Town was provided and three initial routes were introduced, each running every 15 minutes:

- L1 – Braddon Road – Town Centre – Tiverton Road
- L2 – Maxwell Drive – Town Centre – Poplar Road
- L3 – Tynedale Road – Town Centre – Valley Road.

Through CountyLink, Leicester CityBus had built a good working relationship with County Travel who had just acquired a depot in Loughborough on Bishop Meadow Road, the ex Tourmaster depot. It was this base that was used to house the Trippits.

19 July 1987 – a minor but not insignificant event happened on this day when Midland Fox won the tender for Town Service 12 (new numbers 220 & 221) on Sundays causing GK Kinch to withdraw. This marked the first appearance of Midland Fox on Loughborough Town Services. This lasted until 20 December 1987 after which the Sunday timetable was replaced commercially by the Trippit L1 & L2 routes.

20 July 1987 – GK Kinch dramatically increased the frequency of its Town Services 11 & 12 to become half-hourly each, running all day and Saturdays too, now using two buses. Thus in the space of one week Trent had been dealt a double blow with both the Trippits and GK Kinch competing heavily on its core traditional Town Service routes.

▲ *GK Kinch, ex GMPTE, Leyland National HNB 22N on Town Service 11 in July 1987 complete with '20p Maximum Fare' slogan waits at a Trent bus stop at the 'buses only cut through' at the Thirlmere Drive/Nanpantan Road terminus.*

27 July 1987 – In response to the Trippit competition in Loughborough Trent launched two new routes in Leicester against CityBus, the X29 and X37 both running half hourly inter peak. The X29 operated from Beaumont Leys via Marwood Road to the City Centre and the X37 from Beaumont Leys via Mowmacre Hill to the City Centre.

▲ *Trent Leyland National FRA 533V seen in Loughborough at the 'Argos' bus stop on High Street on service 125 to Leicester in July 1987. By this time the 'Trent 125' was superfluous as Midland Fox had increased their own frequency on 126/7 to every 15 minutes without the assistance of their former joint operator.*

30 July 1987 – Not content with their recent Loughborough incursion LCB increased their presence eastwards with the registration of 147, Leicester to Peterborough (4 journeys) after Midland Fox and Cambus withdrew from this route.

17 August 1987 – the new Kinch PS1 to PS4 above must have performed well as they were considerably stepped up in frequency again.

- The PS1 was now extended to start in Shepshed (The Meadows) and offered a half hourly frequency through to Leicester requiring five buses. This was by now becoming a very serious competitor to the established Midland Fox 126/7 route.
- PS2 Barrow to Leicester continued much as before, six journeys each way, but the use of the PS3 service number was dropped.
- PS4 Sileby to Loughborough was increased to hourly or better, now with nineteen journeys a day, using two buses. This was now a serious competitor to Trent route 6 (ex 620) and also County Travel who were operating on the same corridor.

18 August 1987 – Midland Fox was privatised in a management buy-out with two Stevensons Directors taking a 40% share. Stevensons as a result took the Swadlincote garage, its operations and approximately forty buses.

19 August 1987 – County Travel wasted no time in responding to the GK Kinch PS4 competition on their corridor and improved their Loughborough to Sileby route, taken over from Tourmaster which was running every 40 minutes to be:

- 130 every hour Loughborough to Sileby, and
- 167 every hour Loughborough to Sileby and onwards to Leicester, combining with 130 to offer a half hourly Loughborough to Sileby frequency.

Three operators were now locked in competition on the Loughborough to Sileby corridor via Barrow : County Travel, GK Kinch and Trent. The Trent 6 was being squeezed out.

▲ *County Travel Leyland National NEN 957R, ex Lancashire United, at Loughborough Bus Station on the new 167 to Leicester in May 1988.*

Loughborough's Buses | *The deregulated years*

19

Service No:	167	130
Loughborough (Bus Stn.)	05	45
Quorn (Cross)	17	57
Barrow (High Street)	23	03
Barrow (Babington Road)	25	05
Barrow (River View)	27	07
Sileby (Duke of York)	35	15
Sileby (Heathcote Drive)	—	18
Cossington (Royal Oak)	—	—
E. Goscote (Chestnut Way)	45	—
Syston (Health Centre)	52	—
Thurmaston (Canal St.)	58	—
Leicester (Haymarket)	15	—

Service No:	167	130
Leicester (Haymarket)	20	—
Thurmaston (Canal St.)	37	—
Syston (Health Centre)	43	—
E. Goscote (Chestnut Way)	50	—
Cossington (Royal Oak)	—	—
Sileby (Heathcote Drive)	—	27
Sileby (Duke of York)	00	30
Barrow (River View)	06	36
Barrow (Mill Lane)	08	38
Barrow (Babington Road)	10	40
Barrow (High Street)	12	42
Quorn (Cross)	18	48
Loughborough (Bus Stn.)	30	00

▲ *The new, improved half hourly CountyLink 130/167 timetable from 19 August 1987.*

8 September 1987 – LCB introduced two more Trippit routes in Loughborough. New L5 & L6 which operated from Ravensthorpe Drive via the Town Centre to either Tuckers Road [L6] or the Station [L5].

▲ *Trippit D844 CRY seen on new route L6 to Tuckers Road in September 1987.*

September 1987 – GK Kinch successfully applied for an increase in their Operator's Licence, PE214, from 15 to 22 vehicles.

14 September 1987 – Trent introduced its fifth revision in less than a year on Loughborough Town Services abandoning some areas to the Trippits and GK Kinch whilst enhancing others with greater frequencies. Service 6 to Leicester was all but withdrawn except for some occasional 'placing' journeys leaving this corridor to County Travel and GK Kinch. On services 125-7, which was still a one bus working, running in competition with Midland Fox for most of the day, had its morning and evening peak journeys removed - thus the 0715 from Osgathorpe to Leicester terminated at Loughborough at 0804 hrs with the bus not resuming on 125-7 until 0940 hrs with a similar gap from 1534 hrs to 1710 hrs in the afternoon.

12 October 1987 – the Tourmaster Operator's Licence, PE189, was surrendered, (26 vehicles), as the business had been sold to County Travel.

22 November 1987 – County Link routes 121-4, 131 & 144 were extended beyond Kibworth hourly to Market Harborough. This now created an awfully long Derby to Market Harborough route with a running time of 2 hours 55 minutes.

5 December 1987 – Barton withdrew from service 11, Coalville to Nottingham, after suffering competition from Midland Fox X99.

7 December 1987 – GK Kinch stepped up frequencies again:

- PS1 Shepshed to Leicester remained at the same frequency but with some retiming.
- But PS2 & PS4 were now merged into a new '2' running through from Loughborough to Leicester via Barrow & Sileby at a half hourly frequency for most of the day and requiring six buses.

HIGHLIGHTS OF 1987

- *GK Kinch increased competition on Loughborough Town and Leicester routes*
- *Trippit network introduced on Loughborough Town*
- *County Link routes 121-4/144 extended to run from Derby to Market Harborough*
- *Tourmaster sold to County Travel.*

1 January 1988 – Midland Fox acquired the business of Wreake Valley Travel Ltd incorporating the routes between East Goscote and Leicester.

2 January 1988 – Trent sold their Loughborough operations and depot to Leicester CityBus. Wellglade, Trent's parent company took a 5% shareholding in LCB. All Trent services were deregistered and ran for the last time on Saturday 2 January 1988. LCB's Trippits had moved into the ex Trent depot at The Rushes by Sunday 3 January and had vacated the County Travel depot on Bishop Meadow Road. The former Trent Travel Office at The Rushes reopened as the Trippit Travel Shop on Tuesday 5 January.

3 January 1988 – the Trippit network was revised in response to the Trent takeover and new routes were added. The network was now:

- L1 – Braddon Road – Town Centre – Tiverton Road at every 15 minutes
- L2 – Maxwell Drive – Town Centre – Poplar Road at every 15 minutes
- L3 – Tynedale Road – Town Centre – Valley Road at every 15 minutes
- L5/6 – Ravensthorpe Drive – Town Centre - Station [L5] or Tuckers Road [L6] at every 15 minutes splitting to every 30 minutes
- plus Works Services L5A, L11, L21, L31 & L51 and school buses 5, 9 & 10.

A new Operator Licence was applied for in the name of Loughborough Coach & Bus (LC&B) for 31 vehicles (PE929).

4 January 1988 – CountyLink, operated by LC&B, launched ambitious new services 7 & 8 which linked Ashby with Loughborough and then onwards to Nottingham via Wymeswold and Keyworth (two trips a day to Nottingham with three trips per day to Ashby) employing two all day buses.

▲ The ex Trent depot on The Rushes now rebranded for the Trippits.

15 February 1988 – GK Kinch cancelled the 10 Wolds Village Service, no doubt because of the new CountyLink routes 7 and 8.

▲ Trippit D854 CRY seen at Wymeswold Church on service 8 from Seagrave to Loughborough in January 1988 just after this new route had started.

February 1988 – GK Kinch applied to increase its Operators Licence from 22 to 32 vehicles.

▲ Typical of GK Kinch competition in August 1987 was this ex Badgerline Bristol RE, EHU 388K, seen at the Argos stop on High Street operating Town Service 12.

22 February 1988 – County Travel revamped their Sileby group of routes again to become:

- 130 Loughborough – Quorn - Barrow – Sileby, hourly
- 137 Leicester - direct – Barrow – Sileby, hourly
- 167 Loughborough – Quorn – Barrow – Sileby – Syston – Leicester, hourly.

This created a three bus per hour headway between Loughborough and Sileby.

7 March 1988 – GK Kinch made further changes to 1, 2, 11 & 12 timetables. The 1 was doubled in frequency to every 15 minutes, now requiring in the order of eleven buses and matched that of Midland Fox 127. The changes to the 2, 11 & 12 were minor in comparison.

▲ Competing GK Kinch Fleetline GOG 564N and Midland Fox Olympian A505 EJF stand together at the Shepshed terminus of routes 1 & 127. Which one would set off for Leicester first?

Loughborough's Buses | The deregulated years

1 April 1988 – Midland Fox acquired Fairtax Coaches Ltd of Melton Mowbray, along with their operations. From 30 April new routes 1-5 were introduced competing with Barton on the Melton Mowbray Town Services using Transits M82-5 in a sand based livery branded as Melton Minis.

2 April 1988 – was the last day of operation for Barton's Stamford depot. This had been operational since February 1961 upon the takeover by Barton of Cream Bus Service. Leicester CityBus set up a two vehicle outstation in the town.

5 April 1988 – CountyLink revamped their services 7 and 8, Ashby to Nottingham via Loughborough, to become 137 Ashby to Nottingham via Loughborough and 138 Loughborough to Stamford via Melton Mowbray and Oakham. This competed directly with Barton 130, 140 between Loughborough and Melton Mowbray over what was very thin bus operating territory.

▲ *At the eastern extremity of the CountyLink empire is Trippit D728 PUJ seen leaving Stamford Bus Station in April 1988 on the long, 45 miles, 138 route back to Loughborough.*

1 May 1988 – more Trippit routes and changes as follows:

- the L3 was changed to run from Tynedale Road to Althorpe Drive.
- a new L4 replaced L5 & L6 from Ravensthorpe Drive and then replaced former L3 to Valley Road.
- the use of number L5 was discontinued.
- L6 became a Town Centre to Station and Tuckers Road route.
- and the Town Centre terminus moved from Granby Street to Devonshire Square where the County Council had invested £20,000 in a dedicated terminus.

3 May 1988 – Trent surprisingly returned to Loughborough with a one bus working on CountyLink service 124, jointly with County Travel and Leicester CityBus. Trent operated the 0705, 1115 & 1515 hrs ex Derby and the 0915, 1315 & 1715 hrs ex Leicester from their Derby depot. From this date the long Derby to Market Harborough route was split in half at Leicester with the Leicester to Derby section becoming 121-124 and the Leicester to Fleckney section becoming 141 and 142. Operation beyond Fleckney to Kibworth and Market Harborough was restricted now to just one school bus. The section of route between Loughborough and Derby was increased to hourly with 123 running via Sutton Bonington and Kegworth and 124 via Long Whatton and Diseworth.

29 June 1988 – Loughborough Coach & Bus still of Abbey Park Road, Leicester (PE929) took over the Loughborough area registrations from the main Leicester CityBus licence (PE225). These were for the Trippit 'L' routes plus the rural routes 137 and 138.

18 July 1988 – GK Kinch cut back route 1, Shepshed – Loughborough – Leicester to be Loughborough, Old Ashby Road to Leicester and reduced the frequency to every twenty minutes, now requiring seven buses instead of the previous eleven.

3 August 1988 – due to the competition from CountyLink 138, Barton withdrew their long standing 130 and 140 routes between Loughborough and Melton Mowbray. It is interesting to record here that Wymeswold, one of the biggest villages between Melton Mowbray and Loughborough, was never on the Barton route, which took the B676 direct to Burton on the Wolds. Wymeswold historically was served by Trent on its Nottingham to Loughborough route and since 26 October 1986 by the LCC contracted Wolds Villages service 10 operated by GK Kinch.

5 September 1988 – Trippits introduced a new route L5, University to the Station with a forty minute frequency and the L6, Town Centre to Tuckers Road was also extended to start back at the University providing a joint (with L5) twenty minute frequency to the Town Centre. Extra journeys were also added to the 138 between Loughborough and Melton Mowbray.

26 October 1988 – Midland Fox acquired the businesses of Astill & Jordan of Ratby and County Travel of Leicester. With the Astill & Jordan business came routes 94, 94A, 633, 634 & 635 and with the County Travel business came routes:

- 121-124 Leicester – Loughborough – Derby (joint with LCB and Trent)
- 130 Loughborough – Sileby, hourly
- 132 Leicester – Market Harborough, Mon-Sat evenings tendered
- 137 Loughborough – Sileby, hourly
- 141/142 Leicester – Fleckney, every 30 minutes (joint with Leicester CityBus [LCB])
- 167 Loughborough – Sileby – Leicester, hourly.

It should be noted here that LCB gained a new partner on joint services 121-124 and 141/142, no less than arch rival Midland Fox!

Services 130, 137 & 167 continued to operate from the former County Travel depots at St Ives Road, Leicester and Bishop Meadow Road, Loughborough but services 132, 141 & 142 were transferred to the Midland Fox garage at Wigston and services 121-124 to the Midland Fox garage at Southgates. Midland Fox gained the County Travel depot at St Ives Road as part of the deal but the remaining part of the County Travel business not sold, the coaching arm, moved to the ex Astill & Jordan depot at Ratby.

31 October 1988 – Midland Fox changed the Sileby routes inherited from County Travel. Services 130 & 137 were withdrawn and 167, Loughborough – Sileby – Leicester was increased to every half-hour. This change had been planned by County Travel and indeed a County Travel leaflet had been issued in readiness. Midland Fox was now locked in competition with GK Kinch route 2 on this corridor.

7 November 1988 – GK Kinch retracted slightly on route 1 by pulling back the Loughborough terminus to Schofield Road from Old Ashby Road and reduced the Saturday frequency from every twenty to every thirty minutes. Service 11 was increased to every fifteen minutes by withdrawing service 12.

27 November 1988 – the Trippit network was revised again. The routes were now:
- L1 – Braddon Road – Town Centre – Tiverton Road every 15 minutes.
- L2 – Maxwell Drive – Town Centre – Poplar Road every 15 minutes.
- L3 – Tynedale Road – Town Centre – Valley Road every 15 minutes. (ie, back to its original route)
- L5 – University – Town Centre - Station every 20 minutes.
- L6 – Tuckers Road – Town Centre every 30 minutes.
- L7 – Althorpe Drive – Town Centre every 30 minutes
- L8 – Ravensthorpe Drive - Town Centre every 30 minutes
- L9 – Osgathorpe – Belton – Shepshed – Nanpantan – Town Centre, occasional journeys
- plus Works Services L11, L21, L22, L31 and L51.

28 November 1988 – the Loughborough Coach & Bus rural network stretching from Ashby and Nottingham to Stamford came to an abrupt end. Stamford outstation closed and all that remained from this date was the 138, now truncated to run between Loughborough and Melton Mowbray only with six through journeys each way.

16 January 1989 – GK Kinch reversed the service 11 & 12 changes made on 7 November with both routes becoming every 30 minutes once again, using four buses.

HIGHLIGHTS OF 1986
- *Trent sell their Loughborough operation to Leicester Citybus*
- *CountyLink extend to Ashby, Nottingham and Stamford*
- *County Travel sell out to Midland Fox.*

28 January 1989 – GK Kinch introduced a new Saturday service 5 from the Town Centre to Alan Moss Road at every 30 minutes and from 11 February extended this to run Mondays to Saturdays.

19 February 1989 – substantial changes were made to CountyLink 121-124 with much thinning out made on the Loughborough to Leicester section. It remained hourly Derby to Leicester but with only occasional extra shorts between Loughborough and Leicester. The Trent participation remained the same but Midland Fox (which was ex County Travel share) ceased. LCB and LC&B participation remained.

March 1989 – By now LCB were experiencing financial difficulties and the loss making Loughborough Coach & Bus subsidiary, apparently £150,000 in the last year, was advertised for a quick sale. The deadline date for bids was 15 March for the seventeen Trippits and two double deck vehicle business. Among the operators approached were Barton, South Notts, GK Kinch and Midland Fox.

▲ *Loughborough Echo – 10 March 1989*

▲ *Trippit E858 ENR seen in May 1989 passing Pilkington Library within the Loughborough University campus on route L5.*

Loughborough's Buses | *The deregulated years*

13 March 1989 – GK Kinch started new route 4 which ran direct between Shepshed and Loughborough at every half hour, requiring two buses. By this time the fleet numbered thirty buses and three coaches. Of the buses, twenty were second-hand double decks being a mixture of Atlanteans, Fleetlines and Bristol VRs. The ten single decks comprised seven Leyland Nationals, one Bristol RE and two Leopards modified for the Access contract.

▲ GK Kinch ex Eastern National Leyland National HWC 87N seen in May 1989 at Shepshed Bull Ring on new service 4 which ran 'direct' to Loughborough with 'Lower Fares' as proclaimed by the windscreen boards. A Midland Fox DMS on service 127 sits patiently behind.

1 April 1989 – Midland Fox, masquerading as Green Bus, and trading as Fairtax of Melton Mowbray started new route G2, Loughborough to Leicester via Sileby half hourly, competing directly, five minutes in front of GK Kinch 2. Ten Leyland Olympians in a green livery had been acquired for the purpose from Crosville Wales (MTU 116-9/21Y and A131-5 SMA).

6 May 1989 – Midland Fox started new competitive Loughborough Town Services 11 and 12, both half hourly, running three minutes ahead of GK Kinch 11 and 12. These too were marketed as Green Bus, again using the ex Crosville Wales green Olympians which were not in Midland Fox livery.

◀ The Midland Fox 'Green Bus' leaflet for services 11 and 12 starting on 6 May 1989 which were timed three minutes ahead of GK Kinch 11 and 12.

13 May 1989 – GK Kinch reported Midland Fox to the Office of Fair Trading over its antics on service 2 from 1 April and also on services 11 and 12 from 6 May. A leaflet fully explaining this was widely circulated to Kinch customers urging them to 'Be Proud to stand back and wait for Kinch'. An emergency timetable came in on this day too for service 2 moving certain journeys by 15 minutes to get them away from the Midland Fox G2 buses.

▲ A Midland Fox ex Crosville Wales Olympian A134 SMA 'Green Bus' and a GK Kinch ex United Counties Bristol VR CBD 778K compete for business on service 2 from Loughborough Bus Station in May 1989.

BUS RIVALS IN FRESH FLARE-UP
Unmarked buses slammed by Kinch

A LOCAL BUS boss this week has slammed one of Leicestershire's biggest bus companies, accusing it of restrictive practices and of trying to put him out of business.

Old rivals G. K. Kinch and Midland Fox have once again come head-to-head in the latest episode in what has become a long and bitter bus war.

The latest conflict is over the Loughborough-to-Leicester route, which serves Barrow-upon-Soar, Sileby, Cossington and Birstall. Fairtax, a subsidiary of Midland Fox, has begun to run the route formerly only served by Kinch's.

Fairtax is using unmarked green and white double deckers and, according to Mr. Gilbert Kinch, is trying to "pass off as Kinch's," Mr. Kinch said.

"They're using unmarked buses, picking up customers from our bus stand at Loughborough station and have even put our route number, no. 2, on their buses after the Traffic Commissioner gave them their own, no. 106."

He also accused them of running their buses "below cost", which means that the service actually loses money in order to attract customers.

A spokesman for Midland Fox dismissed the allegations as "nonsense" and "totally unfounded". He described the route as commercially viable for Fairtax and said that "the suggestion that the company is trying to price Kinch's out of business by half is nonsense".

The low prices reflected the company's aim to give the customer the best possible service for providing high quality transport and competitive fares."

In answer to the allegation of "passing off" as Kinch's, the spokesman said that the green and white livery of the Fairtax buses is quite different to the blue and yellow of Kinch's.

He also said that bus companies are not legally bound to display the route number given by the Traffic Commissioner and can display any numbers they wish.

"The council-owned bus stands are allocated according to routes, not companies," he added.

■ Leicester CityBus has decided who the future owner of Loughborough's Trippits is to be. But it is keeping the identity of the buyer secret, while the decision waits for the approval of the Secretary of State.

● A Kinch's no. 2 rubs shoulders with competitor Fairtax, displaying the same number.

▲ From the Loughborough Echo on 7 April 1989

25 May 1989 – Loughborough Coach & Bus, PE929, was acquired by Midland Fox. The 15 x Optare City Pacers, D844-854 CRY and E855-858 ENR were acquired and become M844-858. The deal also included The Rushes depot.

30 June 1989 – Loughborough Coach & Bus, now owned by Midland Fox, withdrew all Trippit routes and a new network was introduced on 1 July as follows:

- G2 – Loughborough to Leicester via Sileby every 30 minutes.
- L3 – Tynedale Road to Town Centre every 15 minutes.
- G4 – Shepshed to Loughborough every 30 minutes
- L5 – Town Centre to University (operationally linked to L3) at every 30 minutes (from new term 2 October).
- L9 – Nanpantan to Tuckers Road via Town Centre every hour.
- L2 – Shelthorpe to Thorpe Acre via Town Centre every 10/20 minutes.
- 121/2/3 – the three operators on this route were now Midland Fox (Mercedes minibuses), LC&B (Citypacers) and Trent (Leopards).
- 138 – transferred to Fairtax operation.
- in addition the use of Devonshire Square was abandoned much to the anger of the local Council. The revised routes ran from the already congested Market Place stop and caused 'Bus Chaos' as reported by the local press.

2 July 1989 – Wellglade Ltd, the parent of Trent, acquired the vehicles and operations of Barton. Barton now traded as Barton Buses Ltd as a sister company to Trent Buses under the Wellglade umbrella.

17 July 1989 – GK Kinch cancelled Town Service 11 in the face of intense competition from Midland Fox 11 and 12 masquerading as Green Bus and from the following day cancelled Town Service 5 too.

24 July 1989 – LC&B, now owned by Midland Fox, moved out of The Rushes (ex Trent) depot back to the former Bishop Meadow Road depot.

August 1989 – the LC&B City Pacers (ex Trippits) were withdrawn and sold to Derby City Transport and replaced in Loughborough by Ford Transit Fox Cubs and Leyland Nationals.

4 September 1989 – Midland Fox became part of the Drawlane Transport Group plc.

7 October 1989 – after a period of intense competition Midland Fox purchased the GK Kinch bus operations. GK Kinch finished after service on this day. All buses, except those for the Access contracts and the coaches, were sold to Midland Fox. Forty staff were transferred to Midland Fox but fifteen remained with Kinch. Initially Midland Fox ran some of these routes out of the GK Kinch Barrow upon Soar depot, until they could be deregistered. After this period GK Kinch still remained as an operator, still had the Barrow upon Soar depot and still retained the PE214 Operators licence but the only work that remained at this time were coaches and the Access Bus contracts. A clause in the condition of sale prevented GK Kinch from running buses in Loughborough for three years. From 12 October the acquired fourteen ex Kinch double deck buses, comprising five Bristol VRs, five Daimler Fleetlines and four Leyland Atlanteans gained Midland Fox legal lettering. Their maintenance was carried out at Southgates depot, but their lives with Midland Fox were shortlived and all were withdrawn from service by the end of October.

13 October 1989 – Midland Fox G2, Loughborough to Leicester via Sileby was withdrawn. This suggests that the deal on the sale was on the cards at least five weeks earlier in order to comply with the 42 day deregistration period.

27 October 1989 – and up to 21 November, Midland Fox, as the new owner of GK Kinch bus operations, deregistered all of the inherited Kinch routes. Midland Fox and its LC&B subsidiary now had Loughborough to itself having seen off Leicester Citybus (Trippits), County Travel and Kinchbus. It looked like that after a period of intense competition that a one operator monopoly had returned to the town but this was not to be for long.

HIGHLIGHTS OF 1989
- *Competition intensifies between Midland Fox and GK Kinch*
- *GK Kinch reports Midland Fox to the Office of Fair Trading*
- *GK Kinch sells bus operation to Midland Fox*
- *Wellglade acquires Barton*
- *Trippits sold to Midland Fox.*

2 January 1990 – Barton opened an outstation at Castle Donington, initially at the Boyden International Coaches depot but soon moving to Enterprise Park, Trent Lane for 13 vehicles. Most of the operations on services 3, 10 & 310 into Loughborough were now covered by this outstation. In a way it was a long overdue replacement for the former Barton Transport depot at Kegworth which had closed on 21 December 1974.

January 1990 – GK Kinch applied to reduce its Operators licence, PE214, from 32 to 20 vehicles.

27 January 1990 – LC&B under its new Midland Fox ownership made further changes to some of its services as follows:

- L3 – Town Centre – Tynedale Road had a frequency reduction from every 15 minutes to every 20 minutes and was renumbered 3.
- G4 – Shepshed to Loughborough was renumbered 4, with the frequency remaining at every 30 minutes.
- L5 – Town Centre – University was surprisingly withdrawn.
- 6 – a new route, Town Centre – Tiverton Road at every 20 minutes. Sharing a common frequency on Forest Road with the 3 gave a combined 10 minute frequency.
- 9 – Nanpantan – Tuckers Road via Town Centre operating hourly.
- 11 and 12 – new routes every 10 minutes, replacing exactly the Midland Fox 11 and 12 that had operated as a Green Bus spoiler since 6 May 1989.

31 January 1990 – GK Kinch comes back to life after the sale of its operations to Midland Fox by registering an 'out of area' school service, 104 from Bunny to East Leake, Harry Carlton School in Nottinghamshire.

26 March 1990 – Barton took over the Trent Buses 122 working and curtailed it to operate out of Castle Donington outstation. Services 121-124 were now jointly worked by Midland Fox (2), LC&B (1) and Barton (1) with LC&B additionally providing some short Loughborough to Leicester workings.

April 1990 – GK Kinch acquired the vehicles and premises of K&M Gagg of Bunny, Nottinghamshire and thus gets a second operating base, one which is closer to Nottingham.

18 April 1990 – GK Kinch, looking for new markets, registered new service 8 from Nottingham to East Midlands Airport (EMA) and then from 30 April an ambitious X8 from Nottingham to Birmingham via EMA, Ashby and Tamworth. The 8 and X8 offered a half hourly frequency between Nottingham and EMA with the X8 continuing to Birmingham hourly. This new operation required in the order of nine buses and was a very brave commercial venture at the time.

29 April 1990 – Barton closed its Leicester depot. With it came the end of competitive activity in the City of Leicester in return for the outstation parking of the remaining six buses at the Leicester CityBus Abbey Park Road depot. Interestingly the site of the former Barton depot on Highcross Street is now part of the Highcross Shopping Centre and it is possible to sit in Pizza Express in the exact same place where one of the running sheds used to be. The office and Travel Centre is a listed building dating back to 1573 being the original Leicester Free Grammar School and remains, also now a restaurant.

4 June 1990 – a further commercial initiative from GK Kinch, away from the Loughborough homeland, was Clifton to Nottingham in direct competition with Nottingham City Transport (NCT). New service 7 combined with the existing hourly 8 and offered a 15 minute frequency between Clifton and Nottingham, Collin Street. The use of Broadmarsh Bus Station was not initially allowed.

The message to Clifton residents in a leaflet was:

NEW BUS SERVICE

Commencing Monday 4 June 1990 we will be providing A NEW LOW COST SERVICE for you. To begin with we will offer a 15 minute frequency (4 buses per hour) and a promise of a 7 and a half minute frequency (8 buses per hour) if we receive your support. We will begin by operating a Monday - Saturday time service with an hourly service on Sundays (X8). Should we prove popular we will introduce an evening service as soon as possible.

In April this year we took over the coaches and premises of K&M GAGG of Bunny, Notts with the main objective of providing the local community with our low cost buses. We have always been known for operating executive style coaches (past suppliers to Nottingham Forest FC and Notts County FC) but we began local bus services in Leicestershire 3 years ago and eventually operated 25 buses per day, carrying 2 million passengers per year.

We now feel that the time has come to give YOU the passenger, a chance to save on your Bus Fares. Unlike our competitors we operate a non-union policy and therefore our wages costs are lower. We are not allowed at the moment to use Broadmarsh Bus Station (we use Collin Street stand no. 5) so we do not incur any Bus Station Departure Fees. These savings along with others mean we can lower our fares to you.

July 1990 – GK Kinch applied or a second Operators licence in the name of Kinchline Ltd, PE1148 for 20 vehicles. This was subsequently granted.

21 July 1990 – Barton sold its Melton Mowbray Town Services and a number of coaches to Midland Fox. These had been under considerable competitive pressure by Midland Fox using their Melton Minis from their Fairtax base in the town. The out of town routes and the depot remained with Barton.

6 August 1990 – GK Kinch considerably stepped up their Clifton to Nottingham operations. The original service 7 was cancelled and replaced by new familiar service numbers 48 (via Queens Drive) & 67 (via Trent Bridge) together forming a ten minute frequency.

3 September 1990 – GK Kinch added service 49 to the Clifton routes 48 & 67 which provided for a quick link over Clifton bridge to the City.

29 October 1990 – not content with its new Nottingham operations GK Kinch once again turned its attention to Leicestershire and won on tender the Leicester Outer Circle, services 40 and 41, requiring four buses. This was previously operated by Leicester CityBus. This was to run until April 1994.

29 October 1990 – GK Kinch cancelled the 49, Clifton to Nottingham, only introduced on 3 September and changed the 48 and 67 to run on a coordinated every 10 minutes timetable with four 48s and two 67s per hour. Access to Broadmarsh Bus Station was now granted and applied from this date giving GK Kinch a much better City Centre terminal point.

12 November 1990 – Kinchline Ltd (PE1148) registered its first route, the 41, from Clifton via the City to St Ann's, at every 20 minutes, using four buses. This took Kinchline in to new territory north of Nottingham City Centre. This only lasted until 11 March 1991 though, being withdrawn from this date.

HIGHLIGHTS OF 1990

- *GK Kinch starts competing on the Clifton to Nottingham corridor against NCT.*

2 February 1991 – did GK Kinch know of the events to follow next month concerning the sale of South Notts? As a new route 10 was started on this date from East Leake to Nottingham via Gotham at every 30 minutes with 3 buses. This only lasted until 3 May 1991 though, being withdrawn from this date.

13 March 1991 – the South Notts Bus Company was sold to Nottingham City Transport. It was founded on 13 March 1926 and since 1929 Barton had held a 50% shareholding. Operations under its new owners continued much as before from the Gotham depot.

31 May 1991 – GK Kinch entered further new territory a long way from home with the award for the contract for service 58 Market Harborough to Rugby via Lutterworth.

1 July 1991 – LC&B reduced the frequency of Town Services 11 & 12 from every 10 minutes to every 15 minutes consolidating their position as a monopoly operator in the town.

25 August 1992 – Farrows Coaches of Melton Mowbray ceased operation of their tendered services Vale Runner 1-3, requiring three vehicles, from the Vale of Belvoir villages to Melton Mowbray and these were taken over on an emergency contract by Barton.

During the summer of 1992 Kinchline PF1148 was sold to NCT together with all the Clifton and City routes. A number of NCT double deck Titans and Atlanteans passed to GK Kinch as part of the settlement.

1 October 1992 – a major new initiative by GK Kinch started – this time competition against Leicester CityBus on their route 54 between Beaumont Leys and the City Centre. The Kinch route being 54K and running every 10 minutes with double deckers.

15 December 1992 – Midland Fox comes under the ownership of British Bus plc formerly Drawlane Transport Group plc.

18 December 1992 – GK Kinch withdrew from service 58, Market Harborough to Rugby, with the route passing to United Counties.

HIGHLIGHTS OF 1992

- *Kinchline and all Nottingham operations sold to NCT*
- *GK Kinch starts up competition with Leicester CityBus.*

4 January 1993 – in addition to the 54K in Leicester GK Kinch introduced new route 21K in Leicester from Rushey Mead to the City every 10 minutes in competition with Leicester CityBus 21. The 21K was withdrawn however from 16 April 1993.

18 January 1993 – Midland Fox changed the 2 route and timetable. Resources were redistributed to run at every 20 minutes between Loughborough and Sileby, and only continuing to Leicester hourly. The route between Sileby and Leicester was made direct via Cossington and the A6 too. The loss of the link to Fosseway on the edge of Syston, which is situated in Charnwood Borough, to Loughborough was of concern to the County Council and three months later, on 26 April, a tendered service 106 was introduced providing three return trips between Thurmaston and Loughborough. This was operated by LC&B.

▲ *The 18 January 1993 changes to Midland Fox route 2 showing the daytime frequency.*

During 1993 Midland Fox rented some additional parking land from a computer company directly opposite their depot in Bishop Meadow Road, Loughborough. This eased the cramped parking conditions for the Loughborough Coach & Bus fleet and also enabled the small Midland Fox outstation, which had been set up on Belton Road after moving out of The Rushes depot, to move there too.

4 May 1993 – GK Kinch tentatively stepped back into Loughborough with the registration of local school routes 174 and 175 won on tender from Midland Fox. By this time the fleet numbered thirty nine buses and four coaches.

24 August 1993 – LC&B cancelled routes 6 and 9 which provided the link to Loughborough from Osgathorpe and Belton (9) and then a half hourly Town Service to Tiverton Road (6). These were won on tender by Stevensons, operating out of their Swadlincote garage with one minibus in operation all day Mondays to Saturdays incorporating a lunchtime driver break.

11 October 1993 – at around this time Leicester CityBus was preparing itself for privatisation and Midland Fox looking to undermine the sale process registered six directly competitive services. These were the 816, 821, 822, 825, 837 & 853 totalling in the order of thirty one buses (!) competing with LCB's 16, 21, 22, 25, 37 & 153. In response LCB registered against Midland Fox on their routes 104 to Queniborough as a 204, 47/8/9 to Wigston as a 245 and on 126/7 to Loughborough (Braddon Road) as a 226 running every 20 minutes. The latter was obviously designed to hurt the Midland Fox 126/127. Sense eventually prevailed in Leicester, with CityBus being sold to GRT Holdings of Aberdeen, and the competitive activity was scaled back including the withdrawal of the 226.

This April 1993 view shows the typical vehicle that Loughborough Bus & Coach, despite its new Midland Fox livery, were using on service 121 at the time. This coach, GNN 223N, is ex Barton and passed to Midland Fox as part of the sale of Melton Mowbray Town Services on 21 July 1990. It had just been repainted out of Fairtax livery and hence it looking very smart here. It was to stay in the fleet until January 1994.

HIGHLIGHTS OF 1993

- *GK Kinch steps up competition in Leicester with new 21K*
- *GK Kinch gains Leicester Inner Circle routes 10 & 11*
- *the Midland Fox/Leicester CityBus battle spills over into Loughborough.*

12 October 1993 – GK Kinch registered commercially the Monday to Friday daytime timetable on the previous Leicester CityBus contracted Inner Circle route 10 and 11. This required six buses.

7 January 1994 – GK Kinch cancelled service 54K in Leicester, bringing the Leicester competition to an end.

9 January 1994 – GK Kinch acquired the LC&B operation from Midland Fox. The LC&B Operators licence PF7157 passed to Kinch ownership as Kinchbus Ltd. As part of the deal GK Kinch gained two all day bus workings on Midland Fox route 126/7 Leicester to Shepshed via Loughborough almost mirroring the Midland Red/Trent joint working arrangement from years before. Kinchbus was now running routes 2, 3, 4, 11, 12, 121/3/4 & 126/7 acquired from LC&B and Midland Fox. Kinchbus re-registered the 2 and reverted the route to every 30 minutes throughout running via Birstall village and Fosseway again, reversing the Midland Fox changes of January 1993.

9 January 1994 – not only did Midland Fox sell LC&B to Kinchbus on this day but there was a major reorganisation of routes in Leicester with GRT owned CityBus too. Leicester routes 8, 27, 27A, 29, 30, 31, 53, 53A, 113 and 114 became exclusively operated by Midland Fox whilst routes 61, 67, 72, 77, 74A, 81, 94 and 94A became exclusively operated by CityBus. The competitive 837 was withdrawn by Midland Fox and routes 37 and 37A became jointly operated. So to the north of the City both Birstall and Anstey passed to CityBus.

27 March 1994 – a further route exchange between CityBus and Midland Fox occurred on this date when Barlestone routes 152 & 153 passed to Midland Fox. This sadly meant the closure of the CityBus, ex Gibsons, Barlestone depot some fifteen years after it was first acquired.

22 April 1994 – Leicester Outer Circle routes 40/41 were deregistered by GK Kinch. These routes had been operated since 29 October 1990. By May 1994 the fleet totalled 49 vehicles, now all buses, the last of the coaches having been disposed of.

On the Operators licence front Kinchbus PF7157, bought from Midland Fox, was decreased from 30 to 15 vehicles. And the existing GK Kinch Operators licence PF7030 continued with 20 vehicles.

June 1994 – British Bus Group Ltd acquired Midland Fox and the Stevensons shareholding.

HIGHLIGHTS OF 1994

- *GK Kinch withdraws from Leicester competitive routes*
- *Midland Fox sells Loughborough Coach & Bus back to GK Kinch*
- *large scale route exchanges between Midland Fox and CityBus.*

23 September 1995 – Midland Fox closed its Leicester Sandacre garage for the second time.

2 October 1995 – Kinchbus started a new route 5 in Loughborough. This cross town service, requiring two buses, linked Ravensthorpe Drive with Hazel Road Estate. Apart from some minor route changes this service continues to the present day.

1 November 1995 – the GK Kinch Operators licence PF7030 was surrendered upon the grant of a new Operators licence, PF1582, in the name of Kinch GK & J (t/a Kinchbus) for 20 vehicles. Thus two Operators licences were now being used: PF7157 for Kinchbus Ltd for 15 vehicles and PF1582 for GK & J Kinch for 20 vehicles. Routes registered to the new PF1582 were:

- 9922/1582 – 10/11 Inner Circle Mon to Fri
- 9921/1582 – 126/127 Shepshed – Loughborough – Leicester Mon to Sat
- 9924/1582 – 175 Loughborough Schools
- 9925/1582 – 174 Loughborough Schools
- 9926/1582 – S4 Woodhouse Eaves to Barrow School (sch)
- 9920/1582 – 2 Loughborough to Leicester via Barrow & Sileby Mon to Sat
- plus Access Bus services.

New bus service welcomed

THE chairman of Charnwood Borough Council's public services committee, Coun Max Hunt, was on hand to officially launch the new Kinchbus service number five

The new hail and ride service covers Beacon Road, Pytchley Drive, Belvoir Drive, Grasmere Road, Atherstone Road, Fairmeadows Way, Laurel Road, The Osiers and Hazel Road on one stretch and Alan Moss Road, with the new hospital, Thorpe Hill, Schofield Road, Sharpley Road and Ravensthorpe Drive area.

Coun Hunt said: "The borough council welcomes new initiatives from the bus companies, such as the new Kinch service using good efficient vehicles."

He added that good public transport not only helped people get from A to B, but also protected the environment."

"A good bus service can help reduce car pollution and traffic congestion," said Coun. Hunt.

"We will certainly be playing our hand much more strongly in the future and have recently formed a Loughborough Quality Bus Partnership bringing together bus companies, the county council and ourselves," he said.

Coun. Hunt said local people will soon see some new borough bus shelters and information boards, improvements to bus stops in the centre of the town.

He said the county council would also be introducing bus priority lanes, after a highway study.

The service will operate every 30 minutes until 5.45pm from Monday to Saturday and timetables are available from Loughborough library and John Storer House and more information is available from Kinchbus on Loughborough 816161.

Coun Max Hunt, picured with Tony Kirk from the public transport unit at County Hall and Brian Greensmith from Kinchbus. 6743/15.

▲ From the Loughborough Echo on 13 October 1995

Other routes on the Kinchbus Ltd PF7157 licence were:

- 3601/7157 – 3 Tynedale Road to Town Centre
- 3603/7157 – 4 Shepshed to Loughborough
- 4038/7157 – 11/12 Thorpe Acre – Shelthorpe
- 8454/7157 – 121-124 Derby to Leicester
- 9759/7157 – 5 Hazel Road Estate to Ravensthorpe Drive (new from 2 October 1995)
- 10347/7157 – 14 & 15 Loughborough Works Services (new from 20 May 1996).

May 1996 – the Kinchbus Operators licence PF7157 was increased from 15 to 20 vehicles.

20 May 1996 – Kinchbus extended service 3 (inherited from LC&B), which required one bus running between the Town and Tynedale Road only, across Town to Bishop Meadow Road Industrial Estate via the Station increasing the requirement to two buses.

7 September 1996 – Paul S Winson Coaches started a competitive Loughborough Town Service 12C similar to Kinchbus 12. The new 12C was a two bus operation running Mondays-Saturdays. Kinchbus introduced a 'shadow' route 12X also requiring two buses on the same date!

Paul S Winson's smartly turned out Leyland National PIJ 8104 seen on the competitive service 12C in Shelthorpe in 1996.

John Bennett

Loughborough's Buses | The deregulated years

▲ A Kinchbus newspaper advertisement for the introduction of service 12X designed to run in front of the new Paul S Winson 12C.

▲ Two Kinchbus, ex NCT Atlanteans parked in Loughborough Bus Station between school duties. RNU 426X has a board showing service 123 and is equipped with a Wayfarer 3 ticket machine whilst RNU432X is dressed for school contract S303.

▲ Kinchbus HIL 7771, a Leyland Leopard Willowbrook Warrior re-body, originally Northern General TUP 582V, seen in Loughborough Bus Station awaiting departure on service 2 to Leicester. Barton Leyland National VCH 479S loads for service 10 to Nottingham behind.

▲ A local newspaper advertisement for the new Paul S Winson Town Service 12C which was shortly to start on 7 September.

1 August 1996 – Cowie Group plc acquired British Bus Group Ltd.

2 December 1996 – Kinchbus started new route 7 from the University Campus to Town Centre every half hour using one bus.

19 May 1997 – Kinchbus started new route 8, Melton Mowbray to Loughborough via Wymeswold requiring one bus. This replaced Midland Fox 138 which had been operated from the Melton Mowbray garage but which had just been closed.

18 August 1997 – Kinchbus introduced new route 10, Town Centre to parts of Thorpe Acre not covered by 11 & 12, half hourly requiring one bus.

18 August 1997 – Kinchbus won the Leicestershire CC contract for Vale Runner, the Vale of Belvoir villages to Melton Mowbray using two buses Mondays to Saturdays. This had previously been operated by Farrows Coaches and later Barton. From the same date Kinchbus also won the Rutland CC contract for Rutland Flyer, Melton Mowbray to Corby via Oakham, a two bus operation, Mondays to Saturdays. Two dedicated, route branded, Mercedes Vario midibuses 827 & 828 were acquired for this contract.

18 August 1997 – Kinchbus changed their routes 3 & 4. The 3 pulled in the Empress Road section of service 4 between the Town Centre and the Station. The 4 which had run every 30 minutes from Shepshed to alternatively Tuckers Road or the Station was cut back to the Town Centre but the resource freed up was used to increase the frequency from every 30 minutes to every 20 minutes to Shepshed. However this soon proved to be too ambitious and the frequency once again reverted to every 30 minutes from 4 September.

6 November 1997 – Cowie Group plc renamed to Arriva plc.

1 February 1998 – Wellglade acquired Kinchbus Ltd. The Operators licence PF7157 for Kinchbus Ltd was acquired but the other Operators licence PF1582 was not. Hence all registrations on PF1582 were reregistered to PF7157. All buses were taken into stock and the business carried on trading as before from the Barrow upon Soar depot. The routes and their associated vehicle requirements at the time of takeover were - see table 2, page 51. All 73 staff were transferred but it soon became apparent that there were a number who failed to materialise and Wellglade faced a driver shortage from day one. This was to prove difficult to overcome. Another issue that Wellglade faced from day one was vehicle parking at Barrow depot. The depot was of insufficient size to cope with its current run-out of 49 vehicles plus spares and at night vehicles were being parked all over Hayhill Industrial Estate which was causing problems with neighbours. An urgent solution was required to resolve this.

20 April 1998 – a first review by Wellglade of its new Kinchbus operation soon revealed that new Town route 10 was a very poor performer, and in any case its route was well covered by 11 and 12, so this was route withdrawn saving one bus. This saved bus was immediately put to use however on service 7, the University Shuttle, which was running to capacity. In addition to bolstering the frequency of the 7 from every 30 minutes to every 20 minutes it was also extended across the Town to the Station where a large untapped demand for students wanting to connect with trains, primarily to and from Leicester, was met. This move soon proved to be a great success.

29 June 1998 – Arriva started a new service 757, funded by East Midlands Airport and Midland Mainline & Central Trains from Loughborough Station to East Midlands Airport running approximately hourly, daily.

3 August 1998 – Paul S Winson decided to withdraw from the competing Town route 12C with the Kinchbus 'shadow' 12X following suit.

14 September 1998 – a bold joint attempt was made by Trent Buses & Kinchbus to run a Derby to Leicester hourly express via the M1. One Mercedes coach seated Vario in a branded livery called Pegasus was provided by each operator to cover the distance between the two cities in just 45 minutes. Each alternate journey, the Trent Buses operated one, continued at Derby to Bakewell on the opposite hour to Transpeak to provide an hourly service between Derby and Bakewell. Reliability wasn't all it should have been with the M1 occasionally causing severe delays and the A6 north of Derby causing timekeeping issues too. The service was withdrawn after its year long trial period on 3 October 1999. This was the second attempt by Trent to run a Derby to Leicester express, the first being the 207 from 10 May 1982 which lasted until October 1986. It was then replaced by an ambitious Derbyshire contracted route X44 from 26 October 1986 being jointly operated by Trent and East Midland every two hours between Sheffield and Leicester via Chesterfield, Derby and EMA. But this only lasted until 2 May 1987, being withdrawn without replacement – but it did prompt CountyLink to start their new 144 to and from Derby – see 3 May 1987.

from 14th September 1998

A line up of smartly turned out Mercedes 709D minibuses of Kinchbus opposite their Barrow depot.

John Bennett

Loughborough's Buses | *The deregulated years*

16 October 1998 – proved to be the last day of operation of Kinchbus on the Leicester Inner Circle routes 10/11. This had been a six vehicle commercial operation but had recently suffered from a severe driver shortage and had started to become unreliable so the decision was made to withdraw. Although Leicester City Council found other operators to continue with the tendered parts of the route, ie evenings, Saturdays and Sundays there was no Mondays to Fridays daytime service provided until 2 January 1999. Sadly this period of unreliability coupled with no service at all for nearly three months meant that this once commercial service never recovered and was doomed to death by a thousand cuts over the following few years.

26 October 1998 – around this time Rural Bus Grant funding was being made available by the Government to local authorities to fund or improve rural bus services. Leicestershire County Council received a large slice of this grant and funding was made available to Kinchbus to increase the frequency of service 8 between Loughborough and Melton Mowbray to hourly. This involved a second bus. Because there was 25 minutes layover in every hour at Loughborough this time was put to use by introducing a new service 13 between the Town Centre and Tuckers Road via Empress Road (currently served by the 3). The 3 was therefore cut back to run between Tynedale Road and the Town Centre only, thus reducing the requirement on this route to one.

26 October 1998 – Vale Runner, the Leicestershire CC contract run by Kinchbus using two buses between the Vale of Belvoir villages and Melton Mowbray was also the subject of some Rural Bus Grant funding and an evening service was added. This added an extra driver duty causing further strain on already stretched resources for what seemed an almost pointless exercise as very rarely was a passenger ever carried.

31 October 1998 – because Kinchbus had spare buses on a Saturday from the University Shuttle fleet a tender was submitted and won to provide a Knossington (Rutland) to Leicester 'shopper' type service. It was numbered 202 and departed Knossington at 0847 via a very scenic route, returning from Leicester at 1415. This was to operate for over seven years.

By late 1998 – the tendered Stevensons routes 6 & 9 within Loughborough were withdrawn as by now they had very little unique territory and did not provide value of money.

11 January 1999 – further Rural Bus Grant funding was made available to Kinchbus, this time to increase the Loughborough to Leicester frequency of 121-124 to half hourly. The new timetable from this date simplified the route through Charnwood Forest so that all buses ran via Woodhouse Eaves, Swithland, Cropston, Thurcaston, Anstey and County Hall and was thus renumbered 123 for all journeys including those continuing to Derby. The long standing Barton working on service 122, Derby to Leicester, was transferred to Kinchbus. Thus from this date Kinchbus increased their share to half of the Derby to Leicester through hourly journeys with Midland Fox. The villages of Newtown Linford, Markfield and Nanpantan omitted from the new 123 were catered for by a new 120, running hourly, from Leicester to Loughborough, operated under contract to the County Council by Arriva.

6 April 1999 – the Barton routes 3, 10 & 310 had remained little changed from deregulation some 12 years earlier but from this date they were substantially revised to become X3 and 10 both branded as 'Barton Airways'. The X3, running hourly, replaced the 3 and offered a faster journey time between Nottingham and East Midlands Airport and in Loughborough was extended to the Station. The 10 and the Sunday variant 310 remained hourly much as before. This was the first real attempt at trying to serve the Airport properly and also to respond to Arriva's 757.

▲ Barton Buses Dart S941 UAL at Loughborough Bus Station on Barton Airways branded service 10 to Nottingham via East Midlands Airport.

12 December 1999 – Kinchbus moved from the GK Kinch rented premises at 17-21 Hayhill Industrial Estate, Sileby Road, Barrow on Soar to a new Wellglade owned depot in Loughborough on Bishop Meadow Industrial Estate at Swingbridge Road. This resolved the parking problems on Hayhill Industrial Estate which had been festering since the takeover in 1998.

▲ Typical of Arriva allocation for services 126/127 around 1998 is this Volvo Olympian S653 KJU pictured in Swan Street, Loughborough heading for Leicester. This popular stop is now denied to buses since the pedestrianisation of this part of Swan Street.

SUBSTANTIAL IMPROVEMENTS ON THE WAY FROM KINCHBUS

KINCHBUS, now happily relocated in Loughborough, have some exciting news for locals.

From March 6 they will be introducing substantial improvements to two of their major services – and this could be just the start.

Managing director Brian King told The Echo: "There will be good news for passengers from the university to the railway station, which is a particular growth area. And our service between Loughborough and Leicester, via Barrow and Sileby, will be boosted by more modern buses and a new timetable."

Mr King said that these would probably be just the start of a number of developments to further improve Kinchbus' service to local passengers, now they have made the important move from Barrow to Loughborough.

"When the Wellglade group of companies took over Kinchbus from the Kinch family in January 1998, the bus service already had a very good reputation, but there was concern about the cramped facilities near Barrow," he added.

"Now we are based at the former plastic recycling plant on Sullivan Way in Loughborough with new facilities for the buses and their maintenance. We have state-of-the-art modern workshop and all the ancillary facilities necessary for our business, together with parking for 60 buses."

Mr King said that both Barton and Trent, owned by the same company, had won UK best bus company awards in 1999 and he was confident that Kinchbus would soon be regarded as a winner in its field.

"We are well placed to anticipate and stimulate demand in the market by improving the quality of our service," he said.

Providing a reliable service

KINCHBUS run every day of the week – 364 days a year.

The only day they have off in the entire year is Christmas Day itself. You can rely on Kinchbus as your major form of transport on Sundays and each Bank Holiday throughout the calendar.

Timetable

They have 70 staff and currently operate more than 50 vehicles.

If you are in need of a timetable, you can find one on any Kinchbus – or you can ring the customer service number on (01509) 815637.

Kinch staff (from left) Dean Ward, Brian Greensmith, Kelly Matthews, John Watson, Andrew Hardy and Tony Blake. 23163/00.

Investment in the Kinchbus fleet is now bearing fruit.

▲ From the Loughborough Echo on Friday 21 January 2000

▲ The new Kinchbus depot on Swingbridge Road, Loughborough seen here on 28 August 2008.

▲ The former Kinchbus depot at Hayhill Industrial Estate, Barrow as seen here on 24 February 2018. It is now occupied by a new tenant.

30 January 2000 – Barton closed their Castle Donington outstation which had been opened ten years earlier and moved some buses to Nottingham and some to the new Kinchbus depot in Loughborough as a Barton outstation to operate services X3, 10 & 310.

4 March 2000 – proved to be the last day of operation by Kinchbus on the Vale Runner contract running between the Vale of Belvoir villages and Melton Mowbray. The contract was terminated by Leicestershire County Council due to poor performance associated with lost mileage caused by a crippling driver shortage. The route was taken over by Paul James.

6 March 2000 – Kinchbus service 2, Loughborough to Leicester via Sileby, had been remarkably stable since the Wellglade takeover in 1998. Following a review of the route a new timetable was introduced from this date. The route between Sileby and Leicester became fast and direct via Cossington and then the A6 rather than via the Fosseway and Birstall village, this reducing the running time by twenty minutes and making the Sileby to Leicester journey much more attractive. The bus saved in this speeding up exercise was then reintroduced as a 2X running hourly between Loughborough and Sileby, Greedon Rise omitting Quorn but using the A6 by-pass instead. So, Sileby benefitted from having faster journey times to both Leicester and Loughborough. This timetable pattern was very similar to what Midland Fox had tried in January 1993 but had since been reversed by Kinchbus in 1994.

1 April 2000 – the financial performance of Barton X3, Nottingham to Loughborough Station via East Midlands Airport (EMA) was poor and it was withdrawn from this date. Kinchbus however replaced the Loughborough Station, East Midlands Airport to Long Eaton section and branded it as Air-Line Shuttle using two coach seated Mercedes Varios running hourly. It too struggled commercially and was destined to be withdrawn but a lifeline was thrown to it in the autumn of 2002 – see below.

▲ Taking over from Barton X3 was Kinchbus Air-Line Shuttle using two of these coach seated Mercedes Varios. Here we see S290 UAL on arrival at Loughborough Station.

3 April 2000 – as mentioned previously the extension of Kinchbus 7 to Loughborough Station had proved a great success and once again the route was now running to capacity again. (because of the road width within the University campus it was not possible to operate any bus larger than a Mercedes 709D). So from this date the frequency was increased further from every 20 minutes to every 15 minutes. In addition, through a partnership involving Leicestershire County Council, Charnwood Borough Council and the major employers on Bishop Meadow Road Industrial Estate, the main one being AstraZeneca, a trial peak hour extension of the 7, running every 15 minutes, was introduced. This linked the Town but more importantly the Station with the Industrial Estate. This enhancement to University Shuttle 7 moved the number of buses required from two to four. The extension to the Industrial Estates, and AstraZeneca in particular, again proved to be very successful.

▲ Kinchbus Mercedes 709D N816 PJU at Loughborough Train Station showing off its branding for University Shuttle 7. The 7 route was an early pioneer for real time information and the *star trak pole can be seen beside the bus shelter.

10 September 2000 – with the withdrawal of Barton X3 on 1 April, Barton's only presence in Loughborough was the long standing hourly 10. However all this was to change on this date when the 10 got absorbed into a major recast of the Barton Long Eaton to Nottingham corridor where the new rainbow 5 frequency was increased to every 6/7 minutes with one of these buses per hour being made up from the old 10, now as rainbow route 5B. The 5B times in and out of Loughborough remained much the same as did the hourly frequency and route. The buses however lost their red livery and were replaced by a fleet of new Excels in a striking purple rainbow 5 livery. The Barton outstation at the Kinchbus Loughborough depot however remained in place for the operation of this new route.

▲ From 10 September 2000 the Barton 10 route from Loughborough to Nottingham via East Midlands Airport was replaced by rainbow 5B using new Excels in this purple based branded livery. Here S164 UAL is seen departing Loughborough Bus Station for Nottingham.

1 April 2000 – Midland Fox 757, Loughborough Station to East Midlands Airport, under contract to the train companies and EMA, was withdrawn. This had been running since June 1998.

1 September 2001 – proved to be the last day of operation by Kinchbus of the Rutland Flyer. Although the contract still had time to run the crippling driver shortage of the time meant that it made better sense to concentrate resources at home in Loughborough rather than in Rutland. It was taken over by Paul James.

29 September 2001 – Loughborough Bus Station closed after operations on this date to be redeveloped into The Rushes Shopping Centre. Buses were moved to street stands on Baxtergate.

▲ The architecture of the old Loughborough Bus Station can be seen in this April 1987 photograph of a GK Kinch Fleetline, NOB 308M, exiting on to Biggin Street on service 1 to Leicester. To the rear of the bus can be seen one of the old concrete bus shelters and to the right the former multi storey car park.

1 October 2001 – the University Shuttle 7 frequency was increased once again from every 15 minutes to every 10 minutes due to ever increasing demand. This increased the number of buses from four to six. There was a ten minute layover at Loughborough Station which meant, that on a ten minute frequency, there was always a bus on the stop at the station exit which was of even greater benefit to rail customers and annoyance to the taxi drivers. But as ever there was no gain without loss, with service 8 paying the price. The 8, Melton Mowbray to Loughborough via Wymeswold, which had been running to its new hourly timetable since 26 October 1988 was utilising two buses and the Rural Bus Grant funding was proving to be inadequate as passenger growth had been below expectations. Coupled with a continuing crippling driver shortage the decision was made to withdraw from this route. This also included the linked 13 within Loughborough to Tuckers Road. This was taken over by Paul James.

26 November 2001 – by this time the ever expanding Dunn-Line Group had opened a depot in Loughborough, on the Bishop Meadow Road Industrial Estate at 15 Bakewell Road, and had started winning school contracts. But the first local bus work was the award of the LCC contract for service 120, Leicester to Loughborough via Markfield, previously operated by Arriva. This was a two bus contract. This operated until 2 January 2004 by which time the Loughborough operation was closing down. The contract was then taken over by Paul S Winson from 5 January. By 21 February 2005 however the frequency of the 120 was reduced to two-hourly.

25 February 2002 – the Shepshed Sprinter route 4 had seen no change for over four years but a major improvement was introduced by Kinchbus on this date. Joint service 126/127, Shepshed to Leicester, where Kinchbus had two buses running alongside Arriva was performing financially well but development was constrained by the fact that it was a joint operation and neither operator was its own master. Kinchbus therefore decided to develop the Shepshed to Loughborough market by enhancing Shepshed Sprinter from every 30 minutes to every 15 minutes. A fleet of four new branded Solo buses were provided for the route upgrade. Through ticketing across Loughborough Train Station from Shepshed to Leicester was introduced too.

▲ *From 25 February 2002 Kinchbus enhanced route 4, Shepshed Sprinter, to a 15 minute frequency and introduced four new Solos. Here we see Solo FP51 GXY at the Loughborough Station terminus with a Mercedes 709D P822 BNR on route 7 to the University in the background.*

2 April 2002 – by this time Leicestershire County Council were pursuing a policy of a minimum hourly frequency between all towns in the county. Although service 8 was still providing an hourly link between Melton Mowbray and Loughborough there was a poor infrequent service between Melton Mowbray and Grantham. The answer was to introduce a new 8, running hourly, from Grantham to Loughborough. This was now a three bus timetable operated by Paul James (two buses) and West End Travel (one bus).

2 September 2002 – the ambitious Rural Bus Grant frequency enhancement from 11 January 1999 of service 123, between Loughborough and Leicester via Charnwood Forest had proved too optimistic and this section of route reverted to hourly once more.

2 September 2002 – the experimental 2X introduced by Kinchbus on 6 March 2000 hadn't generated enough new business and was withdrawn. The 2 timetable reverted to a half hourly frequency throughout.

14 October 2002 – the joint Midland Fox/Kinchbus service 126/127 had remained little changed since 1994. As explained under the 25 February 2002 heading for Shepshed Sprinter, Kinchbus were anxious to develop the corridor but felt constrained by the joint operation. So, from this date Kinchbus withdrew its two bus workings on joint 126/127 and replaced them with a new 'Leicester Flyer' running hourly from Ravensthorpe Drive and Schofield Road in Loughborough via the town centre then non stop to Leicester via the A6. The Arriva response was to immediately register the two ex Kinchbus workings on 126/127.

▲ *Kinchbus P202 BNR a very early model Optare Excel which was new in October 1996 representing the heavy fleet investment at this time. This bus and its sister P201 BNR were allocated to the two bus share of route 126/127 alongside Midland Fox double decks. The low floor feature was heavily marketed. This bus is seen in Loughborough Swan Street.*

27 October 2002 – the joint Kinchbus/Midland Fox service 123 Leicester to Derby, previously 121-4, had remained little changed, apart from the operators, since CountyLink days back in 1987. However with an end to end running time of 1hour 50 minutes it had become outdated and this no doubt caused Midland Fox to announce their withdrawal from the route. This left Kinchbus in a dilemma as to what to do with the 'other half' of the joint frequency. It was time for a radical rethink. As mentioned previously the Air-Line Shuttle running between Loughborough, East Midlands

Airport (EMA) and Long Eaton was a poor performer and its days were numbered. However EMA was rapidly growing by now and the management there were keen to invest in bus services to their three major cities. So the decision was taken to abandon the EMA to Long Eaton leg of Air-Line Shuttle and go to Derby instead. Thus a new Air-Line Shuttle was launched running from Loughborough Station to EMA and on to Derby every hour using two of the coach seated Varios transferred from the Long Eaton route plus one additional one to make up the new requirement of three buses. The 123 was then truncated to run between Loughborough and Leicester only, still running hourly.

5 April 2003 – the Kinchbus initiative to provide a fast Loughborough to Leicester service as the 'Leicester Flyer' competing with the long standing, but slower, Midland Fox 126/127 had failed to attract enough customers and was withdrawn after operation on this date after only six months experience.

19 April 2003 – Barton sold its remaining Melton Mowbray services to Paul James and closed its depot on North Street which it had taken over from Farrows Coaches on 29 March 1992 after moving out of the rented Barton Transport plc depot on Wilton Road.

31 May 2003 – since the big changes to 123 on 27 October 2002 Kinchbus had been running, commercially, the hourly Loughborough to Leicester via Charnwood Forest route. However the financial return was poor and it was withdrawn after operation on this date. It was initially taken over by Barton from 2 June to 11 October 2003 and then passed to Woods Coaches and then to Centrebus by November 2004. Under Centrebus the route number was changed to 54 which represented the linking up at Beaumont Leys with their existing 54 route into Leicester but this link was broken again in January 2013 when it became 154 with its own unique route in to Leicester once more. It now runs via Strasbourg Drive and Avebury Avenue between Beaumont Leys and the City terminating at St Margaret's Bus Station.

▲ *Seen loading in Baxtergate, Loughborough on 13 March 2018 is CentrebusEnviro YY64 GWJ on service 154 to Leicester via Woodhouse Eaves.*

4 January 2004 – saw Kinchbus Loughborough school services 874 & 875 (formerly 174 & 175) lost on retender to Paul S Winson. By now most of the school contracts inherited by Wellglade in 1998 had been lost on retender too. The local Leicestershire market for school contracts was very competitive at that time.

21 February 2004 – Kinchbus 3, Tynedale Road to the Town Centre, was not a good financial performer and was withdrawn after operation on this date. It was replaced by Centrebus.

23 February 2004 – new service 27 was introduced by Leicestershire County Council to link Thurmaston to Loughborough via Syston, Rothley, Mountsorrel, Sileby, Seagrave, Walton on the Wolds and Barrow. Its frequency was hourly requiring 2 buses and was contracted to Centrebus. It has carried on to the present day, the frequency now however is every 75 minutes representing the ever increasing traffic congestion. It was operated by Centrebus up to 27 January 2008 when the contract was lost to Woods Coaches. However Woods exited local bus operation on 26 August 2008 with the contract returning to Centrebus for a further four years when it was lost once again, this time to Roberts Coaches who remain the current operator.

▲ *Roberts Streetlite MX12 DYW on service 27 on 12 January 2018 seen loading in Loughborough, Lemyngton Street for Thurmaston.*

4 May 2004 – East Midlands Airport together with help from Nottingham City Council funded a Nottingham to EMA direct via the A453 'skylink' route which was operated by Nottingham City Transport. This was to remain in place, and during this time generated much new business to the Airport, until 25 March 2012.

5 June 2004 – the Kinchbus 4 Shepshed Sprinter which had been running to an enhanced every 15 minute frequency with new buses since 25 February 2002 had failed to capture enough of the Shepshed market from Midland Fox 126/127 and was withdrawn from this date. The strength of 126/127 had been underestimated by Kinchbus who had failed with both Shepshed Sprinter and Leicester Flyer to create a new, profitable, market. Midland Fox were not to have Shepshed to themselves however as Paul S Winson stepped into the gap and introduced their own Shepshed Sprinter but running half hourly instead of the Kinchbus four times an hour. This was to run for the next 11 years, finally being withdrawn on 24 December 2015.

Immaculate Paul S Winson Dart SLF DW05 PSW seen in Loughborough, High Street on 5 January 2006 on Shepshed Sprinter route 4.

By now it is probably opportune to look at the remaining Loughborough operations as the development of today's network (2018) had almost taken place.

- The 2, Loughborough to Leicester, had been through its changes but had now settled into a timetable very recognisable today.
- The 5, not mentioned in this text since 1995, carried on with only very minor amendments.
- The 7, University Shuttle had by now got itself up to a 10 minute frequency from the very poor half hourly frequency in 1998.
- The 11/12, the core four bus Town Service just continued without change.
- Air-Line Shuttle had started to develop the airport market but there was much more to come here in later years.
- So after many years of transition the Kinchbus network had developed into five key commercial brands, the 2, 5, 7, 11/12 and Air-Line Shuttle.
- And for Midland Fox there were by now two key commercial brands the 126/127 Shepshed to Leicester and the 99 Coalville, Loughborough to Nottingham.
- Trent Barton's rainbow 5B and South Notts 1 completed the picture.

Had stability finally arrived?

24 July 2005 – a very close working partnership had by now developed between Kinchbus and EMA and some pump priming subsidy was made available to extend the hours of Air-Line Shuttle from 0400 to 2400 hrs seven days a week.

Cresswells Mercedes Vario S311 DLG seen at Loughborough Market Place bus stop on market day Thursday 5 January 2006 on service 129 to Ashby de la Zouch. Service 129 has remained firmly in the tendered arena and has had a great variety of operators over the years as contracts changed hands including Paul James, Stevensons, Midland Classic, Macpherson and as shown here Cresswells. The current operator, since 2012, is Paul S Winson. Sadly Cresswells is now longer trading.

New Kinchbus low floor Dart SLF P408 BNR demonstrating its kneeling skills at the Loughborough Market Place stop on service 12.

Loughborough's Buses | The deregulated years

30 April 2006 – Air-Line Shuttle was further improved. The pump priming subsidy to increase the operating hours almost a year ago had been very successful in attracting new business to the point where it was no longer required. EMA then reinvested this into further improvements which saw a doubling of the frequency to half hourly and a 24 hour/7 day operation.

▲ Kinchbus Volvo B7RLE/Plaxton Centro YN08 CWU seen at East Midlands Airport on 25 May 2012 on the skylink route between Derby and Leicester via Loughborough. This was one of a batch of six that was part funded by Derby City Council on behalf of EMA to relaunch Air-Line Shuttle as skylink in March 2008.

24 October 2006 – Arriva Fox County Ltd was renamed to Arriva Midlands Ltd.

2 July 2007 – Kinchbus relaunched its core Town Services 11 and 12 with four new Optare Tempo buses in a branded livery.

23 March 2008 – Air-Line Shuttle was rebranded skylink with a new fleet of six yellow Volvo B7RLE/Plaxton Centro single deck buses.

1 April 2009 – EMA had not only been financially assisting the development of skylink to Loughborough and Derby but also a limited-stop hourly service via the M1 to Leicester. This was marketed as Leicester Skylink and had started on 1 October 2006. It was operated by Arriva. However because of the limited-stop nature of the service, and the fact it was routed from Leicester via Braunstone because of regeneration funding made available to the service to enable workers to get to EMA, the subsidy was high and by now was becoming unaffordable and could not continue into the new financial year starting 1 April. Kinchbus proposed a solution which was an hourly extension of their skylink from Loughborough to Leicester which would only use half the resource of the dedicated route and therefore at a much reduced cost. This proposal was accepted by EMA and an hourly extension from Loughborough, non-stop via the A6, to Leicester commenced.

▲ Here we see Kinchbus Tempo 320, YJ07 VSV, on its first day in service at Loughborough Market Place on service 12 on 2 July 2007. The batch of four Tempos for routes 11 and 12 comprised fleet numbers 319 to 322.

▲ Arriva Leyland National Greenway JIL 2198 (previously Ribble SCK703P) is typical of the type of vehicle used on service 99, Coalville to Nottingham. It is seen here in Loughborough Bus Station heading for Nottingham shortly before the route was cut back to run from Coalville to Loughborough only.

38

11 July 2009 – Arriva's Leicester Southgates garage closed. Operations moved to either Wigston or Thurmaston garages. Also on this date the 99 was withdrawn beyond Loughborough to Nottingham leaving this part of the route unserved. The 126 was extended from Shepshed to Coalville half hourly as a replacement for the 99. However new Nottingham based independent Premiere filled the void with a half hourly 'red 9' running between Nottingham and Loughborough via the former 99 route and extended it at peak hours into the University at Loughborough. This new half hourly timetable generated much new patronage and the route was soon quite busy and a successful commercial venture.

26 October 2009 – Paul S Winson started an X27 from Rothley to Loughborough over the same route as Arriva 127.

25 April 2010 – such was the success of the skylink extension from Loughborough to Leicester that just one year later the frequency was doubled to half hourly meaning that skylink had become a half hourly Derby to Leicester service.

13 December 2010 – Premiere were now quite settled in and doing well on the 'red 9' between Loughborough and Nottingham. In Nottingham, Premiere were competing with trent barton on many of their key routes so it was decided that Kinchbus would introduce their own 9 between Loughborough and Nottingham in competition. This ran until 24 March 2012 when Kinchbus withdrew having failed to secure enough of the market on this corridor.

26 March 2011 – Arriva closed their Coalville garage. A new outstation opened at the Roberts depot at Hugglescote.

May 2011 – Centrebus took over West End Travel of Melton Mowbray. West End Travel had a one third share in service 8, Grantham to Loughborough. Centrebus and Veolia (who had bought out Paul James by now) therefore became joint operators of the 8.

October 2011 – Centrebus took over Veolia Transport of Saxby near Melton Mowbray who in turn had previously bought out Paul James so the 8, Grantham to Loughborough, was therefore now 100% operated by Centrebus.

25 March 2012 – continued funding for the Nottingham to East Midlands Airport skylink route operated by NCT became an issue and it was withdrawn from this date. Trent barton started a new commercial 'skylink' route to replace it. This absorbed the existing rainbow 5B but between Long Eaton and Nottingham, ran much more direct omitting Beeston and therefore becoming much quicker. So in Loughborough from this date there were now two 'skylinks', the yellow Leicester to Derby route and the new blue Loughborough to Nottingham route. The new blue skylink was hourly between Loughborough and EMA but then half hourly to Nottingham. But as well as this new Trent Barton skylink to EMA via Long Eaton, Nottingham independent Premiere, ever keen to compete, introduced a new fast link, Red Flyer, to EMA via the A453.

16 April 2012 – by now Kinchbus route 7, the University Shuttle, had been rebranded as 'Sprint' and new slim line Solos had arrived. This route had always been run in close partnership with Loughborough University. The geography of the campus is one of a long thin access road and the distance from one end to the other is quite considerable. A change of policy at the University to make bus use more attractive to students was to introduce free travel on Sprint within the campus. This resulted in a huge increase of students travelling and from this date two extra buses were added to Sprint to provide a 5 minute frequency within the campus.

26 January 2013 – during the previous afternoon Kinchbus was made aware that Premiere, the Nottingham based operator of 'red 9', Loughborough to Nottingham via the A60, was about to cease trading. A hurried application to the Traffic Commissioners was made to start a new 9 from Loughborough to Nottingham the following day on Saturday 26 January. This was a half hourly timetable very similar to Premiere's but without the University peak hour extensions.

▲ *Kinchbus Solo FJ09 MWE on service 5 to Ravensthorpe Drive on 13 March 2018. It is seen waiting for time on High Street now devoid of traffic since it is no longer the A6 following the construction of the Inner Relief Road and pedestrianisation of the Town Centre. This bus will now turn sharp right in to Baxtergate rather than continuing along High Street and Swan Street as previously.*

▲ *Kinchbus Mercedes Citaro BX64 WJD is seen leaving Leicester, St Margarets Bus Station on skylink to EMA and Derby on 9 August 2017. This is one of a batch of eight Citaros delivered in 2014 to further upgrade skylink. Three more arrived in March 2018 to complete the route requirement of eleven buses.*

6 July 2014 – Loughborough Town Centre was pedestrianised and all buses were rerouted away from Swan Street and the Market Place to new bus stops on High Street, Lemyngton Street or Baxtergate.

28 September 2014 – the Leicester to Derby yellow skylink was enhanced to operate from half hourly to every 20 minutes all day.

20 September 2015 – Arriva changed their 16 and 126 services in the Coalville and Shepshed area. The 16 running between Coalville and Thringstone (Hensons Lane) was effectively extended to Loughborough replacing 126 over this section at a new half hourly frequency. The daytime 127 reverted to a Shepshed to Leicester timetable at a 12 minute frequency. By 18 February 2017 the frequency of the 16, Coalville to Loughborough, had dropped to hourly.

27 September 2015 – saw a trent barton return to Coalville after the Barton withdrawal of service 11 in December 1987 some 28 years earlier. EMA by now was attracting staff from Coalville and Shepshed and there was no bus connection so an hourly extension of the blue skylink from Nottingham to EMA to Coalville was introduced. The frequency of the blue skylink was now every 20 minutes to EMA with one hourly leg continuing to Loughborough, another hourly leg forming the new Coalville extension and the third leg terminating at EMA. The trent barton outstation at Kinchbus Loughborough continued to provide a number of buses for this route.

31 January 2016 – trent barton introduced new skylink express, half hourly, between Nottingham and EMA which runs direct via the A453 completing the journey in 33 minutes instead of 58 minutes via Long Eaton on the blue skylink.

25 March 2018 – further Airport development saw trent barton my15, Ilkeston to Old Sawley, extended hourly southwards to East Midlands Airport.

Trent barton FH54 VRX seen loading in Coalville for the skylink route to EMA and Nottingham on 9 August 2017. This batch of Scania/Wright Solar buses have since been replaced by a new fleet of E200s for this route. ▼

Author's collection

Chapter 6
Compare and contrast

That brings us to the end of the story. But it is interesting to compare and contrast this list of current routes below with what was on offer 32 years earlier at Deregulation Day in 1986.

The current routes (as at October 2018) serving Loughborough are:

- 1 – Loughborough to Nottingham via East Leake and Gotham every 20 minutes – South Notts (NCT). Probably one of the most consistent of all of the routes but even this is now running more frequently than it did in1986.
- 2 – Loughborough to Leicester via Barrow and Sileby half hourly – Kinchbus. From the 1986 days of a joint Midland Red/Trent route with Howletts running part way too this route has seen much of the competition but has now settled to its current frequency throughout.
- 3 – Town Centre to Tynedale Road hourly – Paul S Winson. This route did not exist in 1986 and was first introduced by the Trippits in 1987. It has run consistently since but has moved from the commercial to the tendered arena at its lower frequency of hourly.
- 5 – Ravensthorpe Drive to Hazel Road Estate via Town Centre half hourly – Kinchbus. This route existed only in parts in 1986 by other route numbers but the current 5, running half hourly, started in October 1995 serving new areas of the Town.
- 8 – Loughborough to Grantham via Melton Mowbray hourly – Centrebus. Back in 1986 this was an infrequent Barton route and through a chequered history of operators, Rural Bus Grant and sheer determination it is now running hourly, commercially.
- 9 – Loughborough to Nottingham via Bunny half hourly – Kinchbus. There have been dramatic improvements on this corridor from the two-hourly, slow, via the villages 101 prior to deregulation to the half hourly direct service of today. The route number '9' has its origins in the Midland Red X99, which became Midland Fox 99, then Premiere red 9 and finally Kinchbus 9.
- 11 – Thorpe Acre to Shelthorpe via Town Centre clockwise half hourly – Kinchbus. There has been change of operators, service numbers and slight changes to the route but this core Town Service, together with the 12 below, remains as a constant.
- 12 – Thorpe Acre to Shelthorpe via Town Centre anticlockwise half hourly – Kinchbus. See 11 above.
- 13 – Town to Tuckers Road hourly – Paul S Winson. This route has been covered on and off since 1986 but has now settled to an hourly tendered service.
- 16 – Loughborough to Coalville via Shepshed hourly – Arriva. Although there has been changes to route numbers and frequency, the operator and the current hourly frequency is now consistent with 1986.
- X26 – Rothley to Loughborough via Mountsorrel & Quorn hourly – Paul S Winson. This is a new development offering greater choice and frequency on the Mountsorrel to Loughborough corridor.
- 27 – Loughborough to Thurmaston via Seagrave & Syston every 75 minutes – Roberts. This partly replaces a section of service 2 when its route was streamlined but provides greater coverage than pre 1986.
- 120X – Markfield to Loughborough (Thursdays) – Paul S Winson
- 126 – Leicester to Coalville via Rothley, Mountsorrel, Loughborough and Shepshed hourly (evenings and Sundays) – Arriva. See 127 below.
- 127 – Leicester to Shepshed via Rothley, Mountsorrel and Loughborough every 15 minutes – Arriva. Another very consistent core route which has varied in frequency and levels of competition but is still running more frequently now than in 1986.
- 129 – Loughborough to Ashby via Belton two-hourly – Paul S Winson. This link has always been in the tendered arena but the current timetable is more frequent than 1986.
- 154 – Loughborough to Leicester via Woodhouse Eaves and Anstey hourly – Centrebus. A route which has seen enormous changes since 1986 but is now running at hourly again, the same as CountyLink in 1986.
- skylink (blue) – Loughborough/Coalville to Nottingham via EMA each hourly – trent barton. Although now looking dramatically different this is basically the former Barton 10 running at the same frequency.
- skylink (yellow) – Leicester to Derby via Loughborough and EMA every 20 minutes – Kinchbus. If there has been one area of outstanding development it is this route. Formed from the seeds of Barton 3 and CountyLink 144, skylink has developed into a 20 minute frequency Leicester to Derby core route with an all night hourly timetable too.
- sprint – Loughborough Train Station to University via Town Centre every 10 minutes – Kinchbus. This route did not exist in 1986 even though the University did. Much innovation has taken place up to the current time where the frequency is now up to every 10 minutes overall and every 5 minutes within the campus.

▲ The 29 October 2017 skylink Leicester to Derby daytime frequency timetable extract.

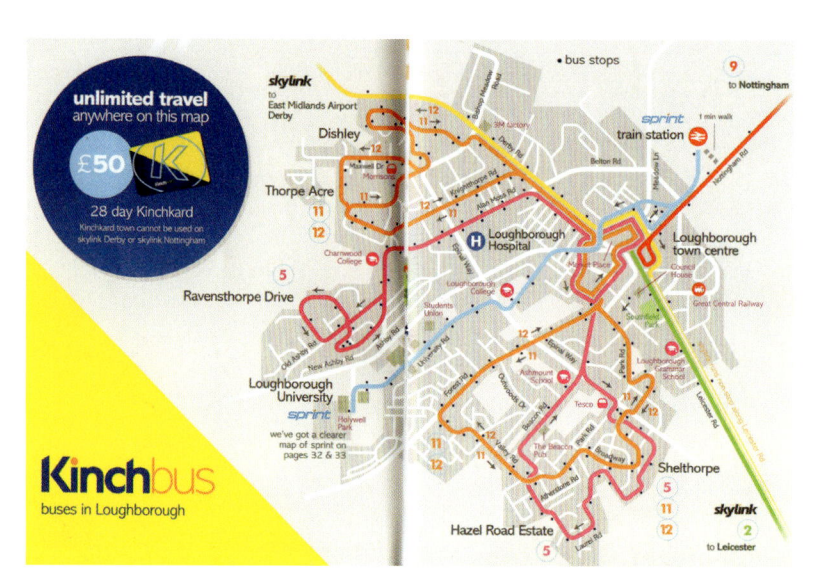

▲ The current Kinchbus Loughborough Town Map in May 2018.

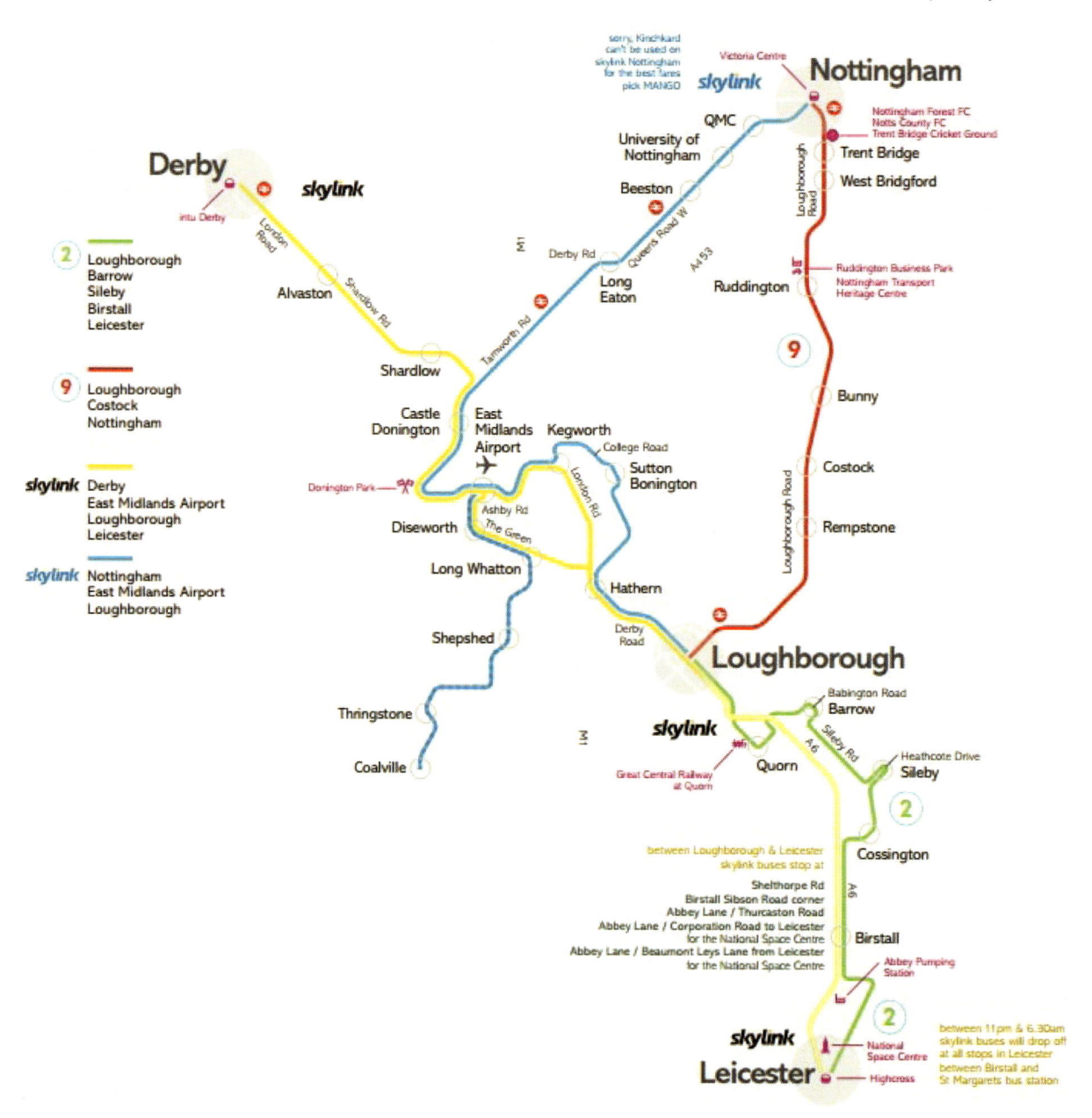

▲ The current Kinchbus skylink map in May 2018.

Chapter 7
The current scene

NCT Enviro 400 YN15 EJE branded for South Notts is seen leaving Loughborough for Nottingham on service 1 on 4 April 2018. Behind the bus can be seen the listed Beacon Bingo building which opened as an Odeon cinema on 21 November 1936.

Mercedes Citaros now form the Kinchbus allocation for route 2, Loughborough to Leicester via Sileby. Here we see 905, BN09 FWY, loading for Leicester in Baxtergate, Loughborough on 4 April 2018. The other four Citaros forming the requirement of five buses are 901, 903, 904 & 906.

Kinchbus allocate two Solos to route 5. Seen here is 478, FJ09 MWD, approaching the Browns Lane bus stop for Hazel Road Estate on 4 April 2018. In the background is Queens Park in which the Carillon Tower is situated.

Loughborough's Buses | *The deregulated years*

43

▶ Route 8, Loughborough to Grantham via Melton Mowbray, used to require three buses to operate it. This was changed during 2017 when buses only operated through to Grantham every 2 hours with a change required at Melton Mowbray on the opposite 2 hours. This enabled Centrebus to link the Melton Mowbray to Nottingham route 19 with that from Grantham following the closure of their Saxby depot. Here we see Enviro YX63 LGJ loading at Loughborough, Baxtergate for Melton Mowbray on 23 January 2018.

▶ A crowd queuing to board the 1045 hrs Kinchbus 9 from Loughborough Baxtergate to Nottingham on 4 April 2018. Kinchbus Solar FJ03 VWG is one of three required for the route.

▶ Kinchbus run four Tempos, 319-322, on the core Town Services 11 and 12. Here is 320, YJ07 VSV, loading at the Swan Street bus stop on route 12 on 4 April 2018.

◀

Routes 3 and 13 interwork as a one bus working by Paul S Winson. Here, Enviro WW13 PSW, is seen loading in Baxtergate for service 13 to Tuckers Road on 4 April 2018.

◀

Arriva's hourly 16, Coalville to Loughborough, is a two bus working from Coalville outstation. Here is VDL/Wright 4770, FJ06 ZRP waiting to turn left out of Baxtergate on to the new Inner Relief Road on 4 April 2018 before heading back to Coalville.

◀

Roberts Coaches operate tendered route 27 between Thurmaston and Loughborough. It is a two bus working on a 75 minute frequency. Streetlite MX12 DYY is seen here passing Loughborough Station on the 0930 hrs from Loughborough to Thurmaston on 4 April 2018. In the background can be seen the 3M Health Care building.

Loughborough's Buses | *The deregulated years*

45

Paul S Winson Volvo ALX400, X16 PSW, is seen at Baxtergate, Loughborough waiting to operate the return trip of the Thursday only 120X to Markfield on 30 March 2017.

Waiting for time on Loughborough, High Street is Arriva 4750, FJ06 ZSV, a VDL/Wright of Thurmaston garage. It is operating service 127 from Leicester to Shepshed on 4 April 2018 (despite the Christmas tree still in situation!). Service 127 is a major trunk route operating every 15 minutes off peak and increasing to every 12 minutes during peak hours.

Between Loughborough and Leicester the Arriva trunk 127 runs via Quorn, Mountsorrel and Rothley. Here, 4751, FJ06 ZSW, another VDL/Wright of Thurmaston garage picks up at Rothley, Green for Leicester on 4 April 2018.

Service 129 between Ashby-de-la-Zouch and Loughborough is a Leicestershire contracted route and is currently operated by Paul S Winson. Here Enviro XX13 PSW is seen arriving in Loughborough, Bedford Square on the 1133 hrs from Ashby on 4 April 2018. The 129 offers five journeys each way and serves the villages of Belton, Osgathorpe and Newbold in between.

Centrebus 154 provides the hourly link between Loughborough and Leicester via the Charnwood Forest villages of Woodhouse Eaves, Swithland and Cropston. Here is Versa767, YJ57 XWD, of the Centrebus Leicester fleet passing through Woodhouse Eaves on 4 April 2018. The route requires two buses to maintain the hourly frequency.

The 'blue' skylink is operated by trent barton from its Nottingham depot and Loughborough outstation. Its origins come from the Barton 10 route and the frequency into Loughborough is still hourly and still via Sutton Bonington. Between East Midlands Airport and Nottingham however the frequency steps up to every 20 minutes and it is joined by the leg from Coalville and Shepshed. Here is new Enviro YX67 VEY at its Loughborough terminus stop on Swan Street on 4 April 2018.

Loughborough's Buses | *The deregulated years*

47

The 'yellow' skylink is operated by Kinchbus and has a requirement of eleven buses to maintain the 20 minute frequency between Leicester and Derby. Three more new Citaros have just joined the original eight '64' registered ones. BF67 WHN represents one of the new order and is seen here pulling out of Baxtergate, Loughborough on its way to East Midlands Airport and Derby on 4 April 2018.

Sprint runs every 10 minutes from Loughborough Station to the University and requires seven of these slim line Solos. Here is number 6, YJ07 EFW, on layover at Loughborough Station on 4 April 2018.

Sprint Solo YJ07 EFW again on 4 April 2018, as it is leaving Loughborough Station via its dedicated bus lane and barrier which gets the bus to the front of the queue of cars exiting the station car park (especially after a London train arrival). In the background can be seen the Station and the Brush works.

It has taken nearly 32 years of deregulation to get to today's network. As can be seen from above text in almost every case the routes are better now than they were in 1986, some dramatically so. There is very little in the way of tendered services now remaining, just the 3, 13, 27, 120X & 129 with all other routes running commercially. Loughborough has seen turbulent times to get to today's position but it can now boast an excellent bus network provided by good quality operators who have not been afraid to invest.

Chapter 8

SCHEDULE OF ROUTES REGISTERED IN LOUGHBOROUGH
in the Special Edition of Notices & Proceedings dated 31 March 1986
to take effect at Deregulation Day on 26 October 1986

Table 1

Operator	Lic. No.	Reg'n No.	Route No.	Details	Days
Barton Transport plc	PE35	PE/0154/35	130, 140	Melton Mowbray to Loughborough	M-S
Barton Transport plc	PE35	PE/0138/35	3	Nottingham to Loughborough via Diseworth	M-S
Barton Transport plc	PE35	PE/0150/35	3c	Nottingham to Melbourne	M-S
Barton Transport plc	PE35	PE/0159/35	11	Nottingham to Coalville via Shepshed	M-S
Barton Transport plc	PE35	PE/0158/35	310	Nottingham to Loughborough via Kegworth	Su
Barton Transport plc	PE35	PE/0145/35	10	Nottingham to Loughborough via Kegworth	M-S
Butlers Coaches Ltd	PE69	PE/0332/69		Willoughby to Loughborough Grammar School	sch
Butlers Coaches Ltd	PE69	PE/0331/69		L'boro Warwick Way to L'boro St Mary's School	sch
County Travel (Leicester Ltd) #	PE96	PE/0802/96	121-124	L'boro - Leicester - Kibworth Beauchamp	D
Housden Caldwell Coaches Ltd*	PE189	PE/0562/189		Shepshed to Leicester City Football Ground	football
Housden Caldwell Coaches Ltd*	PE189	PE/0563/189		Coalville to Quorn Mills via Loughborough	M-F
Housden Caldwell Coaches Ltd*	PE189	PE/0616/189		Loughborough to Sileby	M-S
Housden Caldwell Coaches Ltd*	PE189	PE/0957/189		Coalville to Mablethorpe via Loughborough	summer
Kinch, Gilbert Kenneth	PE214	PE/1109/214	2	Leicester to Barrow	M-F
Kinch, Gilbert Kenneth	PE214	PE/1114/214	LW2	Loughborough to Barrow	M-F
Kinch, Gilbert Kenneth	PE214	PE/1115/214	1	Barrow to Leicester	M-F
Kinch, Gilbert Kenneth	PE214	PE/1190/214	PS1	Loughborough to Leicester via Mountsorrel	M-F
Kinch, Gilbert Kenneth	PE214	PE/1189/214	LW1	Sileby to Loughborough	M-F
Leicester City Transport #	PE225	PE/0304/225	121-124	L'boro - Leicester - Kibworth Beauchamp	D
Massey, GH	PE248	PE/0088/248		Kirkby Muxloe to L'boro Fairfield School	sch
Midland Fox Ltd	PE491	PE/0333/491	X67, 120	Leicester to Loughborough via Sileby	D
Midland Fox Ltd	PE491	PE/0515/491	128	Coalville to Nottingham via Shepshed & L'boro	M-S
Midland Fox Ltd	PE491	PE/0511/491	125-7	Leicester to Coalville via L'boro & Shepshed	D
Midland Fox Ltd	PE491	PE/0938/491	X61	Nottingham to Oadby via L'boro & Leicester	D
Midland Fox Ltd	PE491	PE 0664/491	X61	Oadby to Northampton via Market Harborough	D
Silverdale Tours (Nottm) Ltd	PE340	PE0430/340	1, 2	Tollerton/Ruddington - L'boro High School	sch
South Notts Bus Co Ltd	PE364	PE/0090/364		Nottingham to Loughborough via Gotham	D
Trent Motor Traction Co Ltd	PE392	PE/0315/392	3, 3A	L'boro Swan St - L'boro Swan St via Station	M-S
Trent Motor Traction Co Ltd	PE392	PE/0316/392	6	L'boro to Leicester via Barrow & Sileby	M-S
Trent Motor Traction Co Ltd	PE392	PE/0319/392	5	L'boro Swan St - L'boro Swan St via Dishley Est	M-S
Trent Motor Traction Co Ltd	PE392	PE/0323/392	4	L'boro Swan St - L'boro High St via Shelthorpe	M-S
Trent Motor Traction Co Ltd	PE392	PE/0437/392	1, 2, 2A	L'boro Swan St - L'boro Swan St via Maxwell Drive	M-S
Trent Motor Traction Co Ltd	PE392	PE/0690/392	125-127	Leicester to Coalville via L'boro & Shepshed	D
United Counties Omnibus Co Ltd	PE394	PE/0701/394	X61	Leicester to Nottingham via L'boro	D
West Rushcliffe Parish Opg Grp	PE789	PE/0746/789		East Leake to L'boro	sch & Th

* - trading as Tourmaster
# - joint

KINCHBUS ROUTES AT TAKEOVER DATE BY WELLGLADE LTD

Table 2

Route No.	Description	PVR	Type(s)
2	Loughborough - Sileby - Leicester	7	Titan, LN2, Dart
3	Tynedale Road - Town - Bishop Meadow Ind Est	2	Merc 709D
4	Shepshed Sprinter	2	Merc Vario
5	Hazel Road Est - Town - Ravensthorpe Drive	2	Merc Vario
7	University Shuttle	1	Merc 709D
8	Melton Mowbray - Loughborough	1	Merc 709D
10	Town - Thorpe Acre	1	Merc 709D
10/11	Leicester Inner Circle	6	Merc 709D
11/12	Thorpe Acre - Town - Shelthorpe	4	Dart SLF
12x	Thorpe Acre - Town - Shelthorpe (PSW shadow)	2	Dart
121-4	Leicester - Loughborough - Derby	1	Merc 811D
121-4	Leicester - Loughborough	1	Dart
126/7	Leicester - Loughborough - Shepshed	2	Excel
Vale Runner	Vale of Belvoir villages - Melton Mowbray	2	Merc 709D
Rutland Flyer	Melton Mowbray - Oakham - Corby	2	Merc Vario
Access	Access bus contracts	1	LN2 with lift
Dial-a-Ride	Dial-a-Ride contract in Leicester	1	Iveco 59/10
S174	schools	1	SD
S175	schools	1	SD
S41/S49am, S41/S49 pm	schools	1	DD
S45/S485am, S45/S485 pm	schools	1	SD with seatbelts
S302/S40am, S302?S484 pm	schools	1	DD
S193am, S40/S193 pm	schools	1	DD
S42/S484am, S42 pm	schools	1	DD
S301am, S301pm	schools	1	SD with seatbelts
S46am, S46pm	schools	1	DD
S4 am, S4pm	schools	1	DD
		48	

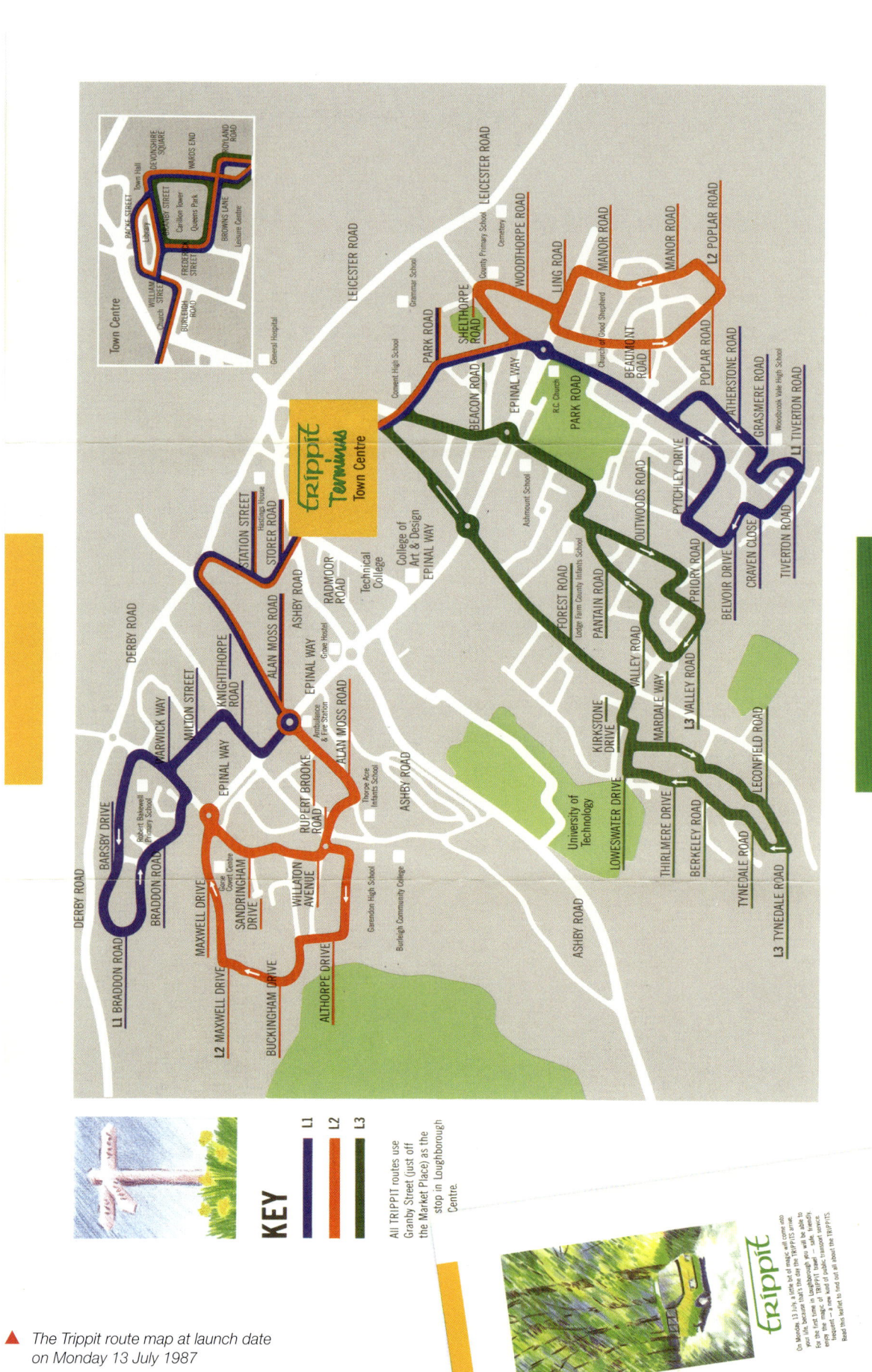

▲ *The Trippit route map at launch date on Monday 13 July 1987*

52

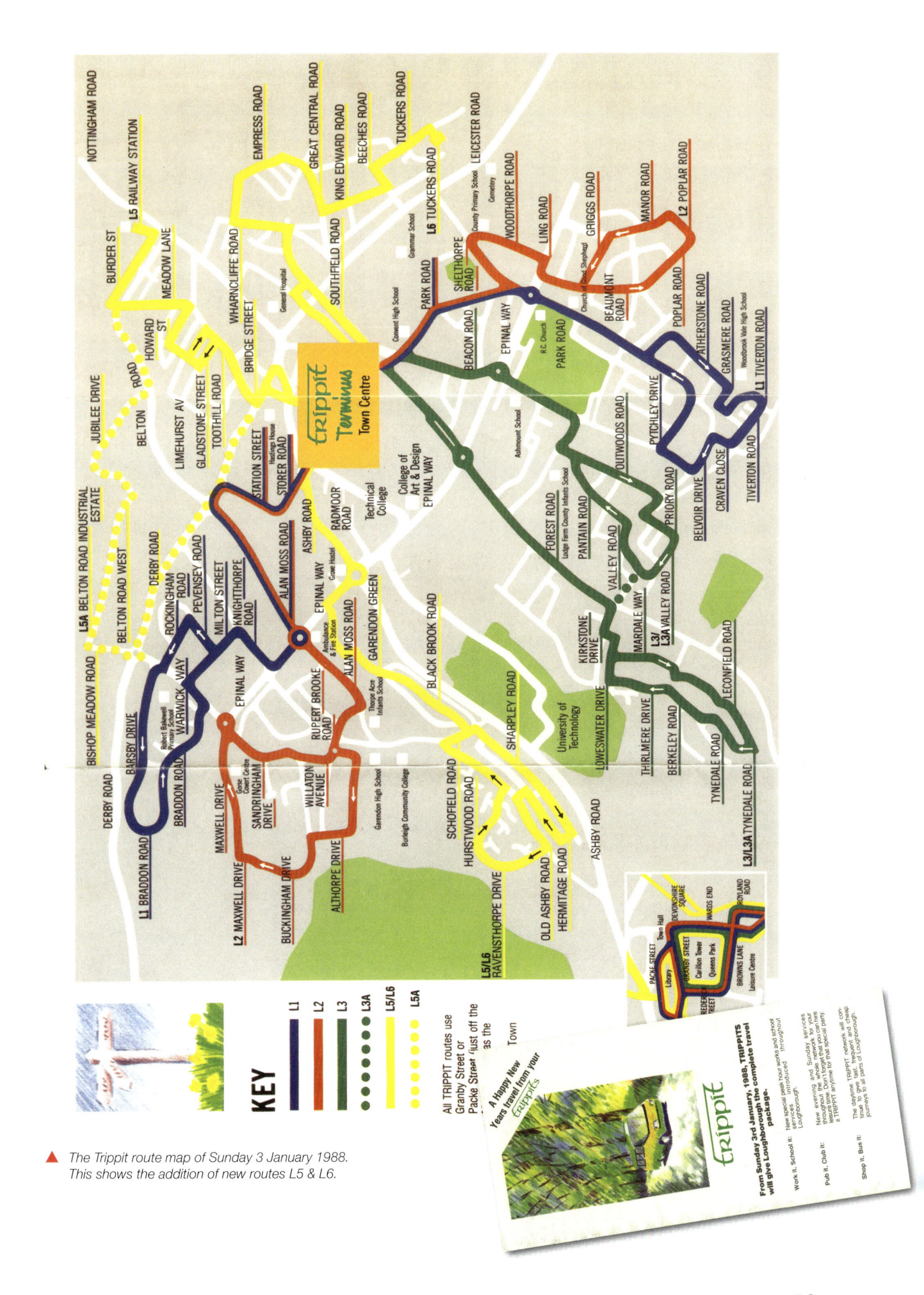

▲ The Trippit route map of Sunday 3 January 1988. This shows the addition of new routes L5 & L6.

Loughborough's Buses | *The deregulated years*

53

▲ *The Trippit route map of Sunday 1 May 1988*

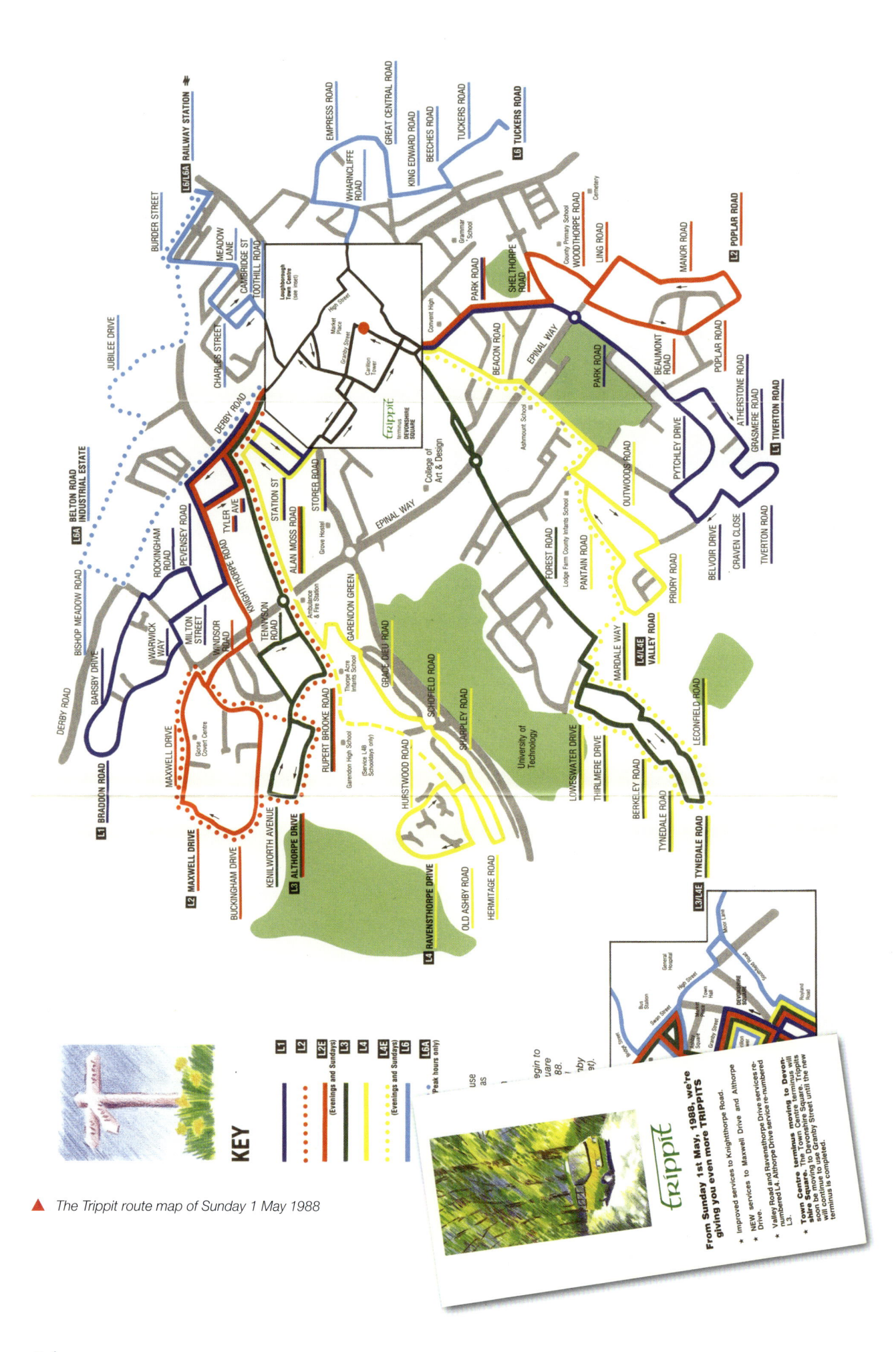

Ashby → Loughborough → Nottingham

CountyLink 7, 8

Monday to Saturday

Code:			NS	SO		NS	SO	NS	NS	NS	SO	
Service No:		7	7	7	8	7	7	7	7	7	7	7
Ashby Market Street	—	—	9.10	10.40	—	1.40	1.40	—	—	—	4.40	6.20
Coleorton	—	—	9.20	10.50	—	1.50	1.50	—	—	—	4.50	6.30
Peggs Green	—	9.23	9.23	10.53	—	1.53	1.53	—	—	—	4.53	6.33
Newbold	—	9.27	9.27	10.57	—	1.57	1.57	—	—	—	4.57	6.37
Worthington	—	9.30	9.30	11.00	—	2.00	2.00	—	—	—	5.00	6.40
Osgathorpe	7.15	9.38	9.38	11.08	—	2.08	2.08	—	—	—	5.08	6.48
Belton	7.22	9.45	9.45	11.15	—	2.15	2.15	—	—	—	5.15	6.55
Shepshed, Bull Ring	7.32	9.55	9.55	11.25	—	2.25	2.25	—	—	—	5.25	7.05
Nanpantan	7.42	10.02	10.02	11.32	1.02	2.32	2.32	—	4.32	—	5.32	7.12
Loughborough, Granby St. arr.	7.55	10.12	10.12	11.42	1.12	2.42	2.42	—	4.42	—	5.42	7.22
dep.	—	10.15	10.15	11.45	1.15	2.45	2.45	4.10	5.05	5.45	5.45	—
Cotes	—	10.23	10.23	11.53	1.23	2.53	2.53	4.18	5.13	5.53	5.53	—
Hoton	—	10.28	10.28	11.58	1.28	2.58	2.58	4.23	5.18	5.58	5.58	—
Wymeswold	—	—	—	12.03	—	3.03	—	4.28	5.23	6.03	6.03	—
Burton-on-the-Wolds	—	10.32	10.32	12.08	1.32	3.08	3.02	4.33	5.28	6.08	6.08	—
Walton-on-the-Wolds	—	—	—	12.13	—	—	—	4.38	—	6.13	6.13	—
Seagrave	—	—	—	12.20	—	—	—	—	—	—	—	—
Wymeswold	—	10.38	10.38	—	1.38	—	3.08	—	—	—	—	—
Wysall	—	10.43	10.43	—	1.43	—	3.13	—	—	—	—	—
Keyworth, Church	—	10.52	10.52	—	1.52	—	3.22	—	—	—	—	—
Plumtree	—	10.57	10.57	—	1.57	—	3.27	—	—	—	—	—
Nottingham, Victoria Bus Stn.	—	11.15	11.15	—	2.15	—	3.45	—	—	—	—	—

Code: NS – Not Saturdays   SO – Saturdays only.
Sorry, there is no Sunday service on this route.
Morning times shown in light type   **Afternoon and Evening times shown in bold type**

Nottingham → Loughborough → Ashby

CountyLink 7, 8

Monday to Saturday

Code:			NS	SO	SO	NS			C	NS	SO	NS	NSX	SO	X
Service No:		7	7	7	7	7	8	7	8	7	7	7	7	7	7
Nottingham Victoria Bus Stn.	—	—	—	—	—	—	11.35	—	2.35	2.35	—	—	4.15	—
Plumtree	—	—	—	—	—	—	11.51	—	2.51	2.51	—	—	4.31	—
Keyworth, Church	—	—	—	—	—	—	11.56	—	2.56	2.56	—	—	4.36	—
Wysall	—	—	—	—	—	—	12.05	—	3.05	3.05	—	—	4.45	—
Wymeswold	—	6.55	—	—	—	—	12.10	—	3.10	3.10	—	—	4.50	—
Seagrave	—	—	—	—	—	—	8.58	—	12.23	—	—	—	—	—	—
Walton-on-the-Wolds	—	—	7.33	7.33	—	8.30	9.05	—	12.28	—	—	—	4.40	—	6.15
Burton-on-the-Wolds	—	7.01	7.38	7.38	8.14	8.35	9.10	12.16	12.33	3.16	3.16	—	—	4.56	—
Wymeswold	—	—	7.43	7.43	8.19	8.40	9.15	—	—	—	—	—	—	—	—
Hoton	—	7.05	7.48	7.48	8.24	8.45	9.20	12.20	—	3.20	3.20	—	—	5.00	—
Cotes	—	7.10	7.53	7.53	8.29	8.50	9.25	12.25	12.40	3.25	3.25	—	—	5.05	—
Loughborough, Granby St. arr.	—	7.18	8.01	8.01	8.37	8.58	9.33	12.33	12.48	3.33	3.33	—	4.58	5.13	6.33
dep.	6.45	—	—	8.05	—	—	9.35	12.35	—	—	3.35	4.15	5.15	5.15	—
Nanpantan	6.55	—	—	8.15	—	—	9.45	12.45	—	—	3.45	4.25	5.25	5.25	—
Shepshed, Bull Ring	7.02	—	—	8.22	—	—	9.52	12.52	—	—	3.52	—	—	5.32	—
Belton	—	—	—	8.32	—	—	10.02	1.02	—	—	4.02	—	—	5.42	—
Osgathorpe	7.14	—	—	8.39	—	—	10.09	1.09	—	—	4.09	—	—	5.49	—
Worthington	—	—	—	8.47	—	—	10.17	1.17	—	—	4.17	—	—	5.57	—
Newbold	—	—	—	8.50	—	—	10.20	1.20	—	—	4.20	—	—	6.00	—
Peggs Green	—	—	—	8.54	—	—	10.24	1.24	—	—	4.24	—	—	6.04	—
Coleorton	—	—	—	8.57	—	—	10.27	1.27	—	—	4.27	—	—	6.07	—
Ashby, Market Street	—	—	—	9.07	—	—	10.37	1.37	—	—	4.37	—	—	6.17	—

Code: C – From Burton this journey operates via Cotes Mill instead of Hoton and Cotes.   NS – Not Saturdays.
X – These journeys operate from Walton via the A60 to Loughborough.   *Sorry, there is no Sunday service*
Morning times shown in light type   **Afternoon and Evening times shown in bold type**

▶ *The new CountyLink 7 & 8 timetable from Monday 4 January 1988. This was operated by Loughborough Coach & Bus and was to run until 4 April when it would be expanded even further.*

New bus services 7, 8

Ashby de la Zouch
Loughborough
The Wolds
Nottingham

CountyLink

Loughborough Coach and Bus

Starting on Monday 4th January 1988

Loughborough's Buses | *The deregulated years*

Ashby→Loughborough→Nottingham (137)
Loughborough→Melton Mowbray→Oakham→Stamford (138)

COUNTY LINK 137, 138

Monday to Saturday

Code:	NS				NS	SO	X	X		Sch	Sch		NS	SO		A	NS	NS	SO
Service No:	138	138	137	138	137	137	138	137	138	138	137	138	137	137	138	138	137	137	137
Ashby, Market Street	—	—	—	—	—	9.10	10.40	—	—	—	—	—	—	1.40	1.40	—	—	—	4.40
Coleorton	—	—	—	—	—	9.20	10.50	—	—	—	—	—	—	1.50	1.50	—	—	—	4.50
Peggs Green	—	—	—	—	9.23	9.23	10.53	—	—	—	—	—	—	1.53	1.53	—	—	—	4.53
Newbold	—	—	—	—	9.27	9.27	10.57	—	—	—	—	—	—	1.57	1.57	—	—	—	4.57
Worthington	—	—	—	—	9.30	9.30	11.00	—	—	—	—	—	—	2.00	2.00	—	—	—	5.00
Osgathorpe	—	—	7.18	—	9.38	9.38	11.08	—	—	—	—	—	—	2.08	2.08	—	—	—	5.08
Belton	—	—	7.25	—	9.45	9.45	11.15	—	—	—	—	—	—	2.15	2.15	—	—	—	5.15
Shepshed, Bull Ring	—	—	7.35	—	9.55	9.55	11.25	—	—	—	—	—	—	2.25	2.25	—	—	—	5.25
Nanpantan	—	—	7.42	—	10.02	10.02	11.32	—	1.02	—	—	—	—	2.32	2.32	—	4.22	—	5.32
Loughborough, Granby St.	—	6.30	7.52	8.45	10.15	10.15	11.42	11.45	1.15	—	—	2.00	2.42	2.45	—	4.35	5.05	5.45	5.45
Cotes	—	6.38	—	8.53	10.23	10.23	—	11.53	1.23	—	—	2.08	—	2.53	—	4.43	5.13	5.53	5.53
Hoton	—	6.43	—	8.58	10.28	10.28	—	11.58	1.28	—	—	2.13	—	2.58	—	4.48	5.18	5.58	5.58
Wymeswold	—	6.48	—	9.03	—	—	—	12.03	—	—	—	2.18	—	—	—	4.53	5.23	6.03	6.03
Burton on the Wolds	—	6.53	—	9.08	10.33	10.33	—	12.08	1.33	—	—	2.23	—	3.03	—	4.58	5.28	6.08	6.08
Wymeswold	—	—	—	—	10.38	10.38	—	—	1.38	—	—	—	—	3.08	—	—	—	—	—
Wysall	—	—	—	—	10.43	10.43	—	—	1.43	—	—	—	—	3.13	—	—	—	—	—
Keyworth, Church	—	—	—	—	10.52	10.52	—	—	1.52	—	—	—	—	3.22	—	—	—	—	—
Nottingham, Victoria	—	—	—	—	11.15	11.15	—	—	2.15	—	—	—	—	3.45	—	—	—	—	—
Walton on the Wolds	—	6.58	—	9.13	—	—	—	12.13	—	—	—	2.28	—	—	—	5.03	—	6.13	6.13
Seagrave	—	7.05	—	9.20	—	—	—	12.20	—	—	—	2.35	—	—	—	5.10	—	—	—
Thrussington	—	7.10	—	9.25	—	—	—	12.25	—	—	—	2.40	—	—	—	5.15	—	—	—
Hoby	—	7.15	—	9.30	—	—	—	12.30	—	—	—	2.45	—	—	—	5.20	—	—	—
Asfordby	—	7.20	—	9.35	—	—	—	12.35	—	—	—	2.50	—	—	—	5.25	—	—	—
Melton Mowbray, Bus Stn.	—	7.35	—	9.50	—	—	—	12.50	—	—	—	3.05	—	—	—	5.40	—	—	—
Burton Lazars	—	7.40	—	9.55	—	—	—	12.55	—	—	—	3.10	—	—	—	5.45	—	—	—
Whissendine	—	7.48	—	10.03	—	—	—	1.03	—	—	—	3.18	—	—	—	5.53	—	—	—
Ashwell	—	7.55	—	10.10	—	—	—	1.10	—	—	—	3.25	—	—	—	6.00	—	—	—
Langham	—	8.05	—	10.20	—	—	—	1.20	—	—	—	3.35	—	—	—	6.10	—	—	—
Oakham, John Street	—	8.10	—	10.25	—	—	—	1.25	—	—	—	3.40	—	—	5.00	6.15	—	—	—
Empingham	—	8.25	—	10.40	—	—	—	1.40	—	—	—	3.55	—	—	5.15	6.30	—	—	—
Great Casterton	8.02	8.32	—	10.47	—	—	—	1.47	—	3.35	3.55	4.02	—	—	5.22	6.37	—	—	—
Stamford, Bus Station	8.10	8.40	—	10.55	—	—	—	1.55	—	3.43	4.03	4.10	—	—	5.30	6.45	—	—	—

Code: A – The journey between Nanpantan and Loughborough does not operate on Saturday. NS – Not Saturday. SO – Saturday only.
Sch – Schooldays only. X – These journeys operated by the same bus, through fares available. Sorry, there are no Sunday services on these routes.

Morning times shown in light type. Afternoon and evening times shown in bold type.

Nottingham→Loughborough→Ashby (137)
Stamford→Oakham→Melton Mowbray→Loughborough (138)

COUNTY LINK 137, 138

Monday to Saturday

Code:			NS	SO			Sch	Sch				NS	SO	A	NS	SO		
Service No:	137	137	137	137	138	137	138	138	138	137	138	137	137	138	137	137	138	138
Stamford, Bus Station	—	—	—	—	6.30	—	7.52	8.12	8.45	—	11.45	—	—	2.00	—	—	4.15	5.45
Great Casterton	—	—	—	—	6.38	—	8.00	8.20	8.53	—	11.53	—	—	2.08	—	—	4.23	5.53
Empingham	—	—	—	—	6.45	—	—	9.00	—	—	12.00	—	—	2.15	—	—	4.30	6.00
Oakham, John Street	—	—	—	—	7.00	—	—	9.15	—	—	12.15	—	—	2.30	—	—	4.45	6.15
Langham	—	—	—	—	7.05	—	—	9.20	—	—	12.20	—	—	2.35	—	—	—	6.20
Ashwell	—	—	—	—	7.15	—	—	9.30	—	—	12.30	—	—	2.45	—	—	—	6.30
Whissendine	—	—	—	—	7.22	—	—	9.37	—	—	12.37	—	—	2.52	—	—	—	6.37
Burton Lazars	—	—	—	—	7.30	—	—	9.45	—	—	12.45	—	—	3.00	—	—	—	6.45
Melton Mowbray, Bus Stn.	—	—	—	—	7.35	—	—	9.50	—	—	12.50	—	—	3.05	—	—	—	6.50
Asfordby	—	—	—	—	7.50	—	—	10.05	—	1.05	—	—	—	3.20	—	—	—	7.05
Hoby	—	—	—	—	7.55	—	—	10.10	—	1.10	—	—	—	3.25	—	—	—	7.10
Thrussington	—	—	—	—	8.00	—	—	10.15	—	1.15	—	—	—	3.30	—	—	—	7.15
Seagrave	—	—	—	—	8.05	—	—	10.20	—	1.20	—	—	—	3.35	—	—	—	7.20
Walton-on-the-Wolds	—	—	7.32	7.32	8.12	—	—	10.27	—	1.27	—	—	—	3.42	—	—	—	7.27
Nottingham, Victoria	—	—	—	—	—	—	—	—	—	—	11.25	—	2.25	2.25	—	—	4.10	—
Keyworth, Church	—	—	—	—	—	—	—	—	—	—	11.48	—	2.48	2.48	—	—	4.33	—
Wysall	—	—	—	—	—	—	—	—	—	—	11.57	—	2.57	2.57	—	—	4.42	—
Wymeswold	—	6.52	—	—	—	—	—	—	—	—	12.02	—	3.02	3.02	—	—	4.47	—
Burton-on-the-Wolds	—	6.57	7.37	7.37	8.17	9.02	—	10.32	12.07	1.32	12.07	3.07	3.07	3.47	—	4.52	—	7.32
Wymeswold	—	—	7.42	7.42	8.22	9.07	—	—	10.37	—	1.37	—	—	3.52	—	—	—	7.37
Hoton	—	7.02	7.47	7.47	8.27	9.12	—	10.42	12.12	1.42	12.17	3.12	3.12	3.57	—	4.57	—	7.42
Cotes	—	7.07	7.52	7.52	8.32	9.17	—	10.47	12.17	1.47	—	3.17	3.17	4.02	—	5.02	—	7.47
Loughborough, Granby St.	6.45	7.15	8.00	8.05	8.40	9.35	—	10.55	12.35	1.55	—	3.25	3.35	4.10	5.15	5.15	—	7.55
Nanpantan	6.55	—	—	8.15	—	9.45	—	—	12.45	—	—	—	3.45	4.20	5.25	5.25	—	—
Shepshed, Bull Ring	7.02	—	—	8.22	—	9.52	—	—	12.52	—	—	—	3.52	—	5.32	5.32	—	—
Belton	—	—	—	8.32	—	10.02	—	—	1.02	—	—	—	4.02	—	5.42	5.42	—	—
Osgathorpe	7.14	—	—	8.39	—	10.09	—	—	1.09	—	—	—	4.09	—	5.49	5.49	—	—
Worthington	—	—	—	8.47	—	10.17	—	—	1.17	—	—	—	4.17	—	5.57	5.57	—	—
Newbold	—	—	—	8.50	—	10.20	—	—	1.20	—	—	—	4.20	—	6.00	6.00	—	—
Peggs Green	—	—	—	8.54	—	10.24	—	—	1.24	—	—	—	4.24	—	6.04	6.04	—	—
Coleorton	—	—	—	8.57	—	10.27	—	—	1.27	—	—	—	4.27	—	—	—	—	—
Ashby, Market Street	—	—	—	9.07	—	10.37	—	—	1.37	—	—	—	4.37	—	—	—	—	—

Code: A – The journey between Loughborough and Nanpantan does not operate on Saturday. NS – Not Saturday. SO – Saturday only.
Sch – Schooldays only. Sorry, there are no Sunday services on these routes.

Morning times shown in light type. Afternoon and evening times shown in bold type.

▲ *The CountyLink 7 & 8 timetable was revised from 5 April 1988, renumbered to 137 & 138 and extended eastwards to Melton Mowbray, Oakham and Stamford a distance of 46 miles. This challenged incumbent operator Barton over the Oakham to Melton Mowbray section and also the Melton Mowbray to Loughborough section. This section was withdrawn by Barton just months later on 3 August.*

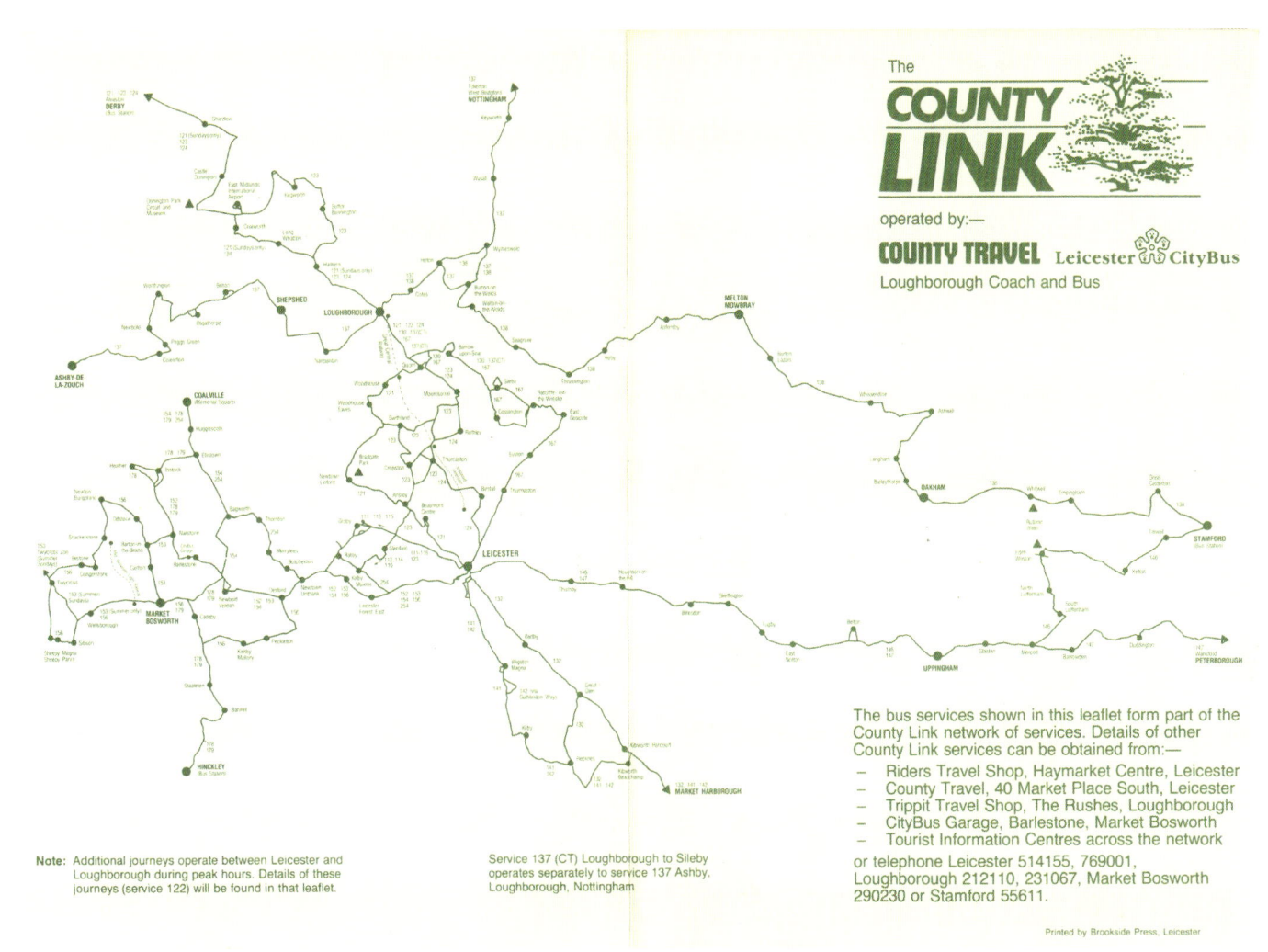

▲ The CountyLink network at its peak in mid 1988. Much of this was to come to an abrupt end on 28 November.

Loughborough's Buses | *The deregulated years*

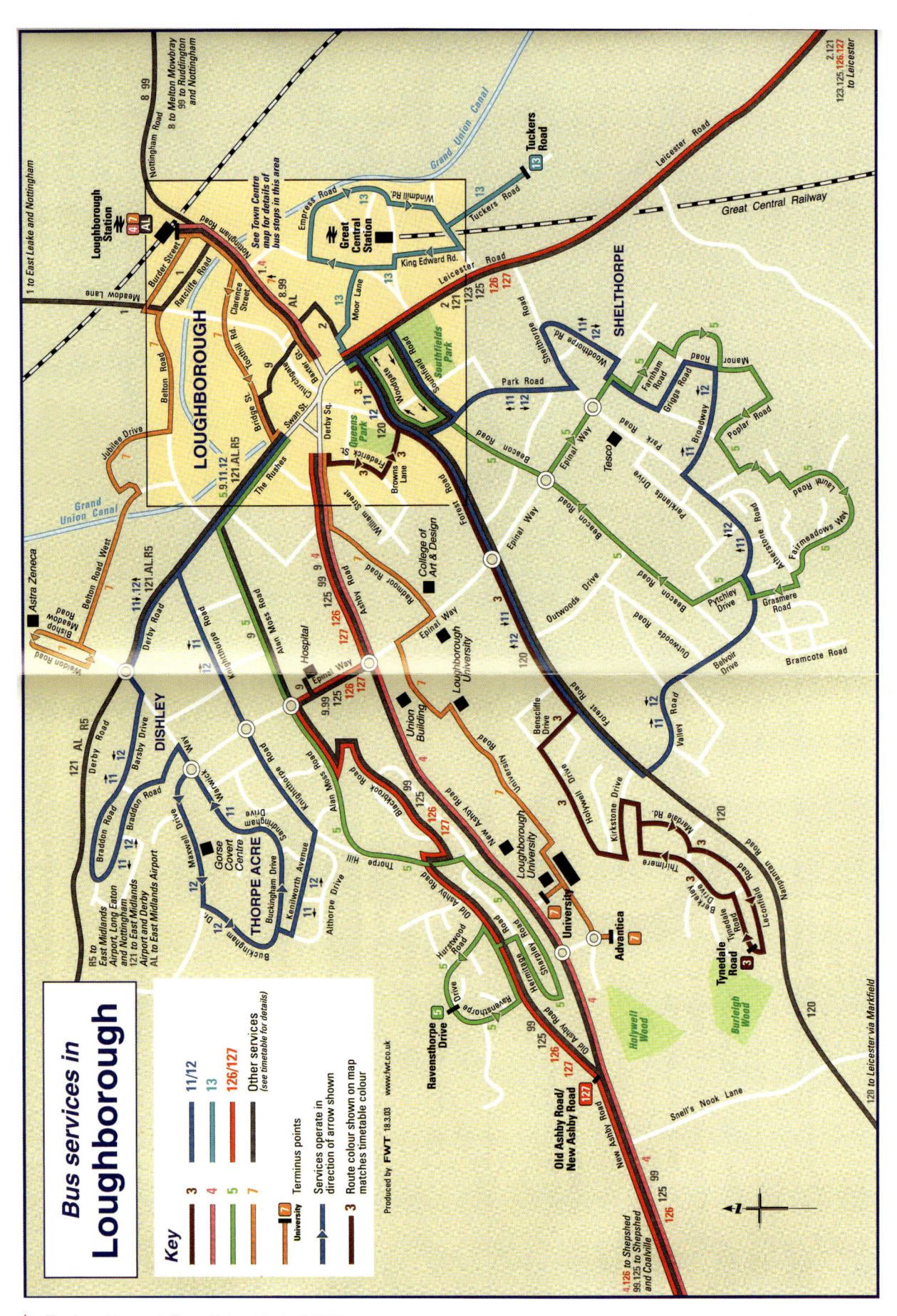

The Loughborough Town Network in April 2003

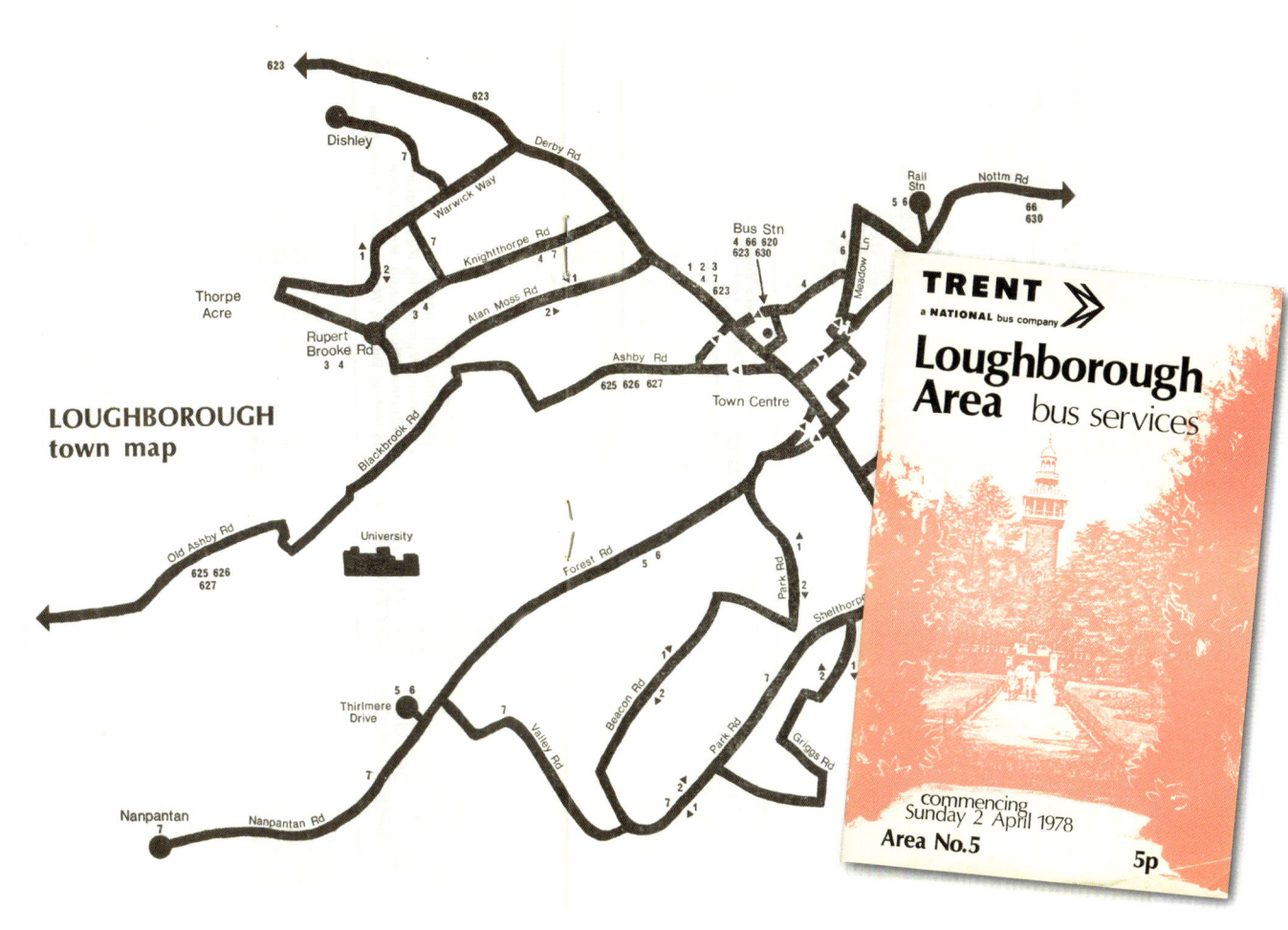

▲ The Trent Loughborough Town Network as at 2 April 1978.

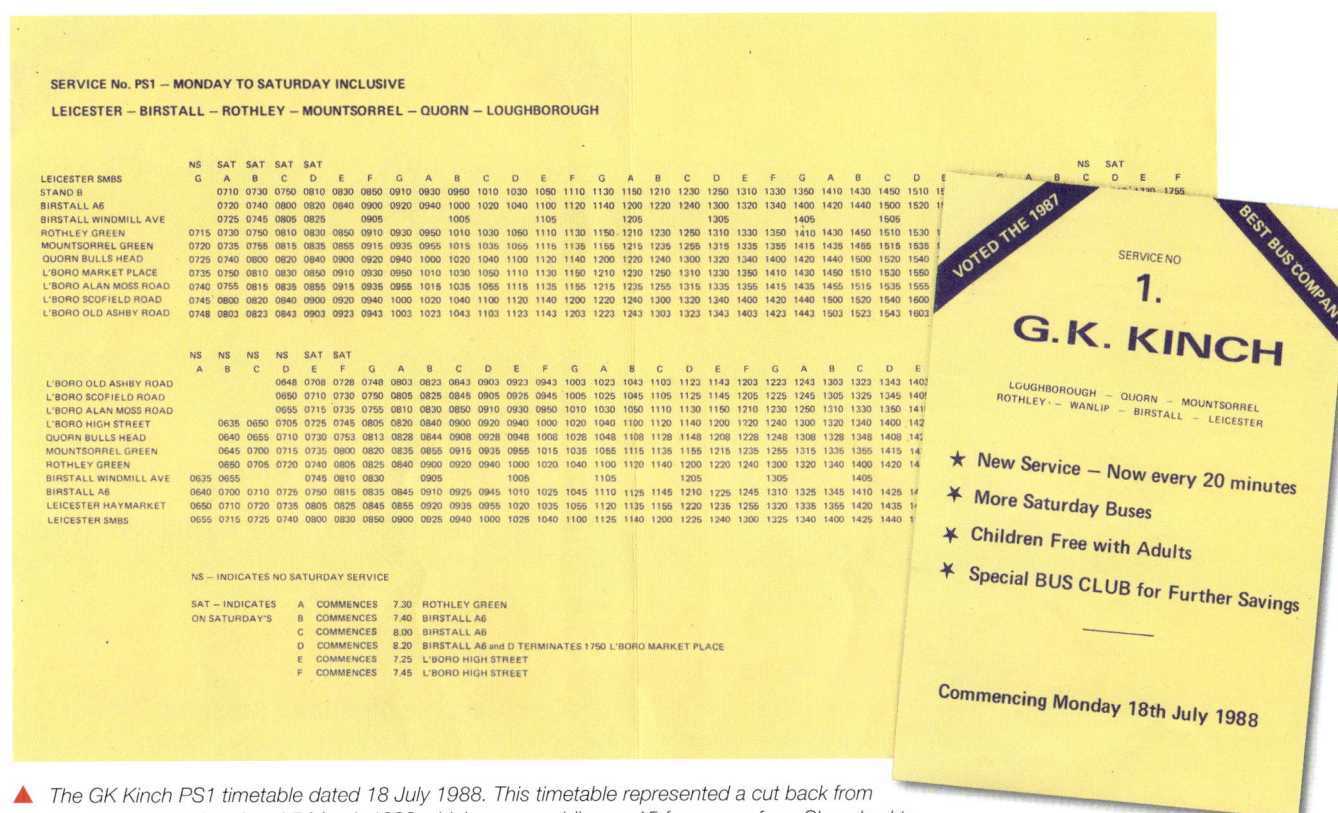

▲ The GK Kinch PS1 timetable dated 18 July 1988. This timetable represented a cut back from the previous version dated 7 March 1988 which was providing a x15 frequency from Shepshed to Leicester. This timetable saved 4 buses, requiring 7 instead of the previous 11. Each bus working, and indeed driver duty as they were the same, is shown by the letter A to G above each journey.

Loughborough's Buses | *The deregulated years*

BUS SERVICE between LOUGHBOROUGH, QUORN, BARROW and SILEBY

MONDAYS TO FRIDAYS

					§																			
LOUGHBOROUGH (Bus Stn)	Dep	0615	0645	0740	0820	0910	0950	1030	1110	1150	1230	1310	1350	1430	1500	1540	1630	1650	1740	1810	1900	2010	2130	2250
QUORN (Cross)	Dep	0625	0655	0750	0830	0920	1000	1040	1120	1200	1240	1320	1400	1440	1510	1550	1640	1700	1750	1820	1910	2020	2140	2300
BARROW (High St)	Dep	0631	0701	0756	0836	0926	1006	1046	1126	1206	1246	1326	1406	1446	1516	1556	1646	1706	1756	1826	1916	2026	2146	2306
BARROW (Babington Rd)	Dep	0633	0703	0758	0848	0928	1008	1048	1128	1208	1248	1328	1408	1448	1518	1558	1648	1708	1758	1828	1918	2028	2148	2308
BARROW (River View)	Dep	0636	0706	0801	0851	0931	1011	1051	1131	1211	1251	1331	1411	1451	1521	1601	1651	1711	1801	1831	1921	2031	2151	2311
SILEBY (Duke of York)	Dep	0640	0710	0805	0855	0935	1015	1055	1135	1215	1255	1335	1415	1455	1525	1605	1655	1715	1805	1835	1925	2035	2155	2315
SILEBY (Heathcote Dr V.G. Store)	Arr	0643	0713	0808	0858	0938	1018	1058	1138	1218	1258	1338	1418	1458	1528	1608	1658	1718	1808	1838	1928	2038	2158	2318

														§										
SILEBY (Heathcote Dr V.G. Store)	Dep	0645	0715	0810	0900	0940	1020	1100	1140	1220	1300	1340	1420	1500	1532	1608	1700	1720	1810	1840	1930	2040	2200	2320
SILEBY (Greedon Rise)	Dep	↓	↓	↓	↓	0944	↓	1104	↓	↓	1304	↓	1424	↓	↓	1612	↓	↓	↓	↓	↓	↓	↓	↓
SILEBY (Unity Hall)	Dep	0649	0719	0814	0904	0947	1024	1107	1144	1224	1307	1344	1427	1504	1536	1615	1704	1724	1814	1844	1934	2044	2204	2324
SILEBY (Duke of York)	Dep	0651	0721	0816	0906	0949	1026	1109	1146	1226	1309	1346	1429	1506	1538	1617	1706	1726	1816	1846	1936	2046	2206	2326
BARROW (River View)	Dep	0655	0725	0820	0910	0952	1030	1112	1150	1230	1312	1350	1432	1510	1542	1621	1710	1730	1820	1850	1940	2050	2210	2330
BARROW (Mill Lane)	Dep	0657	0727	0822	0912	0954	1032	1114	1152	1232	1314	1352	1434	1512	1544	1623	1712	1732	1822	1852	1942	2052	2212	2332
BARROW (Babington Rd)	Dep	0659	0729	0824	0914	0956	1034	1116	1154	1234	1316	1354	1436	1514	1546	1625	1714	1734			1944	2054	2214	2334
BARROW (High St)	Dep	0701	0731	0826	0916	0958	1036	1118	1156	1236	1318	1356	1438	1516	1556	1627	1716	1736						
QUORN (Bulls Head)	Dep	0707	0737	0832	0922	1003	1042	1123	1202	1242	1323	1402	1443	1522	1602	1633	1722	1742						
LOUGHBOROUGH (Bus Stn)	Arr	0720	0750	0845	0935	1015	1055	1135	1215	1255	1335	1415	1455	1535	1615	1645	1735	1755						

§ These journeys operate via Humphrey Perkins School on school days.

SATURDAYS

LOUGHBOROUGH (Bus Stn)	Dep	0700	0740	0820	0900	0940	1020	1100	1140	1220	1300	1340	1420	1500	1540	1620	1700	17
QUORN (Cross)	Dep	0710	0750	0830	0910	0950	1030	1110	1150	1230	1310	1350	1430	1510	1550	1630	1710	17
BARROW (High St)	Dep	0716	0756	0836	0916	0956	1036	1116	1156	1236	1316	1356	1436	1516	1556	1636	1716	17
BARROW (Babington Rd)	Dep	0718	0758	0838	0918	0958	1038	1118	1158	1238	1318	1358	1438	1518	1558	1638	1718	17
BARROW (River View)	Dep	0721	0801	0841	0921	1001	1041	1121	1201	1241	1321	1401	1441	1521	1601	1641	1721	17
SILEBY (Duke of York)	Dep	0725	0805	0845	0925	1005	1045	1125	1205	1245	1325	1405	1445	1525	1605	1645	1725	
SILEBY (Heathcote Dr V.G. Store)	Arr	0728	0808	0848	0928	1008	1048	1128	1208	1248	1328	1408	1448	1528	1608	1648	1728	

SILEBY (Heathcote Dr V.G. Store)	Dep	0730	0810	0850	0930	1010	1050	1130	1210	1250	1330	1410	1450	1530	1610	1650	1730	
SILEBY (Greedon Rise)	Dep	↓	↓	↓	↓	↓	↓	↓	↓	↓	↓	↓	↓	↓	↓	↓	↓	
SILEBY (Unity Hall)	Dep	0734	0814	0854	0934	1014	1054	1134	1214	1254	1334	1414	1454	1534	1614	1654	1734	
SILEBY (Duke of York)	Dep	0736	0816	0856	0936	1016	1056	1136	1216	1256	1336	1416	1456	1536	1616	1656	1736	
BARROW (River View)	Dep	0740	0820	0900	0940	1020	1100	1140	1220	1300	1340	1420	1500	1540	1620	1700	1740	
BARROW (Mill Lane)	Dep	0742	0822	0902	0942	1022	1102	1142	1222	1302	1342	1422	1502	1542	1622	1702	1742	
BARROW (Babington Rd)	Dep	0744	0824	0904	0944	1024	1104	1144	1224	1304	1344	1424	1504	1544	1624	1704	1744	
BARROW (High St)	Dep	0746	0826	0906	0946	1026	1106	1146	1226	1306	1346	1426	1506	1546	1626	1706	1746	
QUORN (Bulls Head)	Dep	0752	0832	0912	0952	1032	1112	1152	1232	1312	1352	1432	1512	1552	1632	1712	1752	
LOUGHBOROUGH (Bus Stn)	Arr	0805	0845	0925	1005	1045	1125	1205	1245	1325	1405	1445	1525	1605	1645	1725	1805	

The Company will make every effort to maintain these Services, and will accept no liability for loss, damage, injury or delay sustained by any pass... by reason of unpunctuality or failure to maintain these services.

▲ The 9 February 1987 Tourmaster timetable for the ex Howletts Sileby to Loughborough route.

Tourmaster COACHES

LOUGHBOROUGH, QUORN, BARROW and SILEBY BUS SERVICE

Revised Timetable
MONDAY, 9th FEBRUARY, 1987

Leicester FLYER — KINCHBUS
£2 day return
Faster... Cheaper... Friendlier... Direct...
from 14th October 2002
www.kinchbus.co.uk
Loughborough to Leicester EVERY HOUR

Loughborough - Leicester — Mondays to Saturdays

	NS	NS	S						
LOUGHBOROUGH (Ravensthorpe Drive)	6.50	7.30	7.45	8.40	9.45		45	3.45	4.50
Schofield Road	6.52	7.34	7.49	8.44	9.49		49	3.49	4.54
Epinal Way/Ashby Road	6.54	7.38	7.53	8.48	9.53	then	53	3.53	4.58
LOUGHBOROUGH (High Street, Argos, stop C)	7.00	7.45	8.00	9.00	10.00	every	00	4.00	5.05
Shelthorpe Road	7.03	7.48	8.03	9.03	10.03	hour	03	4.03	5.10
non stop via A6									
LEICESTER (St Margarets Bus Station)	7.25	8.25	8.25	9.25	10.25		25	4.25	5.35

Leicester - Loughborough

	NS							
LEICESTER (St Margarets Bus Station)	7.50	9.00		00		3.00	4.00	5.10	5.45
non stop via A6									
Shelthorpe Road	8.10	9.20	then	20		3.20	4.20	5.35	6.10
LOUGHBOROUGH (High Street, stop B)	8.25	9.30	every	30	until	3.30	4.35	5.40	6.15
Epinal Way/Ashby Road	8.30	9.35	hour	35		3.35	4.40	5.45	6.20
Schofield Road	8.35	9.40		40		3.40	4.45	5.50	6.25
LOUGHBOROUGH (Ravensthorpe Drive)	8.40	9.45		45		3.45	4.50	5.55	6.30

Code: NS - Not Saturdays   S - Saturdays only

▲ The Kinchbus 'Leicester Flyer' timetable introduced on 14 October 2002.

60

LOUGHBOROUGH → WOODHOUSE EAVES → ANSTEY → LEICESTER → KILBY → FLECKNEY   SERVICE 121

Monday to Saturday

Code:-		NS	S						C			t				
Loughborough (Bus Station)	—	0725	—	0825	0945	1045	1145	1245	1345	1445	—	1600	1645	1745	1845	1945	2135
Quorn Cross	—	0735	—	0835	0955	1055	1155	1255	1355	1455	—	1610	1655	1755	1855	1955	2145
Old Woodhouse	—	0739	—	0839	0959	1059	1159	1259	1359	1459	—	1614	1659	1759	1859	1959	2149
Woodhouse Eaves	—	0742	0742	0842	1002	1102	1202	1302	1402	1502	—	1617	1702	1802	1902	2002	2152
Swithland (Triangle)	—	0745	0745	0845	1005	1105	1205	1305	1405	1505	—	1620	1705	1805	1905	2005	2155
Newtown Linford (Bradgate)	—	0750	0750	0850	1010	1110	1210	1310	1410	1510	—	1625	1710	1810	1910	2010	2200
Anstey (Nook)	0700	0800	0800	0900	1020	1120	1220	1320	1420	1520	—	1635	1720	1820	1920	2020	2210
Leicester (St. Margarets) arr	0715	0815	0815	0915	1035	1135	1235	1335	1435	1535	—	1650	1735	1835	1935	2035	2225
dep	0720	—	0840	0940	1040	—	1240	—	1440	1540	1640	—	1740	—	—	—	—
Wigston (Royal Oak)	0732	—	0852	0952	1052	—	1252	—	1452	1552	1652	—	1752	—	—	—	—
Wigston Magna (Bank)	0737	—	0857	0957	1057	—	1257	—	1457	1557	1657	—	1757	—	—	—	—
Kilby Bridge	0742	—	0902	1002	1102	—	1302	—	1502	1602	1702	—	1802	—	—	—	—
Kilby Village	—	—	0907	—	1107	—	1307	—	1507	1607	1707	—	1807	—	—	—	—
Arnesby	0745	—	—	1005	—	—	—	—	—	—	—	—	—	—	—	—	—
Shearsby	0750	—	—	1010	—	—	—	—	—	—	—	—	—	—	—	—	—
Saddington Turn	0753	—	—	1013	—	—	—	—	—	—	—	—	—	—	—	—	—
Fleckney (Edward Road)	0755	—	0915	1015	1115	—	1315	—	1515	1615	1715	—	1815	—	—	—	—

FLECKNEY → KILBY → LEICESTER → ANSTEY → WOODHOUSE EAVES → LOUGHBOROUGH   SERVICE 121

Monday to Saturday

Code:		tNS	t		C					Sch.		C				
Fleckney (Edward Road)	—	—	0755	0915	1015	1115	—	1315	—	1515	1615	1715	1815	—	—
Saddington Turn	—	—	—	—	—	—	—	—	—	1517	—	—	1817	—	—
Shearsby	—	—	—	—	—	—	—	—	—	1520	—	—	1820	—	—
Arnesby	—	—	—	—	—	—	—	—	—	1525	—	—	1825	—	—
Kilby Village	—	—	0803	0923	1023	1123	—	1323	—	—	1623	1723	—	—	—
Kilby Bridge	—	—	0808	0928	1028	1128	—	1328	—	1528	1628	1728	1828	—	—
Wigston Magna (Bank)	—	—	0813	0933	1033	1133	—	1333	—	1533	1633	1733	1833	—	—
Wigston (Royal Oak)	—	—	0818	0938	1038	1138	—	1338	—	1538	1638	1738	1838	—	—
Leicester (St. Margarets) arr	—	—	0830	0950	1050	1150	—	1350	—	1550	1650	1750	1850	—	—
dep	0620	0720	0845	0955	1055	1155	1255	1355	1455	1555	1655	1755	1855	2045	2235
Anstey (Nook)	0635	0735	0900	1010	1110	1210	1310	1410	1510	1610	1710	1810	1910	2100	2250
Newtown Linford (Bradgate)	0645	0745	0910	1020	1120	1220	1320	1420	1520	1620	1720	1820	1920	2110	—
Swithland (Triangle)	0650	0750	0915	1025	1125	1225	1325	1425	1525	1625	1725	1825	1925	2115	—
Woodhouse Eaves	0653	0753	0918	1028	1128	1228	1328	1428	1528	1628	1728	1828	1928	2118	—
Old Woodhouse	0656	0756	0921	1031	1131	1231	1331	1431	1531	1631	1731	1831	1931		
Quorn (Cross)	0700	0800	0925	1035	1135	1235	1335	1435	1535	1635	1735	1835	1935		
Loughborough (Bus Station)	0710	0810	0935	1045	1145	1245	1345	1445	1545	1645	1745	1845	1945		

Code: t   — On Mondays to Fridays operates via Brush Works and Loughborough Station.
       C   — Passengers wishing to travel beyond Leicester should change buses at Leicester (St. Margarets).
       NS — Not Saturday   S — Saturday only.
       Sch. — This journey diverts in Quorn via Warwick Avenue and St. Bartholomews School on Schooldays.

▲ The new 9 May 1982 timetable for service 121, Loughborough to Fleckney via Leicester which was a joint operation between County Travel and Gibson Bros (now owned by Leicester CityBus). The brand name CountyLink which this route and a number of others would use had not yet been devised. It linked up the fragmented Woodhouse Eaves to Loughborough and Fleckney to Leicester routes of County Travel and now challenged Midland Red East on a number of fronts.

Loughborough's Buses | *The deregulated years*

Thank you...

A special thanks for the help in the preparation of this book to John Bennett for many of the archive photographs and press cuttings, Steve Smith for his Midland Fox and Loughborough Coach & Bus history and the Omnibus Society for the timetable library at Walsall.

Designed and printed by Trait.
Published October 2018

Master Organic Chemistry Reactions effortlessly with this comprehensive guide

Madison R. Wilson

All rights reserved. Copyright © 2023 Madison R. Wilson

Funny helpful tips:

Diversify your reading list; exposing yourself to various genres and cultures broadens your perspective.

Practice empathy; understanding others' perspectives enriches your worldview.

Master Organic Chemistry Reactions effortlessly with this comprehensive guide : Master the Art of Organic Chemistry Reactions with this All-Inclusive and Intuitive Handbook

<u>Life advices:</u>

Practice humility; it's the hallmark of true greatness.

Stay updated with advancements in wireless charging; it's paving the way for more flexible device usage.

Introduction

This is a comprehensive and user-friendly resource designed to help students excel in their study of organic chemistry. The guide begins with a review of general chemistry concepts, providing a solid foundation for understanding the principles of organic chemistry.

The topics covered include electron orbitals, Lewis dot structures, ions, types of bonds, Van der Waals forces, and intermolecular forces. Students are introduced to functional groups and molecular orbital theory, helping them grasp the fundamental building blocks of organic compounds.

The guide then delves into alkanes and cycloalkanes, exploring terminology, classification of carbon and hydrogen atoms, drawing alkanes, and IUPAC nomenclature. Students learn about cycloalkanes, Newman projections, and conformational analysis of cyclohexane, which is essential for understanding the three-dimensional structure of organic molecules.

Next, the guide addresses stereoisomerism and chirality, elucidating the concept of isomers and the R and S convention for chiral molecules. Fischer projections and the relationship between chirality and optical activity are explored, highlighting their significance in the biological world.

The section on acids and bases covers definitions and conventions, the strengths of acids and bases, thermochemistry, and mechanisms related to molecular structure and acidity. This knowledge is crucial for understanding reaction mechanisms in organic chemistry.

The guide then moves on to alkenes, providing insight into the structure and properties of unsaturated hydrocarbons. Students learn about the IUPAC nomenclature for alkenes and the E and Z nomenclature system, which helps differentiate geometric isomers.

Reactions of alkenes are extensively covered, with a focus on Gibbs free energy, energy diagrams, reaction mechanisms, electron pushing, and common mechanisms. Students gain a comprehensive understanding of carbocations and their role in various reactions.

The section on alkynes introduces their properties, IUPAC nomenclature, and methods of preparation. This is followed by a detailed discussion of haloalkanes and radical reactions, exploring their nomenclature and the radical chain mechanism, as well as nucleophilic substitution and β-elimination reactions.

The guide then delves into alcohols and their reactions, with an emphasis on PCC oxidation of alcohols. It covers ethers and epoxides, including nomenclature, physical properties, preparation methods, and ring opening of epoxides.

Overall, this is a valuable resource for students seeking to grasp the fundamentals of organic chemistry and excel in their coursework. It presents complex concepts in a clear and concise manner, making it accessible to beginners in the subject and offering a solid foundation for future organic chemistry studies.

Contents

CHAPTER 1: REVISITING GENERAL CHEMISTRY 1
Organic Chemistry 1
Electron Orbitals 2
Lewis Dot Structures 5
Ions 7
Types of Bonds 8
Van der Waals Forces 10
Intermolecular Forces 11
Functional Groups 11
Molecular Orbital Theory 14
Hybrid Orbitals 16
Resonance (Delocalized Bonding) 18
CHAPTER 2: ALKANES AND CYCLOALKANES 22
Terminology 22
Classification of Carbon and Hydrogen 22
Drawing Alkanes 23
IUPAC Nomenclature 23
Cycloalkanes 28
Newman Projection 29
Strain and Energy 30
Conformations of Cyclohexane 31
Solid and Dashed Wedges 36
Physical Properties of Alkanes 36
CHAPTER 3: STEREOISOMERISM AND CHIRALITY 38

Isomers 38
Chirality 39
R and S Convention 41
Fischer Projections... 43
Plane-Polarized Light, Optical Activity, and RacemicMixtures 45
Chirality in the Biological World 46
CHAPTER 4: ACIDS AND BASES 49
Definitions and Conventions 49
Strengths of Acids and Bases... 50
Thermochemistry and Mechanisms 51
Molecular Structure and Acidity 53
CHAPTER 5: ALKENES 56
Unsaturated Hydrocarbons 56
Structure of Alkenes.. 56
Index of Hydrogen Deficiency (IHD) 58
IUPAC Nomenclature 59
E and Z Nomenclature of Alkenes 64
CHAPTER 6: REACTIONS OF ALKENES 67
Gibbs Free Energy 67
Energy Diagrams 68
Reaction Mechanisms 69
Electron Pushing 69
Common Mechanisms 70
Carbocations 71
Reaction: Addition of H-X to an Alkene – ElectrophilicAddition Reaction 73
Reaction: Acid Catalyzed Hydration of an Alkene 76
Carbocation Rearrangement.. 78

Reaction: Acid Catalyzed Addition of an Alcohol to anAlkene 82
Reaction: Addition of X_2 to Alkene 84
Reaction: Oxymercuration – Reduction of Alkenes 86
Reaction: Hydroboration Oxidation 89
Reaction: Osmium Tetroxide – Oxidation of Alkenes toGlycol (Diol) 91
Reaction: Ozonolysis 94
Reaction: Hydrogenation of Alkenes 97
CHAPTER 7: ALKYNES AND REACTIONS OF ALKYNES 99
Alkynes and their Properties 99
IUPAC Nomenclature 99
Preparation of Alkynes 101
Reaction: Addition of HX to an Alkyne 103
Reaction: Addition of X_2 to an Alkyne 106
Reduction of Alkynes 107
Reaction: Hydroboration – Oxidation of Alkynes 111
Reaction: Electrophilic Addition to Alkynes 114
CHAPTER 8: HALOALKANES AND RADICAL REACTIONS 115
Haloalkanes (aka Alkyl Halide) 115
Nomenclature 118
Radical Chain Mechanism 118
Reaction: Radical Halogenation of Alkanes 119
Reaction: Allylic Bromination of Alkenes 122
Reaction: Radical Addition of HBr to Alkenes 124
Chapter 9: Nucleophilic Substitution and β-Elimination 127
Nucleophilic Substitution 127
Solvents 130
Nucleophilicity and Basicity 131

Summary of S_N2 and S_N1 132

Summary of E2 vs. E1 135

CHAPTER 10: ALCOHOLS AND THEIR REACTIONS 137

Alcohols 137

Reaction: S_N2 Reaction of 1° Alcohol with HX 138

Reaction: S_N1 Reaction of 2° and 3° Alcohol with HX 139

Reaction: S_N2 Reaction of 1° and 2° Alcohol with PBr₃ 141

Reaction of Alcohols with Thionyl Chloride (SOCL₂) 142

Reaction: Dehydration of 2° and 3° Alcohol 143

Reaction: Chromic Acid Oxidation of Alcohols 145

PCC Oxidation of Alcohols 147

CHAPTER 11: ETHERS AND EPOXIDES 149

Nomenclature 149

Physical Properties of Ethers 149

Preparation of Ethers 150

Synthesis of Epoxides 151

Ring Opening of Epoxides 152

CHAPTER 1: REVISITING GENERAL CHEMISTRY

Organic Chemistry

Organic chemistry is the branch of chemistry that specializes in studying carbon compounds. Organic compounds contain both carbon and hydrogen atoms, while inorganic compounds typically lack carbon.

Carbon

- Relatively small atom
- Capable of forming single, double, and triple bonds
- Electronegativity = 2.55
    - Intermediate electronegativity
- Forms strong bonds with C (carbon), H (hydrogen), O (oxygen), N (nitrogen)
    - Also with some metals
- Has 4 valence electrons
    - To fill its outer shell, it typically forms four covalent bonds
    - Carbon is capable of making large and complex molecules because it is capable of branching off into four directions
- Covalent bonds link carbon atoms together into long chains
    - Form the skeletal framework for organic molecules
- Hydrocarbons are molecules containing only carbon and hydrogen

CHAPTER 1: REVISITING GENERAL CHEMISTRY

Organic Chemistry

Organic chemistry is the branch of chemistry that specializes in studying carbon compounds. Organic compounds contain both carbon and hydrogen atoms, while inorganic compounds typically lack carbon.

Carbon

- Relatively small atom
- Capable of forming single, double, and triple bonds
- Electronegativity = 2.55
    - Intermediate electronegativity
- Forms strong bonds with C (carbon), H (hydrogen), O (oxygen), N (nitrogen)
    - Also with some metals
- Has 4 valence electrons
    - To fill its outer shell, it typically forms four covalent bonds
    - Carbon is capable of making large and complex molecules because it is capable of branching off into four directions
- Covalent bonds link carbon atoms together into long chains
    - Form the skeletal framework for organic molecules
- Hydrocarbons are molecules containing only carbon and hydrogen

- Examples: methane (CH₄), ethane (C₂H₆), propane (C₃H₈)
- Hydrocarbon chains are hydrophobic because they consist of nonpolar bonds

Electron Orbitals

Electrons orbit the nucleus of an atom in "orbitals" of increasing energy levels, or shells. Orbitals are mathematical functions that describe the wave-like behavior of an electron in a molecule (calculates the probability of where you might find an electron).

- Electrons in shells closest to the nucleus have the lowest potential energy
    - Conversely, shells farther from the nucleus have higher potential energy

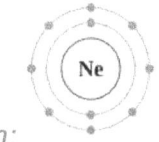

Shell Model of a Neon Atom:

- Orbitals aren't necessarily circular as represented in the shell model
    - In reality, orbitals are "clouds" of various shapes
    - Each orbital can only hold a limited number of electrons
    - An atom can have multiple orbitals of different shapes
- Electrons may move from one energy level to another
    - Happens when they gain or lose energy equal to the difference in potential energy between

energy levels
- First energy level:
    - One spherical s orbital (1s orbital)
    - Holds up to two electrons
- Second energy level
    - One spherical s orbital (2s orbital)
    - Three dumbbell-shaped p orbitals ($2p_x$, $2p_y$, $2p_z$ orbitals)
- Higher energy levels
    - Contain s and p orbitals
    - Contain other orbitals with more complex shapes

Orbital Shapes (s, p, d, f) Top to Bottom:

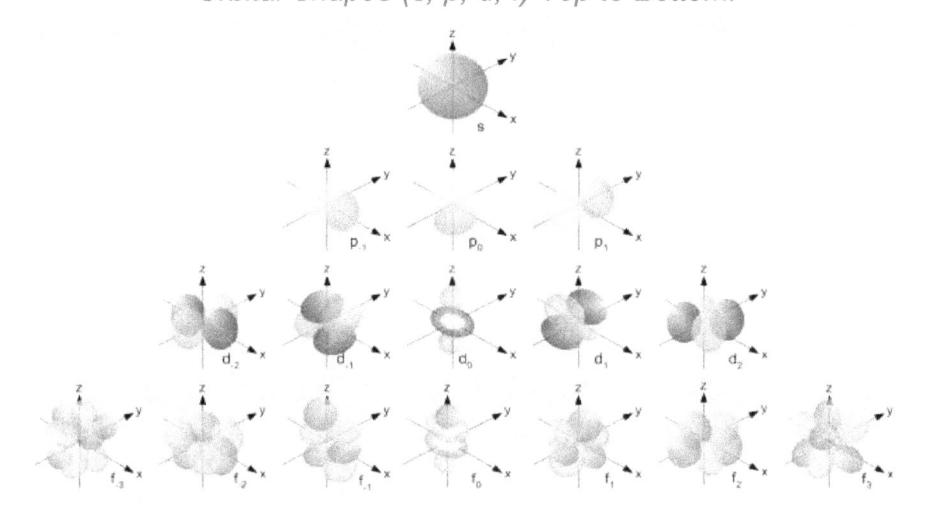

Electron Configuration

The electron configuration of an atom refers to the particular distribution of electrons among the available sub shells in that atom.

- Electronic configuration notation lists subshell symbols (s, p, d, f) sequentially with a superscript to indicate the number of electrons in that subshell
    - Example: Carbon
        - Atomic Number: 6
        - Number of electrons in a neutral carbon atom: 6
            - Number of electrons for a neutral atom is the same as its atomic number
        - 2 electrons in the "1s" sub shell
        - 2 electrons in the "2s" sub shell
        - 2 electrons in the "2p" sub shell
        - Electron Configuration: $1s^2 2s^2 2p^2$
- Configurations can become quite complex as atomic number increases
    - To remedy this, a condensed form of the configuration is often used which utilizes electron configurations of noble gases
        - Noble gases have the maximum number of electrons possible in their outer shell
            - Makes them very unreactive
        - The noble gases are: Helium, Neon, Argon, Krypton, Xenon, and Radon

Table of Condensed Electronic Configuration Examples:

Element	Noble Gas?	Full Electronic Configuration	Condensed Electronic Configuration	Total Number of Electrons
Neon	Yes	$1s^2 2s^2 2p^6$	[Ne]	10
Argon	Yes	$1s^2 2s^2 2p^6 3s^2 3p^6$	[Ar]	18
Krypton	Yes	$1s^2 2s^2 2p^6 3s^2 3p^6 3d^{10} 4s^2 4p^6$	[Kr]	36
Beryllium	No	$1s^2 2s^2$	[He] $2s^2$	4
Magnesium	No	$1s^2 2s^2 2p^6 3s^2$	[Ne] $3s^2$	12
Calcium	No	$1s^2 2s^2 2p^6 3s^2 3p^6 4s^2$	[Ar] $4s^2$	20

- [X] represents the electron configuration of the nearest noble gas that appears before the element of interest on the periodic table
- Keep in mind that you have to adjust the number of electrons and thus the electron configuration for cations and anions of an element

Energy-level Diagrams

- Energy-level diagrams are notations used to show how the orbitals of a sub shell are occupied by electrons
    - Each group of orbitals is labeled by its sub shell notation (s, p, d, f)
    - Electrons are represented by arrows

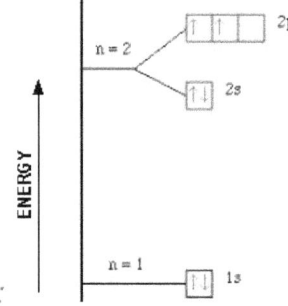

Energy-level Diagram for Carbon:

Lewis Dot Structures

Lewis Dot Structure of Carbon: ·C·

- Symbol of the element represents the nucleus and all the electrons in the inner shells
    - Dots represent electrons in the valence shell
        - Valence shell – outermost electron shell of an atom that is occupied with electrons
        - Valence electrons – electrons in the valence shell
            - These are the electrons primarily involved in chemical bonding and chemical reactions
    - Bonding electron pairs are represented by either two dots or a dash

    Lewis Electron-dot Formula Example:

    H· + :Cl· ⟶ H–Cl: or   H:Cl:

- Rules for Forming Lewis Structures
    - Calculate the number of valence electrons for the molecule
        - Group # for each atom (1-8)
            - Gives valence electron number for each atom
            - Add all numbers up
        - Add the charge of any anions

- - - Example: an anion with a -2 charge has 2 extra electrons, you would add 2 to the total count
  - Subtract the charge of any cations
    - Example: a cation with a +3 charge lacks 3 electrons, you would subtract 3 from the total count
- Place the atom with the lowest group number and lowest electronegativity as the central atom
- Arrange the other elements around the central atom
- Distribute electrons to atoms surrounding the central atom to satisfy the octet rule for each atom
- Distribute the remaining electrons as pairs to the central atom
- If the central atom is deficient in electrons, complete the octet for it by forming double bonds or possibly a triple bond

Ions

Ions are charged atoms or molecules. Ions are formed when atoms or groups of atoms gain or lose valence electrons.

- Monatomic ion – single atom with more or less electrons than the number of electrons in the atom's neutral state
- Polyatomic ions – group of atoms with excess or deficient number of electrons
- Anion – negatively charged ion

- Cation – positively charged ion
- Ionic compounds – association of a cation and an anion

Electronegativity and Ions

Electronegativity is the measure of an atom's ability of to draw bonding electrons to itself in a molecule.

- Electronegativity tends to increase from the lower-left corner to the upper-right corner of the periodic table

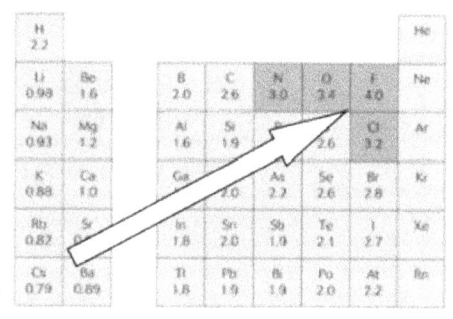

Electronegativity Trend:

Types of Bonds

Covalent Bonds

- Two atoms share valence electrons
- Indicates that atomic orbitals are overlapping
    - Overlapping requires proximity and orientation
- Two Types
    - Non-polar covalent bond – electrons shared equally between atoms
        - Electronegativity of the two atoms is about the same
        - Typically electronegativity difference between the two atoms has to be less

than 0.5 for non-polar bonds
- Electronegativity – an atom's ability to attract and hold on to electrons, represented by a number
- Polar covalent bonds – electrons shared disproportionately between atoms
  - Electronegativity between the two atoms is different by a greater degree than 0.5 but less than 2.0
  - Polarity can be represented using δ+ and δ-
    - δ+ represents the positive end
    - δ- represents the negative end

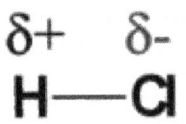

$$\overset{\delta+ \quad \delta-}{H\text{—}Cl}$$

  - Polarity can also be represented by an arrow with a plus sign tail
    - Tip of the arrow represents the negative end
    - Plus sign tail represents the positive end

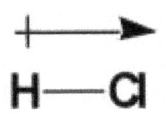

$$\overset{+\longrightarrow}{H\text{—}Cl}$$

- Number of shared pairs
  - Single bond - one shared pair

- Double bond – two shared pair
- Triple bond – three shared pairs

Ionic Bonds

- Electrons are transferred, not shared between atoms
- An atom with high electronegativity will take an electron from an atom with low electronegativity
  - Typically, difference in electronegativity is more than 2.0
- Ion – charged atom or molecule
  - Anion – negatively charged ion
  - Cation – positively charged ion

Hydrogen Bonds

- Attractive force between a hydrogen attached to an electronegative atom of one molecule to a hydrogen attached to an electronegative atom of a different molecule
- Electronegative atoms usually seen in molecules are O, N, and F

Van der Waals Forces

A general term used for the attraction of intermolecular forces between molecules.

Dipole-dipole Interactions

- Interaction between 2 polar groups

London Dispersion Forces

- Interaction between 2 non-polar molecules
- Small fluctuation in electronic distribution

Intermolecular Forces

Forces that act between neighboring particles (can be repulsive or attractive).

- Intermolecular bond strength ranking (strong to weak):
    - Covalent > ionic > hydrogen > van der Waals forces
- Weaker bonds and forces are easily broken or overcome and also re-formed
    - Makes them vital for the molecular dynamics of life
    - Shared electron pair simultaneously fills the outer level of both atoms

Functional Groups

Functional groups are characteristic groups of atoms responsible for the characteristic reactions of a particular compound.

- Functional groups have specific chemical and physical properties that are associated with them
- Are commonly the chemically reactive regions within organic compounds
    - Determine unique chemical properties of organic molecules that they are a part of
    - Consistent properties in all compounds in which they occur

Common Functional Groups

- Hydroxyl group - consist of a hydrogen atom bonded to an oxygen atom

    Hydroxyl Group: $\overset{O-H}{|}$

    - Polar group; oxygen and hydrogen bond is a polar covalent bond
    - Organic compounds with hydroxyl groups are called alcohols
    - Alcohol classification
        - Primary (1°) – 1 carbon atom bonded to the carbon bearing the hydroxyl group
        - Secondary (2°) - 2 carbon atoms bonded to the carbon bearing the hydroxyl group
        - Tertiary (3°) - 3 carbon atoms bonded to the carbon bearing the hydroxyl group

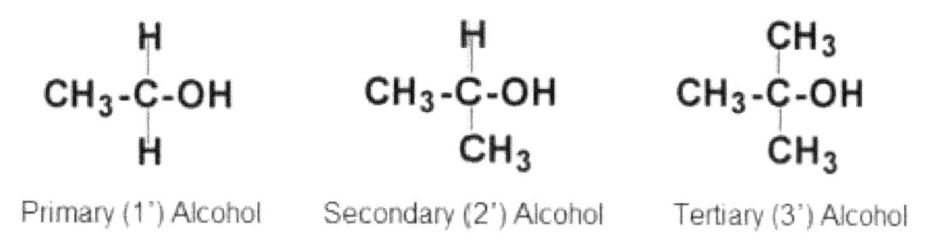

    Primary (1') Alcohol   Secondary (2') Alcohol   Tertiary (3') Alcohol

- Amino group - consists of a nitrogen atom bonded to two hydrogens and to the carbon skeleton

    Amino Group: $-N\begin{smallmatrix}H\\H\end{smallmatrix}$

    - Amines – consist of an amino group bonded to either one, two, or three carbons (1°, 2°, or 3°)

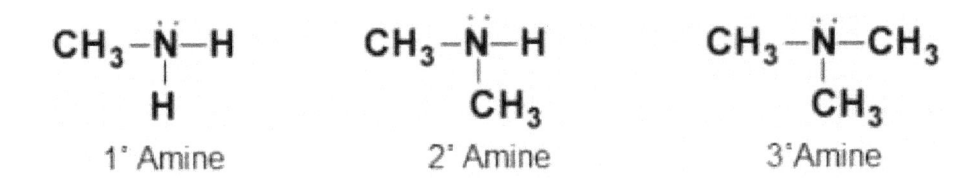

$CH_3-\overset{..}{N}-H$ $CH_3-\overset{..}{N}-H$ $CH_3-\overset{..}{N}-CH_3$
     | | |
     H CH_3 CH_3
  1° Amine   2° Amine   3° Amine

- Carbonyl group - consists of a carbon atom double-bonded to oxygen

  Carbonyl Group: $-\overset{\overset{O}{\|}}{C}-$

- Aldehyde – carbonyl group with a hydrogen attached to the carbon

  Aldehyde Group: $\overset{H}{\diagdown}C=O$

- Ketone – carbonyl group with no hydrogens attached to the carbon

- Carboxyl group – consists of a carbon atom which is attached by a double-bond to an oxygen and single-bonded to the oxygen of a hydroxyl group
  - Group has acidic properties
    - Since it donates H^+
  - Organic compounds with a carboxyl group are called **carboxylic acids**

  Carboxyl Group: $-\overset{\overset{O}{\|}}{C}-OH$

- Ester – derivative of carboxylic acid, where the hydrogen bond is replaced with a carbon bond

- Amide (aka carboxylic acid) – derivative of carboxylic acid in which the hydroxyl group (-OH) is replaced by an amine

   Amide:

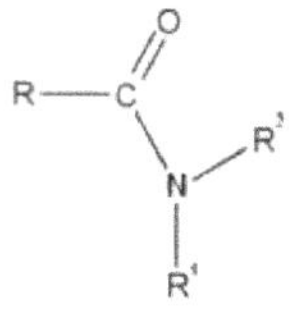

- Sulfhydryl group - consists of an sulfur atom bonded to a hydrogen
    - Organic compounds with a sulfhydryl group are called thiols

   Sulfhydryl Group:

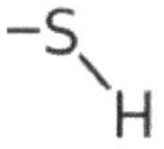

- Phosphate group – consists of a phosphorous atom single bonded to 4 oxygen atoms, and one of those oxygens is attached to the rest of the molecule
    - Acidic properties (loses H^+)
    - Organic phosphates are important part of cellular energy storage and transfer

   Phosphate Group:

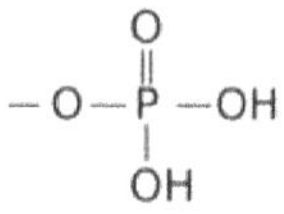

Molecular Orbital Theory

- As atoms approach each other and their atomic orbitals overlap, molecular orbitals are formed
    - Only outer (valence) atomic orbitals interact enough to form molecular orbitals

- Combining atomic orbitals to form molecular orbitals involves adding or subtracting atomic wave functions
- Adding wave functions
    - Forms a bonding molecular orbital
    - Electron charge between nuclei is dispersed over a larger area than in atomic orbitals
    - Molecular orbitals have lower energy than atomic orbitals
        - Reduction in electron repulsion
    - Bonding molecular orbital is more stable than atomic orbital
- Subtracting Wave Functions
    - Forms an antibonding molecular orbital
    - Electrons do not shield one nuclei from the other
        - Results in increased nucleus-nucleus repulsion
    - Antibonding molecular orbitals have a higher energy than the corresponding atom orbitals
    - When the antibonding orbital is occupied, the molecule is less stable than when the orbital is not occupied

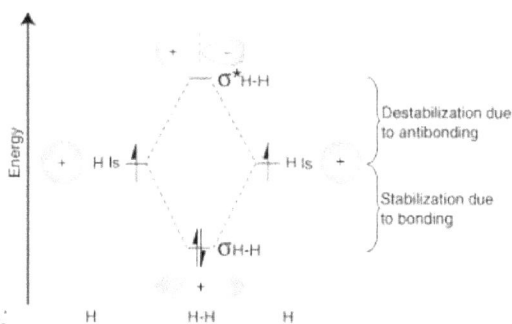

Molecular Orbitals of H₂:

Hybrid Orbitals

- Quantum mechanical calculations show that if specific combinations of orbitals are mixed, "new" atomic orbitals are formed
    - These new orbitals are called hybrid orbitals
- Types of hybrid orbitals
    - Each type has a unique geometric arrangement

Hybrid Orbitals (Hybridization)	Geometric Arrangements	Number of Hybrid Orbitals Formed by Central Atom	Example
sp	Linear	2	Be in BeF_2
sp^2	Trigonal planar	3	B in BF_3
sp^3	Tetrahedral	4	C in CH_4
sp^3d	Trigonal bipyramidal	5	P in PCl_5
sp^3d^2	Octahedral	6	S in SF_6

- Hybrid orbitals are used to describe bonding that is obtained by taking combinations of atomic orbitals of an

- isolated atom
- Number of hybrid orbitals formed = number of atomic orbitals combined
- Steps for determining bonding description
    - Write the Lewis dot formula for the molecule
    - Then use the VSEPR theory to determine the arrangement of electron pairs around the central atom
    - From the geometric arrangement, determine the hybridization type
    - Assign valence electrons to the hybrid orbitals of the central atom one at a time
        - Pair only when necessary
    - Form bonds to the central atom by overlapping singly occupied orbitals of other atoms with the singly occupied hybrid orbitals of the central atom

Multiple Bonds

- Orbitals can overlap in two ways
    - Side to side
    - End to end
- Two types of covalent bonds
    - Sigma bonds (C-C)
        - Formed from an overlap of one end of the orbital to the end of another orbital
    - pi bonds (C=C)

- - Formed when orbitals overlap side to side
    - Creates two regions of electron density
      - One above and one below
- Double bonds always consist of one sigma bond and one pi bond

Covalent Bonding of Carbon

Groups Bonded to Carbon	Orbital Hybridization	Predicted Bond Angles	Types of Bonds to Each Carbon
4	sp^3	109.5°	Four σ bonds
3	sp^2	120°	Three σ bonds One π bond
2	sp	180°	Two σ bonds Two π bonds

Resonance (Delocalized Bonding)

- Structures of some molecules can be represented by more than one Lewis dot formula
  - Individual Lewis structures are called contributing structures
  - Individual contributing structures are connected by double-headed arrows (aka resonance arrows)
  - Molecule or ion is a hybrid of the contributing structures and displays delocalized bonding
    - Delocalized bonding is where a bonding pair of electrons is spread over a

number of atoms
- Some resonance structures contribute more to the overall structure than others
    - How to determine which structures are more contributing:
        - Structures where all atoms have filled valence shells
        - Structures with the greater number of covalent bonds
        - Structures with less charges
            - Formal charges can help discern which structure is most likely (discussed later in this section)
        - Structures that carry a negative charge on the more electronegative atom

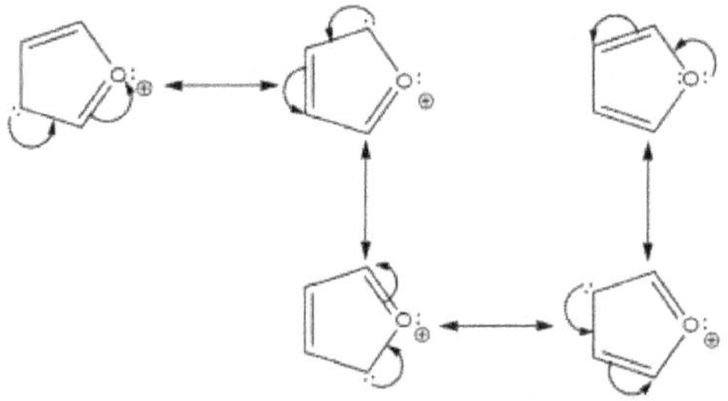

Example of Resonance Structures:

- Curved arrow – symbol used to the redistribution of valence electrons
    - Always drawn as noted in the figure below

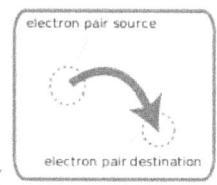

How Curved Arrows are Drawn:

Formal Charge

- An atom's formal charge is:
    - Total number of valence electrons
    - Minus all unshared electron
    - Minus ½ of its shared electrons
- Formal charges have to sum to the actual charge of the species
    - 0 charge for a neutral molecule
    - Ionic charge for an ion
- Lewis structures with the smallest formal charge are the most likely to occur

Formal Charge vs. Oxidation Number

- Formal charges are used to examine resonance hybrid structures
    - Oxidation numbers are used to monitor redox reactions
- **Formal Charge**
    - Bonding electrons are assigned equally to the atoms
        - Each atom has half the electrons making up the bond

- Formal Charge = valence e⁻ − (unbonded e⁻ + ½ bonding e⁻)
- **Oxidation Number**
    - Bonding electrons are transferred completely to the more electronegative atom
    - Oxidation Number = valence e⁻ − (unbonded e⁻ + bonding e⁻)

CHAPTER 2: ALKANES AND CYCLOALKANES

Terminology

- Hydrocarbons - molecules containing only carbon and hydrogen
    - Examples: methane (CH_4), ethane (C_2H_6), propane (C_3H_8)
- Saturated hydrocarbon – hydrocarbon containing only single bonds
- Unsaturated hydrocarbon – hydrocarbon containing at least one double bond
- Alkane (aka aliphatic hydrocarbon) – saturated hydrocarbon whose carbons are arranged in an open chain
    - General formula: C_nH_{2n+2}
- Cycloalkanes – hydrocarbon with a ring of carbon atoms joined by single bonds

Classification of Carbon and Hydrogen

- Primary (1°) Carbon - carbon bonded to one other carbon
    - 1° H - hydrogen bonded to a 1° carbon
- Secondary (2°) Carbon - carbon bonded to two other carbons
    - 2° H - hydrogen bonded to a 2° carbon
- Tertiary (3°) Carbon - carbon bonded to three other carbons
    - 3° H - hydrogen bonded to a 3° carbon

- Quaternary (4°) Carbon - a carbon bonded to four other carbons

Drawing Alkanes

- Line-angle formulas - abbreviated way of drawing structural formulas
    - Each line represents a C-C bond
    - Each vertex and line ending represents a carbon

    Example of a Line-angle Formula: C_1 C_3

        - C_1 is a carbon represented by the end of a line
        - C_3 is a carbon represented by a vertex
    - Hydrogens are not shown, they are assumed to be there
        - C_1 in the example above has 3 hydrogens and is bonded to C_2 (4 total bonds)
        - C_3 in the example above has 2 hydrogens, its bonded to C_2 and C_3 (4 total bonds)
    - Elements aside from hydrogen and carbon are always shown

IUPAC Nomenclature

IUPAC (International Union of Pure and Applied Chemistry) nomenclature is a systematic method of naming organic chemical compounds.

IUPAC - General

- Parent chain – longest carbon chain in a molecule
    - The parent name is used to specify the number of carbon atoms in the parent chain

Parent Name	Number of Carbons	Parent Name	Number of Carbons
Meth-	1	Undec-	11
Eth-	2	Dodec-	12
Prop-	3	Tridec-	13
But-	4	Tetradec-	14
Pent-	5	Pentadec-	15
Hex-	6	Hexadec-	16
Hept-	7	Heptadec-	17
Oct-	8	Octadec-	18
Non-	9	Nonadec-	19
Dec-	10	Eicos-	20

- Infix is used to inform about the type of Carbon-Carbon bonds in the parent chain

Infix	Carbon-Carbon Bonds in the Parent Chain
-an-	All single bonds
-en-	One or more double bonds
-yn-	One or more triple bonds

- Suffix is used to inform about the class of compound

Suffix	Class
-e	Hydrocarbon
-ol	Alcohol
-al	Aldehyde
-amine	Amine
-one	Ketone
-oic acid	Carboxylic Acid

- Substituent – group bonded to the parent chain
    - Alkyl group – substituent derived by removal of a hydrogen from an alkane
        - Alkyl groups are symbolized by the capital letter "R"

Common Alkyl Group Substituents:

Alkyl Group	Substituent Name
CH_3-	Methyl
CH_3CH_2-	Ethyl
$CH_3CH_2CH_2-$	Propyl
$-CHCH_3$ $\;\;\;\mid$ $\;\;CH_3$	Isopropyl
$CH_3CH_2CH_2CH_2-$	Butyl
$-CH_2CHCH_3$ $\quad\quad\mid$ $\quad\;\;CH_3$	Isobutyl
$-CHCH_2CH_3$ $\;\mid$ CH_3	Sec-butyl
$\;\;\;CH_3$ $\;\;\;\mid$ $-CCH_3$ $\;\;\;\mid$ $\;\;\;CH_3$	Tert-butyl

Naming Alkanes

- Suffix –ane specifies an alkane (e.g., eth<u>ane</u>, meth<u>ane</u>)
- Identify the parent chain (longest Carbon chain) and number it (always number sequentially)
    - Example:
        - If there are no substituents, as in the example above, you can begin numbering from either end
    - Number of carbons in the parent chain gives you the parent name, then add the suffix –ane
        - In the example above, there are 6 carbons so the parent name is hex- and you would add the suffix –ane to get "hexane"
- Each substituent has a name and a number (use a hyphen to connect the name and number)
    - Number of the substituent is determined by which carbon it is on
    - Examples:

        Name: 2-methylbutane
        - Methyl group (CH$_3$-) is on C$_2$ so it is named 2-methyl

        Name: 3-methylpropane

- Methyl group is on C_3 so it is named 3-methyl
- Numbering the parent chain must be done so that substituents get the smallest possible numbers
    - Examples:

    Correct Name: 2-methylhexane

    Correct Name: 2,4- dimethylhexane
        - If there are two or more of the same substituent, add a comma to separate the substituent numbers and add a prefix to indicate how many of the substituents you have
            - Two of the same substituent (di-)
            - Three of the same substituent (tri-), and so on and so forth
- If there are two or more different substituents
    - List them in alphabetical order
    - Example:

Name: 4-ethyl-2-methyloctane

- Prefixes (e.g., di-, tri-) are not included in alphabetization
  - Example:

Name: 4-ethyl-2,2-dimethylhexane

Cycloalkanes

- General formula: C_nH_{2n}
  - Five and six-membered rings are the most common
- Structure and nomenclature
  - Add prefix cyclo- to the name of the open-chain alkane containing the same number of carbons
    - Example: six carbon open-chain alkane with no substituents would be called a "hexane," a six carbon ring would be called a cyclohexane

Hexane   Cyclohexane

  - If there is only one substituent in the ring structure, it does not need to be assigned a number
  - If there are two substituents, start numbering from the substituent that comes first

- alphabetically
    - If there are three or more substituents, number the ring so that the substituents have the lowest possible set of numbers

Newman Projection

- Newman projection – way of visualizing chemical conformations of a carbon-carbon bond
    - Conformations - any 3D arrangements of atoms in a molecule that result from rotation around a single bond

Example of Newman Projections

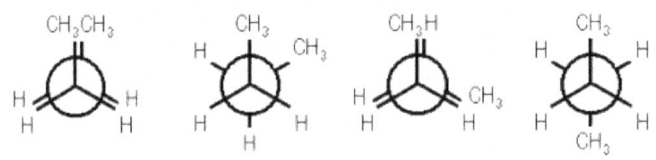

- Newman projection conventions
    - Chemical bond is viewed from front to back
        - Front carbon represented by a dot
        - Back carbon represented by a circle
        - Bonds represented by straight lines
- Staggered conformation – atoms or groups on one carbon are as far apart as possible from the atoms or groups on an adjacent carbon
    - Two types
        - Anti – conformation about a single bond in which the groups on adjacent carbons lie at a dihedral angle of 180°

- Dihedral angle (θ) - angle between two bonds originating from different atoms in a Newman projection

Staggered (Anti) Conformation of Butane:

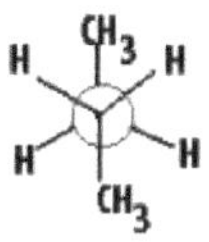

  - Gauche – conformation about a single bond in which two groups on adjacent carbons lie at a dihedral angle of 60°

Staggered (Gauche) Conformation of Butane:

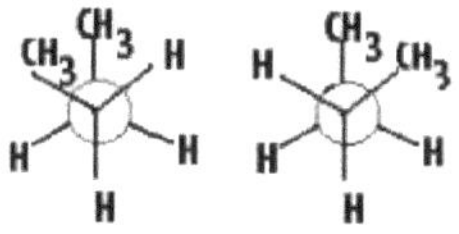

  - Eclipsed conformation - atoms or groups of atoms on one carbon are as close as possible to the atoms or groups of atoms on an adjacent carbon

Eclipsed Conformations of Butane:

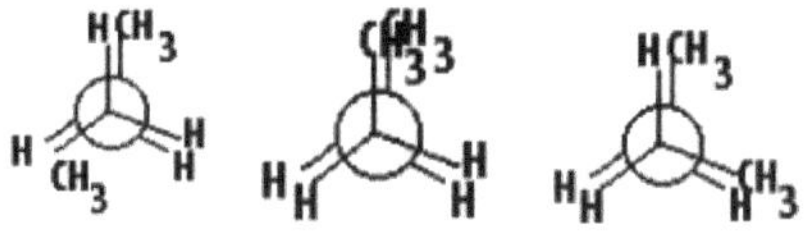

Strain and Energy

Strain energy is the increase in energy that results from the distortion of bond angles and bond lengths from their optimal values.

- Steric strain (aka nonbonded interaction strain) – increases in potential energy of a molecule due to repulsion between electrons in atoms that are not directly bonded to each other

Highest Steric Strain Conformation of Butane:

- Conformation of butane shown above has the highest steric strain out of all the other conformation, since the "bulky" methyl group (-CH3) are closest together in this conformation

- Angle strain – increase in potential energy due to bond angles deviating from their optimal value

- Torsional strain - strain that emerges when non-bonded atoms separated by three bonds are forced from a staggered conformation into an eclipsed conformation

Effect of Dihedral Angle on Energy of Butane:

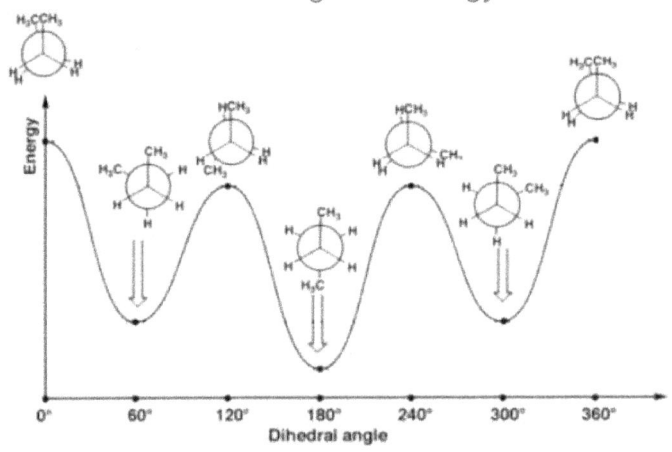

Conformations of Cyclohexane

Flat drawings do not accurately represent the actual 3D shape of a five- or six-membered ring.

Chair Conformation

- Chair conformation – most stable puckered conformation of a cyclohexane ring
    - Most stable conformation that minimizes strain
        - Bond angles are 110.9°
            - Ideal bond angle
        - Bonds on all adjacent carbons are staggered

Cyclohexane Flat (Left) and Chair (Right) Conformations:

- Six of the hydrogens are "axial" and six of them are equatorial
    - Axial hydrogens – hydrogens that are parallel to the axis of the ring
        - Axial bonds are always drawn straight up or straight down

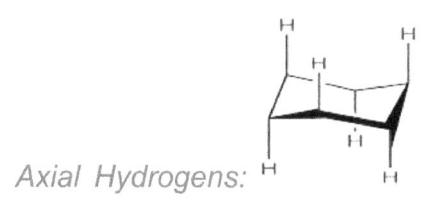

Axial Hydrogens:

    - Equatorial Hydrogens – Hydrogens that are perpendicular to the axis of the ring
        - Equatorial bonds are always drawn parallel to the lines

representing the C-C bonds in the ring

Equatorial Hydrogens:

- There are two chair conformations, one chair conformation can be used to determine the other chair conformation through the process of "flipping the chair" (aka ring flip)

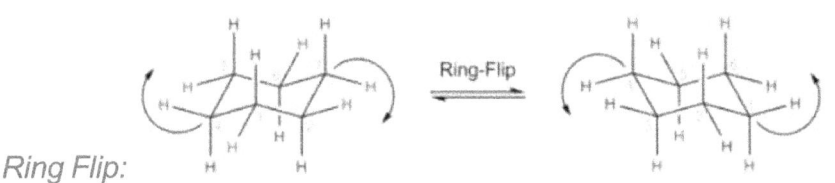

Ring Flip:

  ○ When the chair is flipped, all axial positions become equatorial
    - All equatorial positions become axial
  ○ **IMPORTANT**: Substituents are more stable in the equatorial position
    - Equatorial position is preferred because there is unfavorable steric interactions that occur between axial atoms on the same side
      • This unfavorable interaction is called 1,3–diaxial interaction

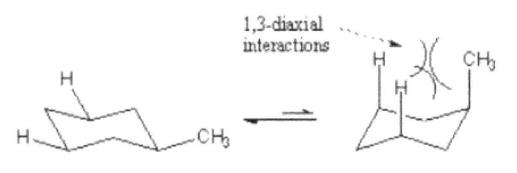

1,3-diaxial Interaction: equatorial methyl   axial methyl

Two Conformations of Methylcyclohexane:

- Conformation for methylclyclohexane on the right is more stable, since the methyl group (-CH₃) is in the equatorial position

Boat Conformation

- Boat conformation – a puckered conformation of a cyclohexane ring where carbons 1 and 4 are bent towards one another

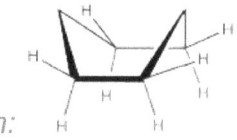

Cyclohexane Boat Conformation:

  ○ Flagpole hydrogens – hydrogens in a 1,4 – relationship in a boat cyclohexane

Flagpole Hydrogens:

- Boat conformation is less stable than chair conformation because the groups involved in the 1,4 relationship create steric strain
- Steric hindrance can be partially relieved with the twist boat conformation

- Twist boat conformation is still less stable than the chair conformation

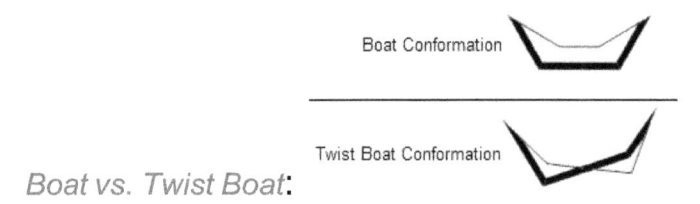

Boat Conformation

Twist Boat Conformation

Boat vs. Twist Boat:

Cis, Trans Isomers

Stereoisomers are compounds that have the same molecular formula, same connectivity, but a different orientation of their atoms in space. Cis and trans isomers are stereoisomers that result from either a ring or a double bond.

- Stereocenter – an atom bearing groups where exchange of two groups produces a different stereoisomer
- Configuration – refers to the arrangement of atoms about a stereocenter
- The following are not isomers:

  H—C(H)(Cl)—C(Cl)(H)—H   H—C(H)(H)—C(Cl)(Cl)—H

  - They are not isomers because there is free-rotation around single bonds

  - The following are isomers:

    (H)(Cl)C=C(Cl)(H)   (H)(Cl)C=C(H)(Cl)

- They are isomers because there is no free-rotation around double bonds
  - Chlorine atoms are locked in their positions
- *Trans* (latin meaning "across") isomers – functional groups are on opposite sides

trans-1,2-dichloroethene:

- *Cis* (latin meaning "on this side") isomers – functional groups are on the same side

cis-1,2-dichloroethene:

Solid and Dashed Wedges

- Solid wedge - symbol used to indicate that a bond is projecting out towards the person viewing the bond
- Dashed wedge – symbol used to indicate that a bond or group is pointed away from the person viewing the bond
- Sold line – symbol used to indicate that the bond lies in the plane of the paper

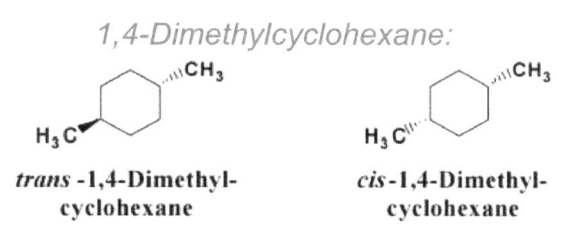

1,4-Dimethylcyclohexane:

trans-1,4-Dimethyl-cyclohexane

cis-1,4-Dimethyl-cyclohexane

Physical Properties of Alkanes

- Not very reactive
- Little biological activity
- Colorless
- Odorless
- Low molecular weight alkanes are gases at room temperature
    - E.g., methane and butane
- Intermediate molecular weight alkanes are liquids at room temperature
- High molecular weight alkanes are solid at room temperature
- Insoluble in water
    - But, dissolve in organic solvents
- Trends
    - Linear alkanes have higher melting/boiling points than their branched counterparts
        - Due to better stacking and surface area contact
    - Highly branched alkanes have **higher** melting points than slightly branched alkanes
        - Due to better stacking
    - Highly branched alkanes have a **lower** boiling point than slightly branched alkanes
        - Due to highly branched alkanes having less surface area

CHAPTER 3: STEREOISOMERISM AND CHIRALITY

Isomers

Isomers are compounds that have the same molecular formula but vary in their structures and properties.

Types of Isomers

- Constitutional isomers (aka structural isomers - differ in the covalent arrangement of their atoms)

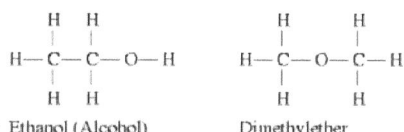

  Structural Isomers: Ethanol (Alcohol)   Dimethylether

- Stereoisomers (aka spatial isomers) - share the same covalent bonds, but differ in their spatial arrangements
    - Two types of stereoisomers
        - Enantiomers – two compounds that are mirror images of each other
            - Can occur when four different atoms or groups of atoms are bonded to the same carbon (chiral carbon/asymmetric carbon)
            - Usually one form of an enantiomer is biologically active while the other is not

  Enantiomers:

- Diastereomers – two compounds that are not mirror images of each other

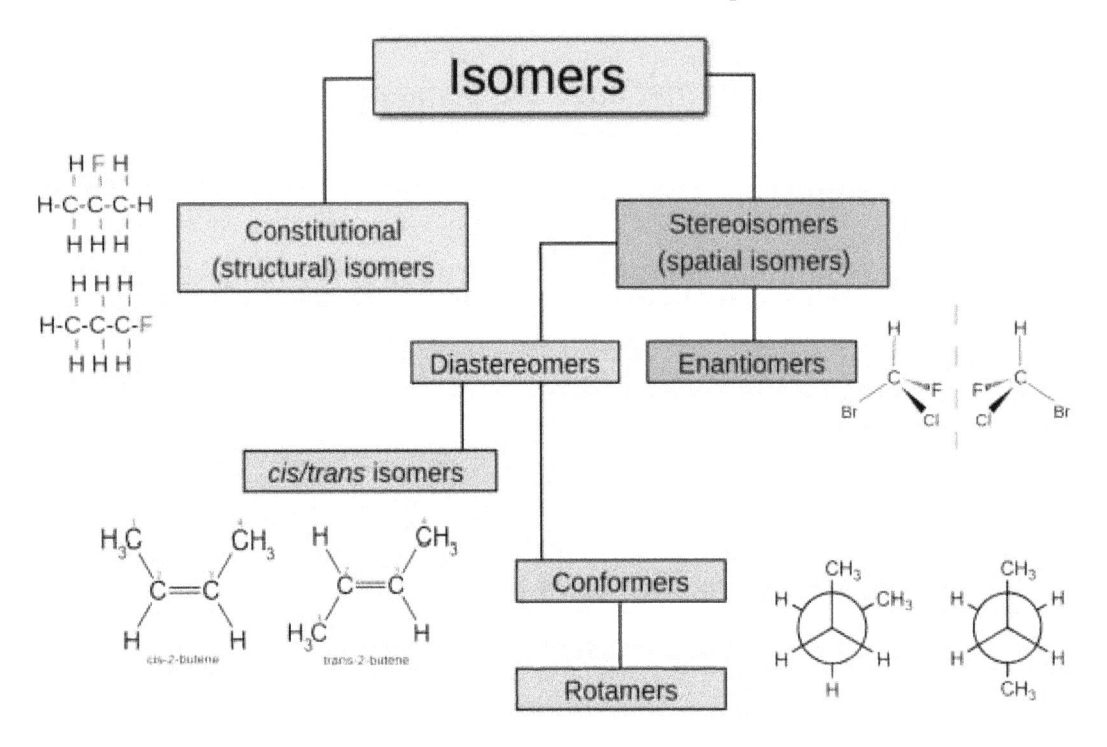

Chirality

- Chiral – an object that is asymmetric in such a way that it is not superposable on its mirror image
- Achiral – an object that lacks chirality
    - Achiral objects have at least one element of symmetry (a plane of symmetry or a center of symmetry)
        - Plane of symmetry – imaginary plane through an object that divides the object into two halves which are mirror images of one another

- Center of symmetry – any point situated in such a manner that identical components of the object are located on opposite sides and equidistant from that point along any axis that passes through that point
- Carbon bonded to four different groups is the most common cause of chirality in organic molecules
    - All chiral centers are stereocenters
        - Not all stereocenters are chiral centers
- For a molecule with *n* chiral centers, the maximum number of stereoisomers is determined by 2^n
    - Examples
        - Molecule with 1 chiral center, 2^1 or 2, stereoisomers are possible
        - Molecule with 2 chiral centers, 2^2 or 4, stereoisomers are possible
- Meso compound – achiral compound with multiple stereoisomers that is superimposable on its mirror image
    - Meso compounds have an internal plane of symmetry
    - Example: consider tartaric acid

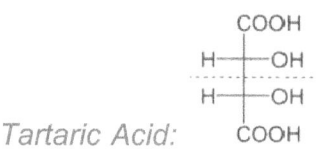

Tartaric Acid:
```
      COOH
   H——OH
   H——OH
      COOH
```

- Has 2 chiral centers, 2^2 or 4, stereoisomers are predicted but really

there are only 3

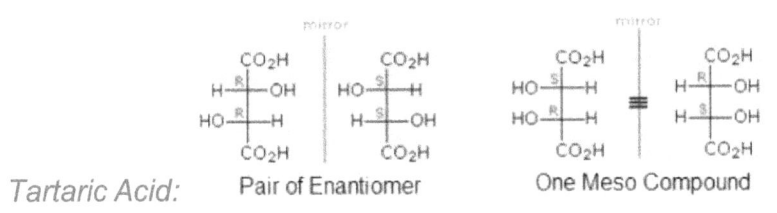

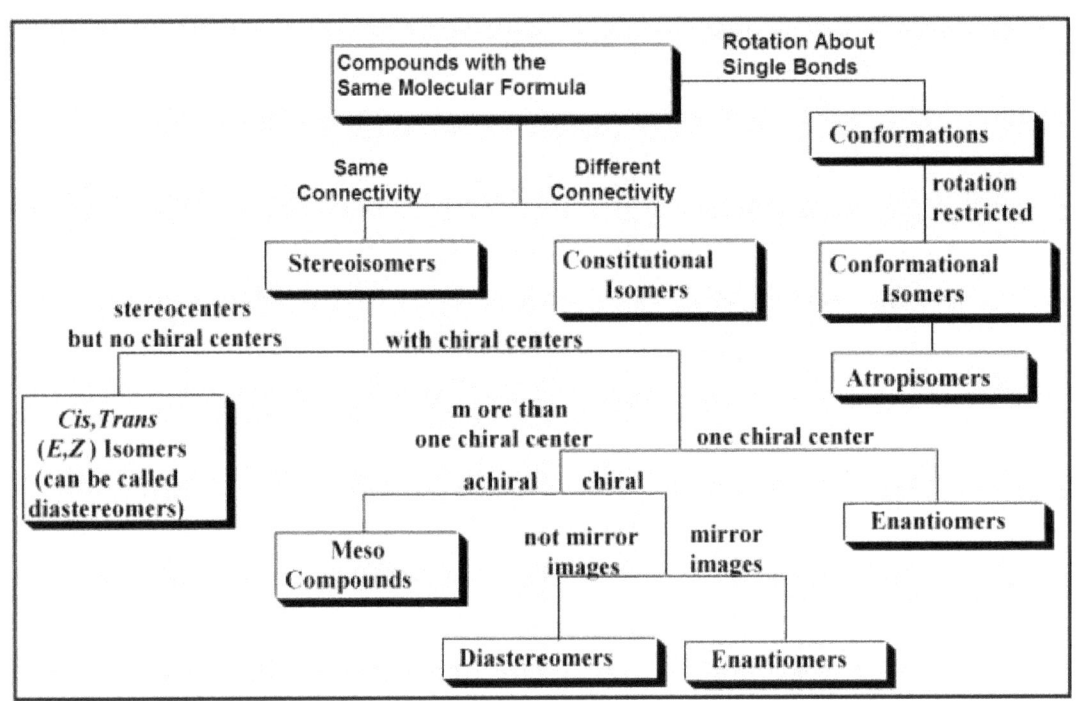

Tartaric Acid: Pair of Enantiomer   One Meso Compound

R and S Convention

Each chiral center is designated as either R or S in the IUPAC system.

Steps

- The four different groups attached to the chiral atom are ranked from 1 to 4
    - Where 1 is the highest priority and 4 is the lowest priority

- Chiral center is reoriented (if required) so that the lowest priority group (4) is placed towards the back (into the plane of the paper, away from you)
    - If the other higher priority groups (1, 2, and 3) are in clockwise order the chiral center is designated as **R**
    - If the other higher priority groups (1, 2, and 3) are in counterclockwise order the chiral center is designated as **S**

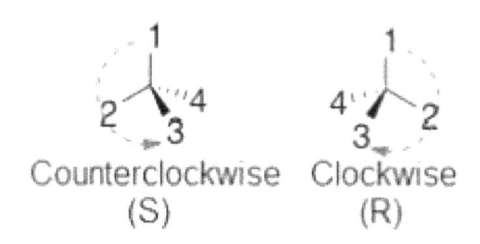

Counterclockwise (S)   Clockwise (R)

Priority Rules

- Each atom bonded to the chiral center is assigned priority based on atomic number
    - Higher priority is given to atoms with higher atomic number

(1) -H   (6) -CH$_3$ (7) -NH$_2$ (8) -OH   (16) -SH   (17) -Cl   (35) -Br   (53) -I

Increasing priority →

- Hydrogen is always the lowest priority group if it is attached to the chiral center
- If two groups have the same atom bonded to the chiral center, look at the next set of atoms

- Priority based on atomic number is assigned at the first point of difference

$$\underset{(1)}{-CH_2-H} \quad \underset{(6)}{-CH_2-CH_3} \quad \underset{(7)}{-CH_2-NH_2} \quad \underset{(8)}{-CH_2-OH}$$

$\xrightarrow{\text{Increasing priority}}$

- Double and triple bonds are treated as if they are a series of single bonds to the same atom

$-CH=CH_2 \xrightarrow{\text{is treated as}} -CH-CH_2$ with C, C

$-\underset{O}{\overset{O}{C}}H \xrightarrow{\text{is treated as}} -C-O$ with O-C, H

$-C\equiv CH \xrightarrow{\text{is treated as}} -C-C-H$ with C, C, C, C

Fischer Projections

Fischer projections are 2D representations of 3D organic molecules with multiple chiral centers.

Fischer Projection of Glucose

- Horizontal segments of a Fischer projection represent bonds that are coming towards you
- Vertical segments of a Fischer projections represent bonds that are direct away from you
- Intersections represent a carbon atom

Steps for Converting Line Diagrams to a Fischer Projection

Let's Convert the Following Line Diagram to a Fischer Projection:

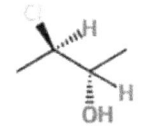

- Number the carbons
    - Makes it easier to keep track of the carbons when you start converting

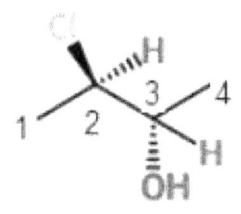

- Identify stereocenters and assign R and S
    - C$_2$ is R
    - C$_3$ is S

- Draw the Fischer projection
    - Chiral carbons are intersection points
    - Draw the groups connected to the chiral carbons
    - Make sure the chiral carbons are R and S in the Fischer projections, as they were when you assigned them on the line angle formula

```
        CH₃
Cl ─────┼───── H
HO ─────┼───── H
        CH₃
```

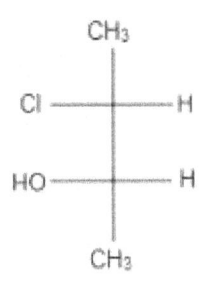

Plane-Polarized Light, Optical Activity, and Racemic Mixtures

- Ordinary light – light that oscillates in all planes perpendicular to its direction of propagation
- Plane-polarized light - light that oscillates only in parallel planes
    - Plane-polarized light is the vector sum of left and right circularly polarized light
        - Circularly polarized light interacts one way with an R chiral center and reacts the opposite way with its enantiomer
- Optically active - refers to a compound that rotates the plane of plane-polarized light
    - Dextrorotatory (+) - refers to a compound that rotates the plane of polarized light to the right
    - Levorotatory (-) - refers to a compound that rotates the plane of polarized light to the left

(S)-(+)-Lactic acid   (R)-(-)-Lactic acid

- Racemic mixture – mixture that has equal amounts of left-handed and right-handed enantiomers of a chiral molecule
    - Contains equal amounts of dextrorotatory and levorotatory molecules
        - Thus, it is optically inactive
        - And there is a net zero rotation of plane-polarized light
- Resolution – separation of a racemic mixture into its enantiomers

Chirality in the Biological World

Enzymes

- Each enzyme has an active site where catalysis takes place
    - Active site - a region on the enzyme which binds substrate
- Act only on a specific substance (substrate)

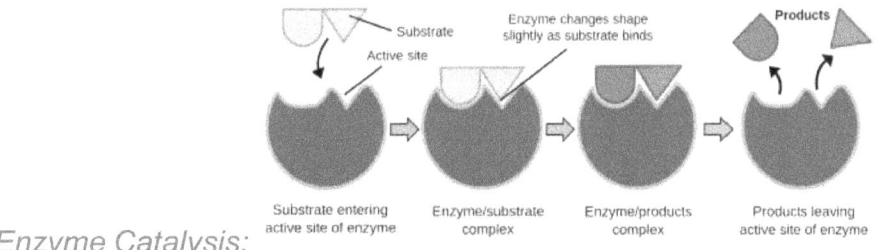

Enzyme Catalysis:

- Left-handed molecule will only fit into a left-handed binding site
- Right-handed molecule will only fit into a right-handed binding site

- Enantiomers have different physiological properties because of the differences in their interactions with other chiral molecules
    - For example, an enzyme may be able to bind with (R)-glyceraldehyde but not with (S)-glyceraldehyde

Amino Acids

- The 20 common amino acids have a central carbon (called the α-carbon)
    - Central carbon is bonded to an amino group (-NH_2) and a carboxylic acid group (-COOH)

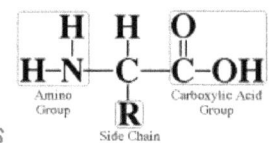

General Structure of Amino Acids

- α-carbon is chiral in 19 out of the 20 common amino acids
    - Glycine does not have a chiral α-carbon
- α-carbon has an S configuration in 18 out of the 19 common amino acids
    - Cysteine has an R configuration
- Zwitterion – molecule or ion that has separate positively and negatively charged groups
    - In amino acids, there is an internal transfer of a hydrogen ion (H^+) from the carboxylic acid group to the amino group

① H₂N−ᵅC(H)(R)−C(=O)OH   ② H₃N⁺−ᵅC(H)(R)−C(=O)O⁻

Amino Acid Zwitterion:

CHAPTER 4: ACIDS AND BASES

Definitions and Conventions

Acid-base reactions are a type of chemical process typified by the exchange of one or more hydrogen ions (i.e. exchange/transfer of a proton).

- Arrhenius definition
    - Acid – substance that produces H^+ ions in aqueous solution
        - We now know that H^+ reacts immediately with a water molecule to produce a hydronium ion (H_3O^+)
    - Base – substance that produces OH^- ions in aqueous solution
- Bronsted-Lowry definition
    - Acid – proton donor
    - Base – proton acceptor
    - Bronsted-Lowry definition does not require water as a reactant
- Conjugate acids and bases
    - Conjugate base – species that is formed when an acid donates a proton to a base
    - Conjugate acid – species that is formed when a base accepts a proton from an acid
    - Conjugate acid-base pair – pair of molecules or ions that can be interconverted through the transfer of a proton

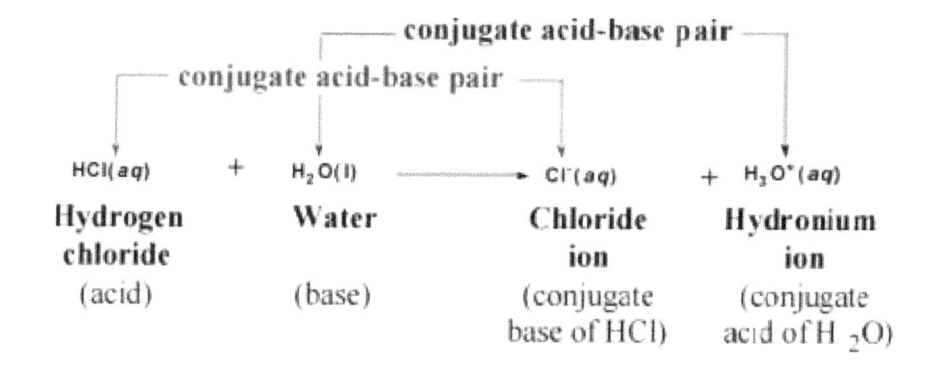

```
                          ┌──── conjugate acid-base pair ────┐
           ┌──── conjugate acid-base pair ────┐
           ▼           ▼                      ▼              ▼
        HCl(aq)   +   H₂O(l)  ⟶  Cl⁻(aq)  +  H₃O⁺(aq)
```

Hydrogen chloride	Water	Chloride ion	Hydronium ion
(acid)	(base)	(conjugate base of HCl)	(conjugate acid of H₂O)

- Curved arrows are used to show the flow of electrons in an acid-base reaction

$$CH_3-C(=O)-\ddot{O}-H + :N H_3 \rightleftharpoons CH_3-C(=O)-\ddot{O}:^- + H-\overset{+}{N}H_3$$

Acetic acid	Ammonia	Acetate ion	Ammonium ion
(proton donor)	(proton acceptor)		

- Resonance and Acids
    - There are many organic molecules that have two or more sites that can act as proton acceptors
        - Preferred site of protonation is the site where the charge is more delocalized

Strengths of Acids and Bases

- Strength of an acid is expressed by an equilibrium constant
    - Equilibrium expression for the dissociation of an uncharged acid (HA)

$$HA + H_2O \rightleftharpoons A^- + H_3O^+$$

$$K_{eq} = \frac{[H_3O^+][A^-]}{[HA][H_2O]}$$

- K_a, the acid dissociation constant, is given by:

$$K_a = K_{eq}[H_2O] = \frac{[H_3O^+][A^-]}{[HA]}$$

- pK$_a$ and Trends
    - $K_a = 10^{-pKa}$
    - $pK_a = -\log(K_a)$
        - Lower the pK$_a$, the stronger the acid
            - Higher the pK$_a$, the weaker the acid
        - Lower the pK$_a$, the weaker the conjugate base
            - Higher the pK$_a$, the stronger the conjugate base
    - Equilibrium favors the side of the weakest acid and weakest base
        - Equilibrium favors the side with the highest pK$_a$
            - Thus, pK$_a$ can be used to predict in which direction equilibrium lies

Thermochemistry and Mechanisms

- Reaction mechanism – step-by-step description of how a chemical reaction is occurring
- Thermochemistry – study of energy of the entire system at each step and every instant of a reaction
- Many chemical reactions occur through collisions
    - When collisions occur, the structure of a molecule becomes distorted
        - Higher energy collisions create greater distortions in structure
    - When collisions occur, the kinetic energy of the reactants is converted to potential energy
        - It becomes stored in chemical structures as structural strains
    - During a collision, a transition state (‡) is formed
        - In the transition state, there are partially broken and partially formed bonds
- Reaction coordinate diagram – graph showing the energy changes that occur during a chemical reaction

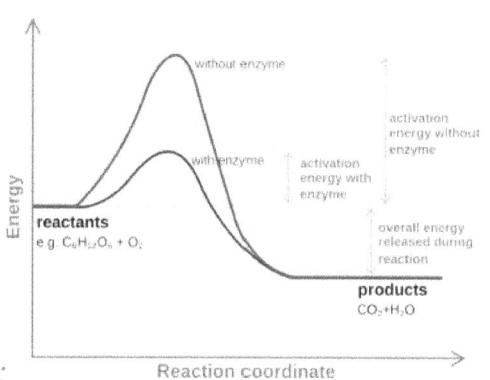

Reaction Coordinate Diagram:

- Progress of the reaction (time) is indicated on the x-axis
- Energy is indicated on the y-axis
    - For reaction occurring at a constant pressure, the change in Gibbs free energy, $\Delta G°$ is shown
        - $\Delta G° = -RT \ln(K_{eq})$
        - Free energy of activation – difference in energy between reactants and the transition state

Spontaneous vs. Non-spontaneous Reactions

- Spontaneous if ΔG_{rxn} is negative

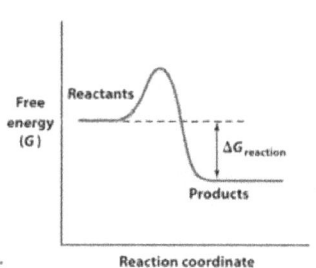

General Spontaneous Reaction Diagram:

- Non-spontaneous if ΔG_{rxn} is positive

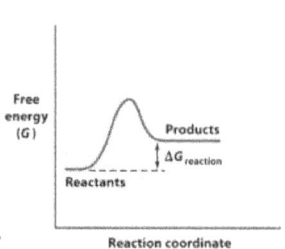

General Non-spontaneous Reaction Diagram:

Molecular Structure and Acidity

- Most important principle in determining the relative acidities of uncharged organic acids is the stability of the anion (A⁻) resulting from the loss of a proton
- The acidity of the acid (HA) is greater if the resulting anion (A⁻) is more stable
- Anions can be stabilized by having the negative charge:
    - On a more electronegative atom
        - Electronegativity – an atom's ability to attract and hold on to electrons, represented by a number
        - Higher electronegativity means the atom holds on to its electrons more strongly which stabilizes the anion
    - On a larger atom
        - There is a greater dispersal of charge
    - Delocalized through resonance
        - Negative charge is disperse over multiple atoms
    - Delocalized by the inductive effect
        - Atoms with high electronegativity are electron withdrawing
            - They pull electron density towards them
            - Electron density on the more electronegative atom is stabilizing as discussed earlier

- Stabilization by the inductive effect becomes lesser the farther the electronegative atom is from the site of negative charge in the conjugate base
  - In an orbital with more s character
    - Remember from general chemistry that there are different types of hybrid orbitals, or look back at chapter 1 of this guide to review
      - Types: sp, sp^2, sp^3, sp^3d, sp^3d^2
        - sp hybridized orbital has 50% *s* character
        - sp^2 hybridized orbital has 33.33...% *s* character
        - sp^3 hybridized orbital has 25% *s* character, and so on and so forth
        - *s* character (highest to lowest): sp, sp^2, sp^3, sp^3d, sp^3d^2
      - The greater the percentage of *s* character the more stable the anion

CHAPTER 5: ALKENES

Unsaturated Hydrocarbons

Unsaturated hydrocarbons contain at least one or more double or triple bonds.

- Alkene – contains at least one C-C double bond
  - General formula: C_nH_{2n}
- Alkyne – contains at least one C-C triple bond
  - General formula: C_nH_{2n-2}
- Arenes – aromatic hydrocarbons (most commonly based on benzene and its derivatives)

Benzene:

Structure of Alkenes

- Alkene double bonds consists of:
  - One sigma bond
    - Formed by the overlap of sp^2 hybrid orbitals
  - One pi bond
    - Formed by the overlap of parallel 2p orbitals
  - Two carbon atoms of a double bond and the four atoms bonded to them have bond angles of ~120°

Cis, Trans Isomers (Review)

Cis and trans isomers have the same connectivity but a different arrangement their atoms in space due to the presence of either a ring or a double bond.

- The following are not isomers:

$$H-\underset{\underset{Cl}{|}}{\overset{\overset{H}{|}}{C}}-\underset{\underset{H}{|}}{\overset{\overset{Cl}{|}}{C}}-H \qquad H-\underset{\underset{Cl}{|}}{\overset{\overset{H}{|}}{C}}-\underset{\underset{Cl}{|}}{\overset{\overset{H}{|}}{C}}-H$$

  - They are not isomers because there is free-rotation around single bonds
  - The following are isomers:

  - They are isomers because there is no free-rotation around double bonds
    - Chlorine atoms are locked in their positions
  - *Trans* (latin meaning "across") isomers – functional groups are on opposite sides

    trans-1,2-dichloroethene:

- *Cis* (latin meaning "on this side") isomers – functional groups are on the same side cis-1,2-dichloroethene:

Index of Hydrogen Deficiency (IHD)

The index of hydrogen deficiency (IHD) is the sum of the number of rings and pi bonds in a molecule.

- IHD for neutral molecules must be an integer
- To determine the IHD, we begin by comparing the number of hydrogens in an unknown compound with the number of hydrogens in a reference hydrocarbon
    - Reference hydrocarbon has:
        - Same number of carbons as the unknown compound
        - No rings or pi bonds
        - Molecular formula of C_nH_{2n+2}
- IHD Formula

    $$IHD = \frac{(H_{reference} - H_{molecule})}{2}$$

    - Things to take into account:
        - For each atom of a Group 7 element (F, Cl, Br, I), you have to add one hydrogen to the reference hydrocarbon
        - No correction has to be made for each atom of a Group 6 element (O, S) to the reference hydrocarbon

- For each atom of a Group 5 element (N,P), you have to add one hydrogen to the reference hydrocarbon

IUPAC Nomenclature

IUPAC – General (Review)

- Parent chain – longest carbon chain in a molecule
    - The parent name is used to specify the number of carbon atoms in the parent chain

Parent Name	Number of Carbons	Parent Name	Number of Carbons
Meth-	1	Undec-	11
Eth-	2	Dodec-	12
Prop-	3	Tridec-	13
But-	4	Tetradec-	14
Pent-	5	Pentadec-	15
Hex-	6	Hexadec-	16
Hept-	7	Heptadec-	17
Oct-	8	Octadec-	18
Non-	9	Nonadec-	19
Dec-	10	Eicos-	20

- Infix is used to inform about the type of Carbon-Carbon bonds in the parent chain

Infix	Carbon-Carbon Bonds in the Parent Chain
-an-	All single bonds
-en-	One or more double bonds
-yn-	One or more triple bonds

- Suffix is used to inform about the class of compound

Suffix	Class
-e	Hydrocarbon
-ol	Alcohol
-al	Aldehyde
-amine	Amine
-one	Ketone
-oic acid	Carboxylic Acid

- Substituent – group bonded to the parent chain
    - Alkyl group – substituent derived by removal of a hydrogen from an alkane
        - Alkyl groups are symbolized by the capital letter "R"

    Common Alkyl Group Substituents:

Alkyl Group	Substituent Name
CH₃-	Methyl
CH₃CH₂-	Ethyl
CH₃CH₂CH₂-	Propyl

-CHCH₃
  |
  CH₃
	Isopropyl

CH₃CH₂CH₂CH₂-	Butyl

-CH₂CHCH₃
     |
     CH₃
	Isobutyl

-CHCH₂CH₃ | CH₃	Sec-butyl

CH₃
  |
-CCH₃
  |
  CH₃
	Tert-butyl

Naming Alkenes

- Suffix –ene specifies an alkene (e.g., hex<u>ene</u>, pent<u>ene</u>)
- Identify the parent chain (longest carbon chain) and number it (always number sequentially)
    - Numbering must also be done in the direction that gives the carbons of the double bond the lowest number possible
        - Example: (numbered 4-2-3-1) NOT (numbered 1-3-2-4)
    - Two carbons define the location of the double bond
        - But only the first carbon (lowest number carbon) is used in naming

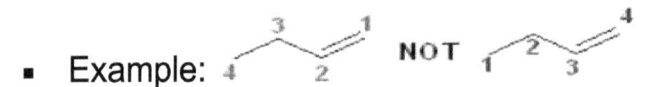

- Number of carbons in the parent chain gives you the parent name, then add the suffix –ene, and you add the number of the first carbon with a hyphen in front of the parent name
    - So for the alkene above, there are 4 carbons so the parent name is but- and you would add the suffix –ene to get "butene" and then you add the number of the first carbon with a hyphen in front of the parent name to get "1-butene"
- Each substituent has a name and a number (use a hyphen to connect the name and number)
    - Number of the substituent is determined by which carbon it is on
        - Example:
        - Methyl group (CH_3-) is on C_3 so the substituent would be named 3-methyl
        - You combine the name and number of the substituent with the parent name so the name of the compound would be "3-methyl-1-butene"
    - If there are two or more of the same substituent, add a comma to separate the substituent numbers and add a prefix to indicate how many of the substituents you have
        - Two of the same substituent (di-)
        - Three of the same substituent (tri-), and so on and so forth

- If there are two or more different substituents:
  - List them in alphabetical order
- Unlike alkanes where numbering the parent chain must be done so that substituents get the smallest possible numbers, alkenes must always be numbered so the carbons in the double bonds get the smallest possible numbers
- For alkenes containing two or more double bonds the infix "-en" is changed
  - –adien- for two double bonds

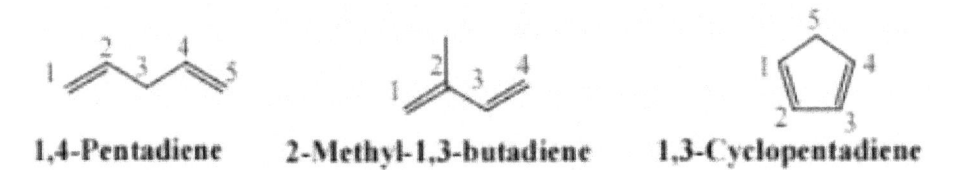

1,4-Pentadiene   **2-Methyl-1,3-butadiene**   **1,3-Cyclopentadiene**

- –atrien- for three double bonds, and so on and so forth

Assigning *Cis* and *Trans*

- Many alkenes exist in two isomeric forms, yet have the same connectivity of atoms (constitutional isomers)
  - These isomers differ in the orientation of groups and are geometric isomers
    - Example: 2-butene

cis-2-butene   *trans*-2-butene

- To determine *cis* or *trans*, use the double bond as a reference plane
    - If the two alkyl groups are on the same side of the double bond then it is *cis*
    - If the two alkyl groups are on the opposite side of the double bond then it is *trans*

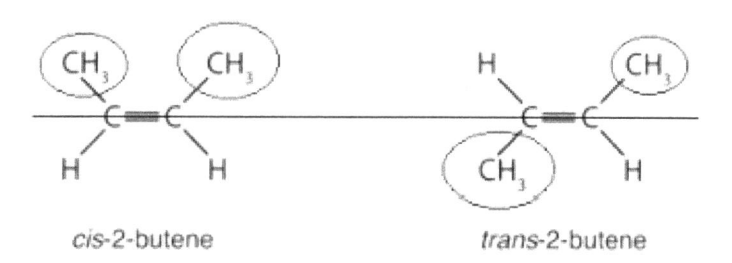

cis-2-butene   *trans*-2-butene

E and Z Nomenclature of Alkenes

The E and Z nomenclature is more reliable and more suited than the *cis* and *trans* system to be applied to tri- or tetra-substituted alkenes, especially when the substituents are not alkyl groups.

- This system uses priority rules that were discussed in Chapter 3 of this guide
    - Each atom bonded to the chiral center is assigned priority based on atomic number
        - Higher priority is given to atoms with higher atomic number

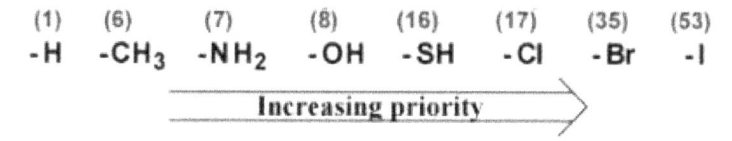

(1)	(6)	(7)	(8)	(16)	(17)	(35)	(53)
-H	-CH$_3$	-NH$_2$	-OH	-SH	-Cl	-Br	-I

Increasing priority →

- Hydrogen is always the lowest priority group if it is attached to the chiral center
  - If two groups have the same atom bonded to the chiral center, look at the next set of atoms
    - Priority based on atomic number is assigned at the first point of difference

$$\underset{\text{Increasing priority} \longrightarrow}{\overset{(1)\qquad\qquad (6)\qquad\qquad (7)\qquad\qquad (8)}{-CH_2-H \quad -CH_2-CH_3 \quad -CH_2-NH_2 \quad -CH_2-OH}}$$

  - Double and triple bonds are treated as if they are a series of single bonds to the same atom

$$-CH=CH_2 \quad \text{is treated as} \quad \overset{C\ \ C}{-CH-CH_2}$$

$$\overset{O}{\underset{-CH}{\parallel}} \quad \text{is treated as} \quad \underset{H}{\overset{O-C}{-C-O}}$$

$$-C\equiv CH \quad \text{is treated as} \quad \underset{C\ \ C}{\overset{C\ \ C}{-C-C-H}}$$

- If the higher priority groups are on the same side, the configuration is Z
- If the higher priority groups are on the opposite side, the configuration is E

High Priority H₃C   CH₃ High Priority | High Priority H₃C   H Low Priority
         C═══C | C═══C
Low Priority H   H   Low Priority | Low Priority H   CH₃ High Priority
        (Z)-2-butene | (E)-2-butene

CHAPTER 6: REACTIONS OF ALKENES

Gibbs Free Energy

Gibbs free energy can be used to determine the direction of the chemical reaction under given conditions.

- $\Delta G = \Delta H - T\Delta S$ or $\Delta G = G_{products} - G_{reactants}$
    - G = Gibbs free energy (J/mol)
    - H = enthalpy (J/mol) - total energy content of a system
    - S = entropy (J/K*mol) - measure of disorder or randomness (how energy is dispersed)
    - T = Temperature (K)
        - As T increases so does S
- $+\Delta G$ means energy must be put into the system
    - Indicates that a process is **nonspontaneous or endergonic**
    - Indicates that the position of the equilibrium for a reaction favors the products
- $-\Delta G$ means energy is released by the system
    - Indicates that a process is **spontaneous or exergonic**
    - Indicates that the position of the equilibrium for a reaction favors the reactants
- $\Delta G = 0$ indicates that the system is at equilibrium

Important: ΔG only indicates if a process occurs spontaneously or not, but does **not** indicate anything about how fast a process occurs.

Energy Diagrams

Energy diagrams are graphs showing the changes in energy that occur during a chemical reaction.

- Transition state (‡)
    - Unstable species with high energy formed during a reaction
- Activation energy ($\Delta G^{\ddagger}$) – difference in Gibbs free energy between reactants and a transition state
    - If $\Delta G^{\ddagger}$ is large; the reaction occurs slowly
        - Few collisions occur with sufficient energy to reach the transition state
    - If $\Delta G^{\ddagger}$ is small; the reaction occurs quickly
        - Many collisions occur with sufficient energy to reach the transition state
- One-step reaction

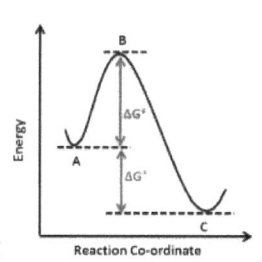

One-step Reaction Energy Diagram:

    - One transition state
    - Two-step reaction

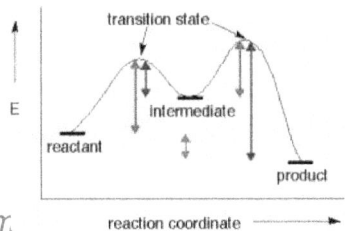

Two-step Reaction Energy Diagram

- Two transition states
- One intermediate

Reaction Mechanisms

A reaction mechanism is step-by-step description of how a chemical reaction is occurring. It shows the following:

- Which bonds are broken
- Which bonds are formed
- Order and relative rated of the various bond-breaking and bond-forming steps
- If the reaction occurs in a solution, the role of the solvent
- If there is a catalyst, the role of a catalyst
- Position of all atoms
- Energy of the entire system during the reaction

Electron Pushing

Electron pushing (aka arrow pushing) is used to depict the flow of electrons during a chemical reaction.

- Arrows are used to indicate movement of electrons

curved, two-barbed arrow: *two electron movement*

curved, single-barbed ('fish-hook') arrow: *single electron movement*

- Arrows are never used to indicate the movements of atoms
    - Make sure an arrow starts from electrons or bonds, never from an atom
- Arrows always start at an electron source
    - Electron source – most commonly, either a pi bond or a lone pair of electrons
- Arrows always end at an electron sink
    - Electron sink – an atom or ion that can accept a new bond or a lone pair of electrons
        - Keep in mind, bonds may have to be broken to avoid overfilling the valence shell of an atom serving as an electron sink

Patterns of e- Movement

- Electrons are moved for these typical reasons:
    - Redistribution of pi bonds and/or lone pairs
    - Forming a new sigma bond from a lone pair or a pi bond
    - Breaking a sigma bond to form a pi bond or a new lone pair

Common Mechanisms

These are four of the most common mechanism elements to consider when predicting the individuals steps of a chemical reaction:

- Attack of the nucleophile
    - Make a new bond between a nucleophile (electron source) and an electrophile (electron sink)
- Departure of the leaving group
    - Break a bond so that a relatively stable ion or molecule is formed
- Add a proton
    - Used when there is no suitable nucleophile-electrophile reaction
    - But a molecule has a strongly basic functional group
    - Or a strong acid is present
- Remove a proton
    - Used when there is no suitable nucleophile-electrophile reaction
    - But a molecule has a strongly acidic proton
    - Or a strong base is present

Carbocations

A carbocation is a carbon atom with only six electrons in its valence shell and a positive charge.

- Are electrophiles ("electron loving")
- Are Lewis acids

- Are classified depending on the number of carbons that are attached to them
    - 1° carbocation – carbocation attached to one carbon
    - 2° carbocation – carbocation attached to two carbons
    - 3° carbocation – carbocation attached to three carbons
- Use sp² hybrid orbitals to form sigma bonds from carbon to the three attached groups
    - Unhybridized 2p orbital lies perpendicular to the sigma bond framework and contains no electrons

Carbocation Stability

- Carbocation stability: 3° > 2° > 1°
    - 3° is more stable than 2°
    - 2° is more stable than 1°

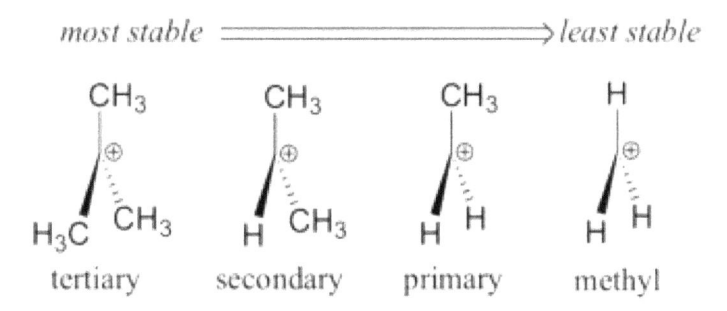

most stable ⟶ *least stable*

| tertiary | secondary | primary | methyl |

- Alkyl groups bonded to a positively charged carbon help delocalize the positive charge of the cation (this is their "electron-releasing" ability)

Alkyl Group Stability Effect (Most Stable Carbocation to the Least Stable):

$$R_3C^+ > R_2CH^+ > RCH_2^+ > CH_3^+$$

- Electron-releasing ability of alkyl groups is due to:
    - Inductive effect
        - Positively charged carbon polarizes electrons of adjacent sigma bonds toward it
        - Positive charge on the carbocation becomes delocalized over nearby atoms
        - Stability of the cation increases with the amount of volume over which the charge is delocalized
    - Hyperconjugation
        - Partial overlap of the sigma-bonding orbital of an adjacent C-H or C-C bond with the vacant 2p orbital of the carbocation that gives an extended molecular orbital that increases the stability of the system

Reaction: Addition of H-X to an Alkene – Electrophilic Addition Reaction

- X is a stand-in for a Group 7 element (e.g., Cl, Br)
- Addition is regioselective
    - Regioselective reaction – addition or substitution reaction in which one product is preferred above all other

- ○ ***Important*:** Markovnikov's Rule – the addition of HX or H$_2$O to an alkene results in hydrogen adding to the carbon of the double bonds that has the greater number of hydrogens
- Mechanism steps:
  - ○ **Step 1:** Add a proton
    - Proton transfer from HX to the alkene gives a carbocation intermediate

    [Probability #1: H$_3$C–CH(H)–C$^+$(H)(H) with :Br:$^-$ — 1° Carbocation Intermediate]

    [Probability #2: H$_3$C–C$^+$(H)–CH$_2$(H)(H) with :Br:$^-$ — 2° Carbocation Intermediate]

    - There are two possibilities in terms of which carbon the positive charge can end up on

- Probability #2 is more likely because a 2° carbocation is more stable than a 1° carbocation
  - **Step 2:** Attack of the nucleophile
    - Reaction of the cation with the anion completes the reaction

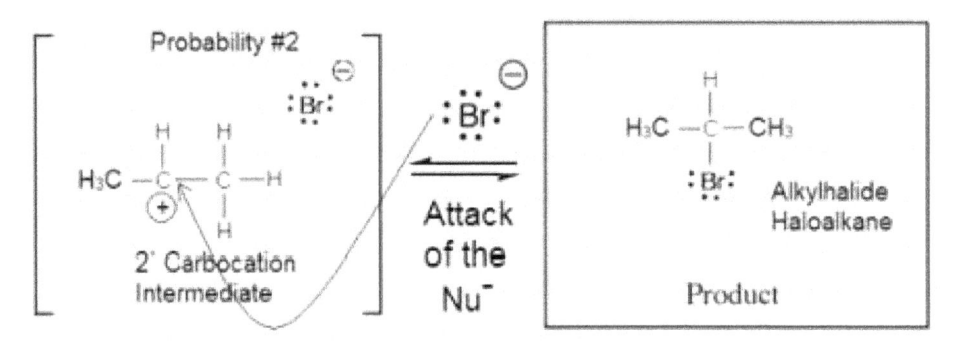

- Reaction Summary: pi bond is protonated in the first step to form a carbocation. The most stable carbocation is formed. The anion attacks the carbocation to give an alkylhalide (aka haloalkane).

$$\text{Alkene} \xrightarrow{HX} \text{Alkylhalide (Haloalkane)}$$

  - Reaction starts with an alkene
    - Transformed to an alkylhalide (aka haloalkane) by the end of the reaction
  - Regioselectivity: Markovnikov
    - Hydrogen adds preferentially to the less substituted carbon of the double bond (the carbon atom bearing the greater number of hydrogens)

- Stereoselectivity: Not a stereoselective reaction
- Carbocation rearrangement is possible (carbocation rearrangement is discussed later in this chapter)

Reaction: Acid Catalyzed Hydration of an Alkene

- Addition of water (H_2O) is called hydration
- Mechanism steps:
    - **Step 1:** Add a proton
    - **Step 2:** Attack of the nucleophile

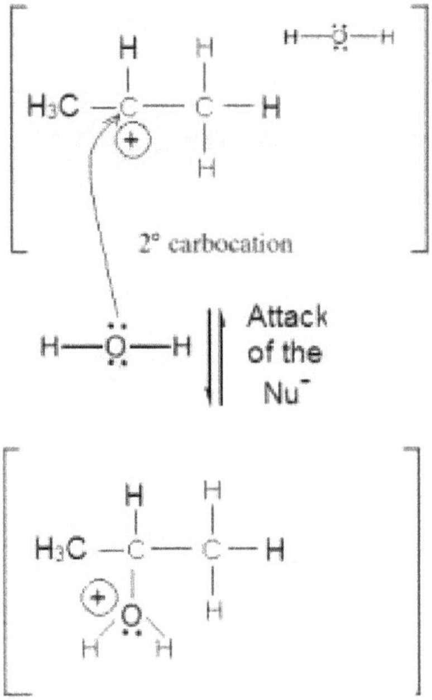

$$\left[H_3C - \overset{\overset{\displaystyle H}{|}}{\underset{\underset{\displaystyle H}{|}}{C}}\!\!\!\!\!\!{}_{\oplus} - \overset{\overset{\displaystyle H}{|}}{\underset{\underset{\displaystyle H}{|}}{C}} - H \quad\quad H-\overset{..}{\underset{..}{O}}-H \right]$$

2° carbocation

H—Ö—H ⇅ Attack of the Nu⁻

$$\left[H_3C - \overset{\overset{\displaystyle H}{|}}{\underset{\underset{\displaystyle \overset{\oplus}{O}\diagdown }{|}}{C}} - \overset{\overset{\displaystyle H}{|}}{\underset{\underset{\displaystyle H}{|}}{C}} - H \right]$$

- **Step 3:** Remove a proton

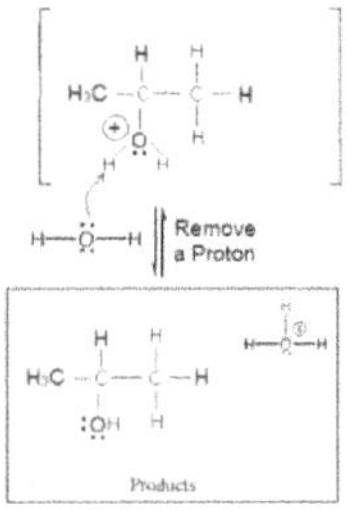

  [figure showing removal of a proton to yield products]

- Reaction Summary: pi bond adds a proton to give a stable carbocation. Carbocation reacts with the nucleophile, water, to give an oxonium ion intermediate. The oxonium ion intermediate loses a proton to form an alcohol.

$$\text{Alkene} \xrightarrow[\text{cat } H_2SO_4]{H_2O} \text{Alcohol}$$

  - Reaction starts with an alkene

- Transformed to an alcohol by the end of the reaction
- Reaction is catalyzed by H_2SO_4
  - H_2SO_4 provides the hydrogen needed to convert water (H_2O) to hydronium (H_3O^+)
    - Note that in the first step the proton is being added from hydronium
- Regioselectivity: Markovnikov
  - Hydrogen adds preferentially to the less substituted carbon of the double bond (the carbon atom bearing the greater number of hydrogens)
- Stereoselectivity: Not a stereoselective reaction
- Carbocation rearrangement is possible

Carbocation Rearrangement

In electrophilic addition to alkenes, there is the possibility for rearrangement if a carbocation is involved.

- Rearrangement – change in connectivity of the atoms in a product compared with the connectivity of the same atoms in the starting material
- Driving force in a carbocation rearrangement is that a less stable carbocation is rearranged to a more stable carbocation

Reaction: Carbocation Rearrangement – Addition of H-X to an Alkene – 1,2 Methyl Shift

- A methyl group can move with its electrons from one atom to another adjacent electron deficient carbocation
    - Driving force for this is that a less stable carbocation is converted to a more stable carbocation
- Mechanism steps
    - **Step 1:** Add a proton

    - Step 2: 1,2 Methyl Shift – Carbocation Rearrangement

○ Step 3: Attack of the nucleophile

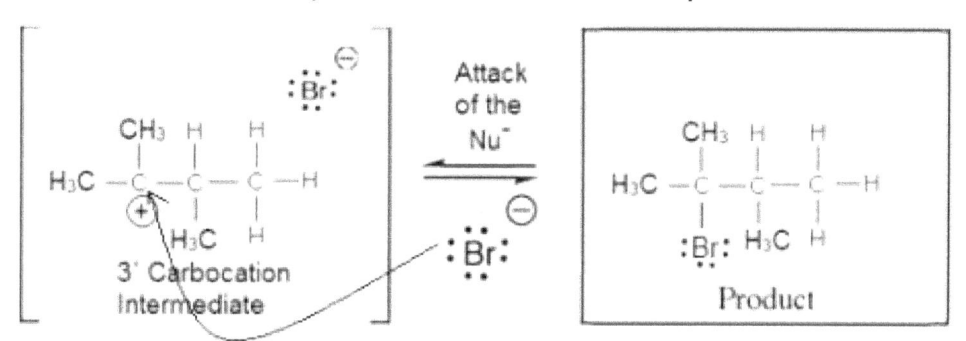

Reaction: Carbocation Rearrangement - 1,2 Hydrogen Shift - Acid Catalyzed Hydration of an Alkene

- Carbocation can rearrange if moving an adjacent hydrogen atom leads to a more stable carbocation
- Mechanism steps
    ○ **Step1:** Add a proton
    ○ **Step 2:** 1,2 Hydrogen Shift – Carbocation Rearrangement

$$\left[\begin{array}{c} \text{CH}_3\quad \text{H}\qquad\text{H}-\overset{..}{\text{O}}-\text{H} \\ \text{H}_3\text{C}-\overset{|}{\underset{|}{\text{C}}}-\overset{+}{\text{C}}-\text{CH}_3 \\ \text{H} \\ 2°\ \text{carbocation} \end{array} \right]$$

Rearrangement ⇅ 1,2 Hydrogen Shift

$$\left[\begin{array}{c} \text{CH}_3\quad \text{H}\qquad\text{H}-\overset{..}{\text{O}}-\text{H} \\ \text{H}_3\text{C}-\overset{|}{\underset{+}{\text{C}}}-\overset{|}{\underset{|}{\text{C}}}-\text{CH}_3 \\ \text{H} \\ 3°\ \text{carbocation} \\ (\text{more stable}) \end{array} \right]$$

- **Step 3:** Attack of the nucleophile

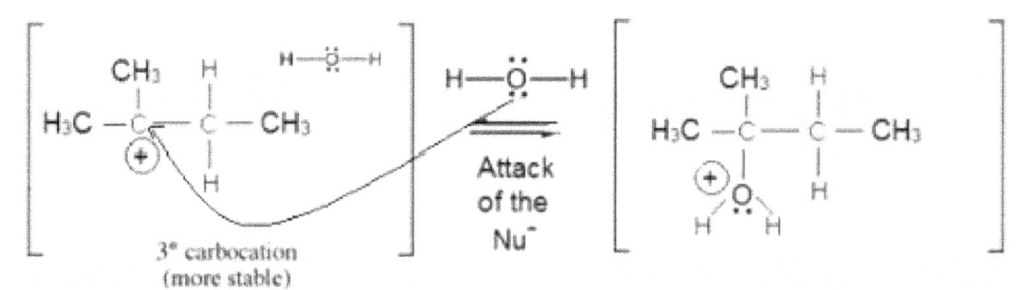

$$\left[\begin{array}{c} \text{CH}_3\ \ \text{H}\quad \text{H}-\overset{..}{\text{O}}-\text{H} \\ \text{H}_3\text{C}-\overset{|}{\underset{+}{\text{C}}}-\overset{|}{\underset{|}{\text{C}}}-\text{CH}_3 \\ \text{H} \\ 3°\ \text{carbocation} \\ (\text{more stable}) \end{array} \right] \xrightleftharpoons[]{\text{Attack of the Nu}^-} \left[\begin{array}{c} \text{H}-\overset{..}{\text{O}}-\text{H} \\ \\ \text{CH}_3\ \ \text{H} \\ \text{H}_3\text{C}-\overset{|}{\underset{+\text{O}}{\text{C}}}-\overset{|}{\underset{|}{\text{C}}}-\text{CH}_3 \\ \text{H}\ \ \text{H} \end{array} \right]$$

- **Step 4:** Remove a proton

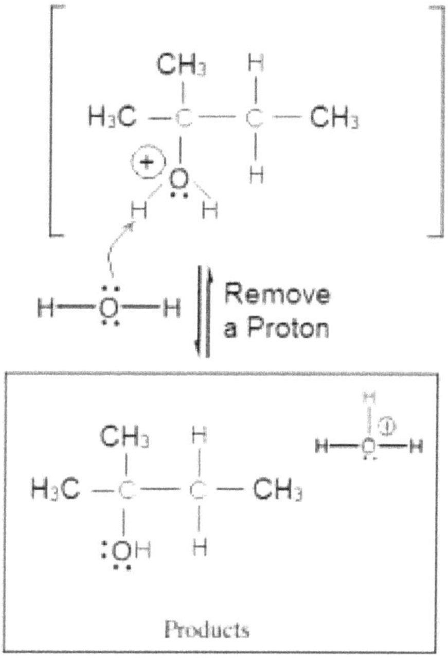
Remove
a Proton
Products

Reaction: Acid Catalyzed Addition of an Alcohol to an Alkene

- Mechanism steps
  - **Step 1:** Add a proton

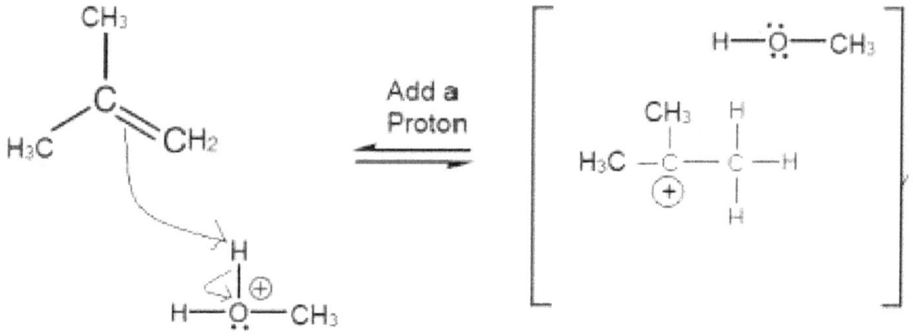
Add a
Proton

  - **Step 2:** Attack of the nucleophile

[Reaction scheme showing carbocation intermediate with methanol (H—Ö—CH₃) attacking, producing protonated ether intermediate via "Attack of the Nu⁻"]

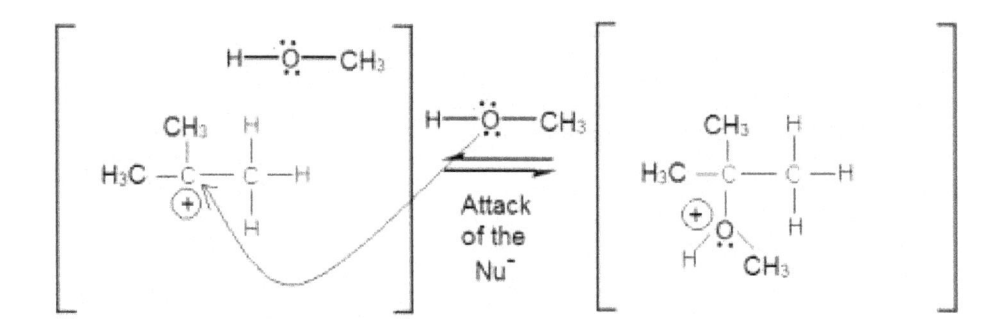

- **Step 3:** Remove a proton

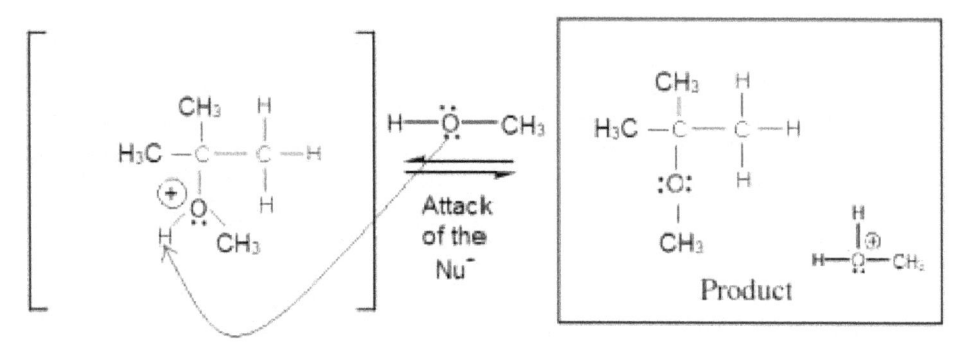

[Reaction scheme showing protonated ether intermediate with second methanol attacking to remove the proton, yielding the neutral ether product and CH₃OH₂⁺]

Product

- Reaction Summary:

$$\text{Alkene} \xrightarrow[\text{cat } H_2SO_4]{ROH} \text{Ether}$$

  - Reaction starts with an alkene
    - Transformed to an ether by the end of the reaction
  - Reaction is catalyzed by H_2SO_4
    - H_2SO_4 provides the hydrogen needed to convert CH_2OH to CH_3OH^+
      - Note that in the first step the proton is being added from

CH₃OH⁺

- Regioselectivity: Markovnikov
    - Hydrogen adds preferentially to the less substituted carbon of the double bond (the carbon atom bearing the greater number of hydrogens)
- Stereoselectivity: Not a stereoselective reaction
- Carbocation rearrangement is possible

Reaction: Addition of X₂ to Alkene

- Typically this is an addition of Cl₂, Br₂, or I₂
- Carried out with either pure reagents or in an inert solvent such as CH₂Cl₂
- Mechanism steps
    - **Step 1:** Electrophilic addition
        - Electrophilic addition is a reaction between an electrophile and a nucleophile, adding to double or triple bonds
        - One of the pi bonds is removed and creates two new sigma bonds
        - A bridged bromonium ion intermediate is formed

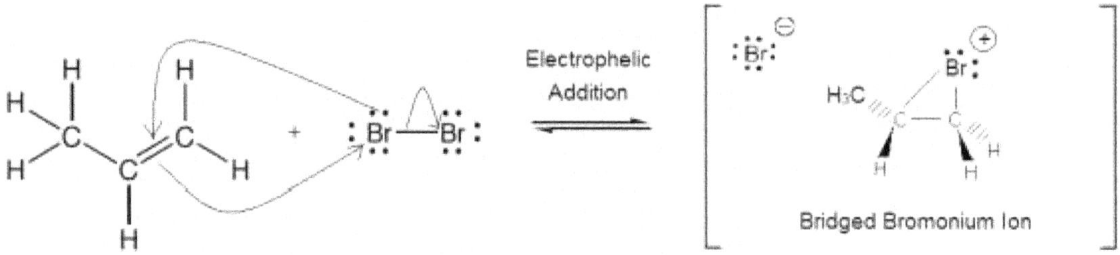
Electrophelic
Addition
Bridged Bromonium Ion

- **Step 2:** Attack of the nucleophile
  - The halide ion (the nucleophile) attacks from the **opposite** side of the bromonium ion and opens the three-membered ring to create the product

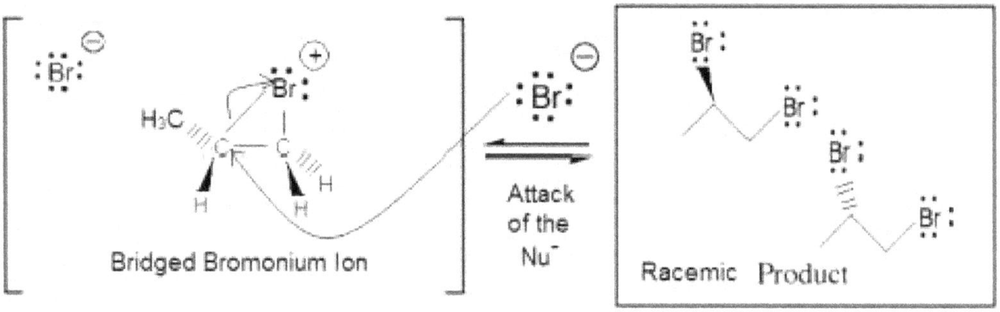
Bridged Bromonium Ion
Attack
of the
Nu⁻
Racemic Product

- Reaction Summary:

$$\text{Alkene} \xrightarrow[CH_2Cl_2]{X_2} \text{Vicinal Dihalide}$$

- Reaction starts with an alkene
  - Transformed to a vicinal dihalide by the end of the reaction
    - Vicinal – refers to any two functional groups bonded to two adjacent carbon atoms

- CH$_2$Cl$_2$ is an inert solvent
  - May not be used in some cases
- Regioselectivity: Non-Markovnikov
  - No addition of hydrogen
- Stereoselectivity: Anti-product
  - Halide ion always attacks from the **opposite** side of the bromonium ion because it is sterically hindered from attacking from the same side
- No carbocation rearrangement in this reaction

Reaction: Oxymercuration – Reduction of Alkenes

- First step of the reaction requires Hg(OAc)$_2$, mercury (II) acetate

$$H_3C-\overset{\overset{O}{\|}}{C}-O-Hg-O-\overset{\overset{O}{\|}}{C}-CH_3$$

Hg(OAc)$_2$

Hg(OAc)$_2$ with OAc Identified:

- Mechanism steps
  - The following occurs before the first step in the mechanism that you are likely to be responsible for:

- **Step 1:** Attack of the nucleophile
  - Creates a mercurinium ion intermediate

- **Step 2:** Attack of the nucleophile

- **Step 3:** Remove a proton

- **Step 4:** Chemist opens the flask and adds a reagent (in this reaction, NaBH₄)
  - Whenever a step has a chemist adding a reagent, you are not responsible for the

mechanism that takes place to create the next intermediate or product, you only need to know the result of the step

- Typically, this is because the mechanism of the step is too complicated to be covered in the first semester of an organic chemistry course

▪ Result of this step: NaBH₄ is a reducing agent, the bond with mercury is replaced with a hydrogen

$$\left[\begin{array}{c} \text{CH}_3 \quad \text{Hg—OAc} \\ | \qquad | \\ \text{H—C—C—H} \\ | \qquad | \\ \text{HO:} \quad \text{H} \end{array}\right]$$

NaBH₄ ⇅ (Chemist opens flask and adds new reagent)

$$\begin{array}{c} \text{CH}_3 \quad \text{H} \\ | \qquad | \\ \text{H—C—C—H} \\ | \qquad | \\ \text{HO:} \quad \text{H} \end{array}$$

Products

- Reaction Summary: pi bond attacks the mercury acetate cation and gives a bridged mercurinium ion intermediate. H₂O (a nucleophile) attacks the more substituted carbon from the opposite side. Removal of the proton and reduction with NaBH₄ gives the final product, an alcohol.

$$\text{Alkene} \xrightarrow[\text{2) NaBH}_4]{\text{1) Hg(OAc)}_2} \text{Alcohol}$$

- Reaction starts with an alkene
    - Transformed to an alcohol by the end of the reaction
- Regioselectivity: Markovnikov
    - Hydrogen adds preferentially to the less substituted carbon of the double bond (the carbon atom bearing the greater number of hydrogens)
    - Also note that the OH group of the final product is added to the other carbon (the more substituted Carbon)
- Stereoselectivity: Overall, not a stereoselective reaction
- No carbocation rearrangement in this reaction

Reaction: Hydroboration Oxidation

- First step of the reaction requires BH₃, borane
- Mechanism steps
    - **Step 1:** Simultaneous bond formation
        - Regioselective and stereoselective addition of B and H to the carbon-carbon double bond

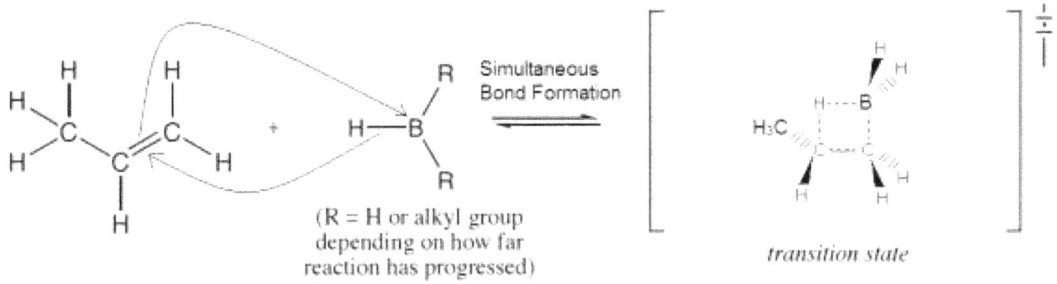

- In the figure above, you are looking at the transition state and not the intermediate
    - Dashed bond lines (not to be confused with dashed wedges) are showing bonds that are forming and bonds that are breaking
- Boron adds to the carbon with less steric hindrance

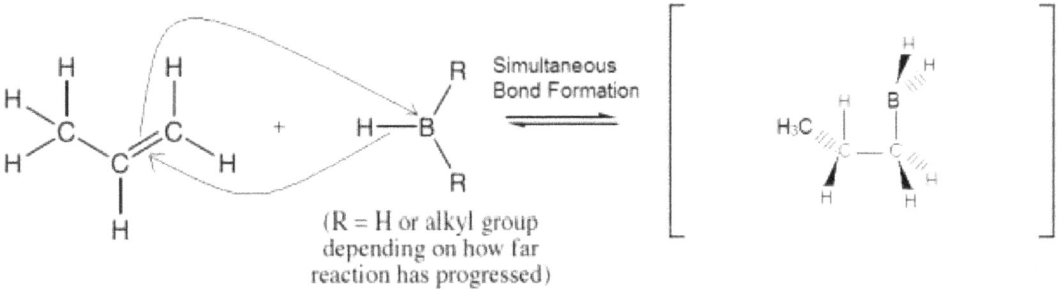

- In the figure above, you are looking at the intermediate
  - **Step 2:** Chemist opens the flask and adds H_2O_2/OH^-

- Result of this step: bond with boron is replaced with a hydroxyl group (-OH)

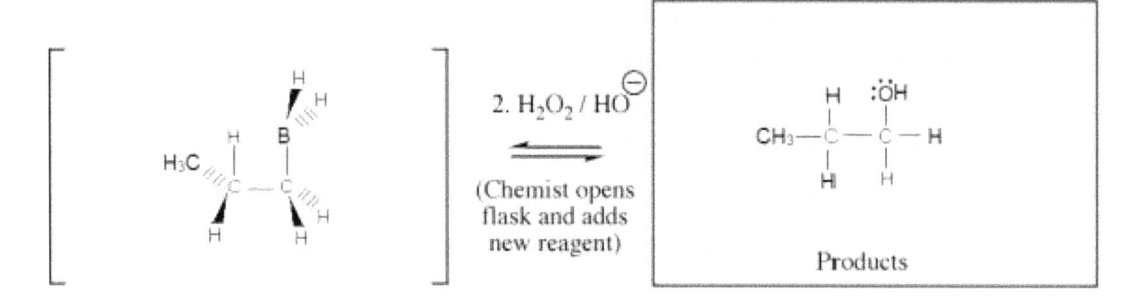

- Reaction Summary: there is simultaneous addition of the boron and the hydrogen on the same side of the double bond. H_2O_2 (hydrogen peroxide) replaces the boron with an OH group to produce an alcohol.

  - Reaction starts with an alkene
    - Transformed to an alcohol by the end of the reaction
  - Regioselectivity: Non-Markovnikov
  - Stereoselectivity: Syn-product
    - Hydroxyl group (-OH) and the hydrogen add to the same side
  - No carbocation rearrangement in this reaction

Reaction: Osmium Tetroxide – Oxidation of Alkenes to Glycol (Diol)

- Osmium tetroxide (OsO_4) oxidizes an alkene to a glycol

- Glycol (aka diol) – compound with OH groups on adjacent carbons
- OsO_4 is expensive and highly toxic
  - So it is used in catalytic amounts with another oxidizing agent to reoxidize its reduced forms
    - Recycles OsO_4
- Mechanism steps
  - **Step 1:** Electrophilic addition
    - Forms a cyclic osmate ether intermediate

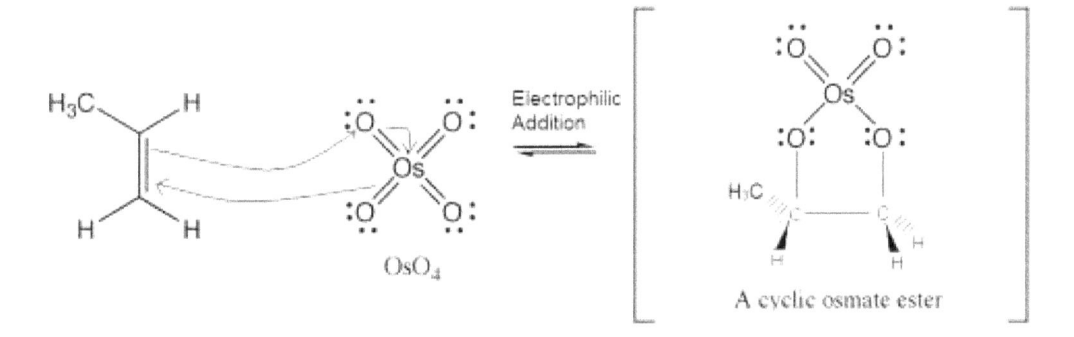

  - **Step 2:** Chemist opens the flask and adds the reducing agent ($NaHSO_3/H_2O$)
    - Result of this step: cyclic osmate intermediate is reduced by the reducing agent which cleaves the osmium-oxygen bond to give a vicinal diol
      - Vicinal – refers to any two functional groups bonded to two adjacent carbon atoms

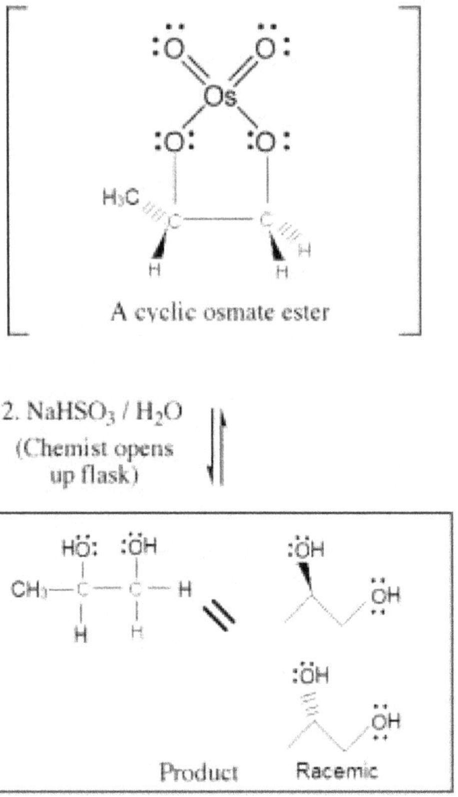

[A cyclic osmate ester structure shown]

2. NaHSO₃ / H₂O
(Chemist opens up flask)

[Product structures: vicinal diol with CH₃, and racemic mixture shown]

Product   Racemic

- Reaction Summary: alkene and OsO₄ form a cyclic osmate intermediate. Cyclic osmate intermediate is reduced by the reducing agent which cleaves the osmium-oxygen bond to give a vicinal diol
  - Vicinal – refers to any two functional groups bonded to two adjacent carbon atoms

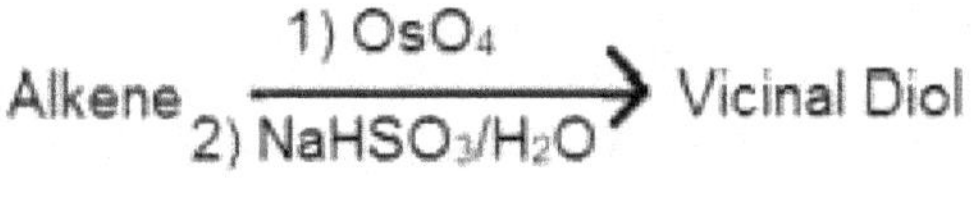

$$\text{Alkene} \xrightarrow[\text{2) NaHSO}_3/\text{H}_2\text{O}]{\text{1) OsO}_4} \text{Vicinal Diol}$$

  - Reaction starts with an alkene

- - Transformed to a vicinal diol by the end of the reaction
  - Regioselectivity: Non-Markovnikov
  - Stereoselectivity: Syn-product
    - Both hydroxyl groups (-OH) add to the same face
  - No carbocation rearrangement in this reaction

Reaction: Ozonolysis

- First step of the reaction requires ozone (O_3)
- Mechanism steps (this is a partial mechanism)
  - **Step 1:** Electrophilic addition
    - Creates a malozonide complex

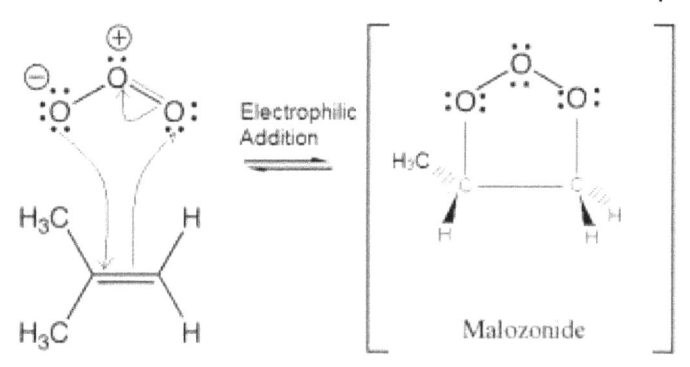

  - **Step 2:** Two-step rearrangement
    - Carbon-carbon bond is broken
    - Malozonide complex rearranges in two steps to an ozonide complex

Rearrangement in two steps | Carbon-Carbon Bond is Broken

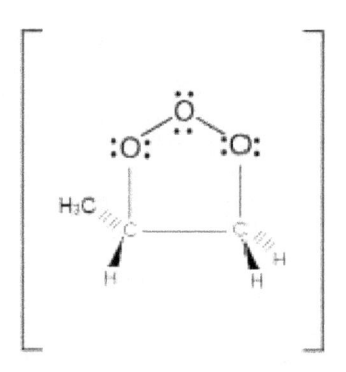

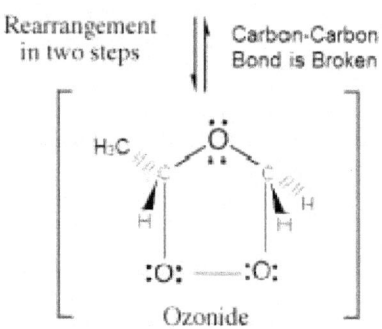

Ozonide

- **Step 3:** Chemist opens flask and adds the reducing agent
    - Reducing agent of this reaction is $(CH_3)_2S$, dimethyl sulfide
    - Result of this step: ozonide complex is reduced by dimethyl sulfide into an aldehyde

$$\left[\begin{array}{c} \text{H}_3\text{C} \diagdown \text{C} \diagup \overset{..}{\underset{..}{\text{O}}} \diagdown \text{C} \diagup \text{H} \\ | | \\ \text{H} \text{H} \\ :\!\overset{..}{\text{O}}\!: \text{———} :\!\overset{..}{\text{O}}\!: \end{array} \right]$$

2. $(CH_3)_2S$
(Chemist opens up flask)

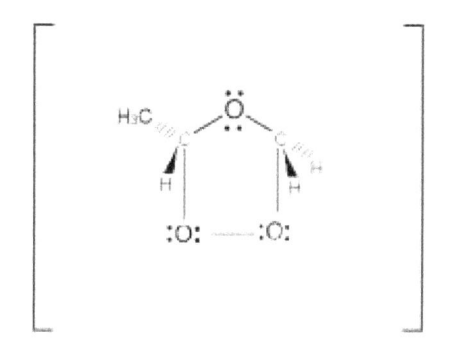

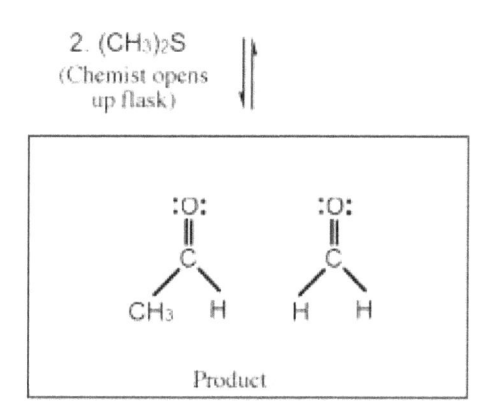

:O: 　　　　:O:
‖ 　　　　‖
C 　　　　C
CH₃ H 　H H

Product

- Reaction Summary: oxidation of alkenes

Alkene $\xrightarrow[\text{2) (CH}_3)_2\text{S}]{\text{1) O}_3}$ Aldehyde/Ketone

- Reaction starts with an alkene
  - Transformed to aldehyde/ketone by the end of the reaction
  - The original C-C double bond is completely gone by the end of the reaction
  - If this reaction occurs with a double bond inside a ring structure, the loss of the C-

Ozonolysis with a Ring-Structure: C double bond opens up the ring structure

- Regioselectivity: Non-Markovnikov
- Stereoselectivity: Not a stereoselective reaction
- No carbocation rearrangement in this reaction

Reaction: Hydrogenation of Alkenes

- This reaction is also known as "reduction of alkenes" and "catalytic hydrogenation
- In the presence of a transition metal catalyst, most alkenes react with H_2 to produce alkanes
    - Common transition metal catalysts are: Pt, Pd, Ru, and Ni
- Reduction of an alkene to an alkane is exothermic
    - Net conversion of one pi bond to two sigma bonds
    - A *trans* alkene is more stable than a *cis* alkene
- Mechanism

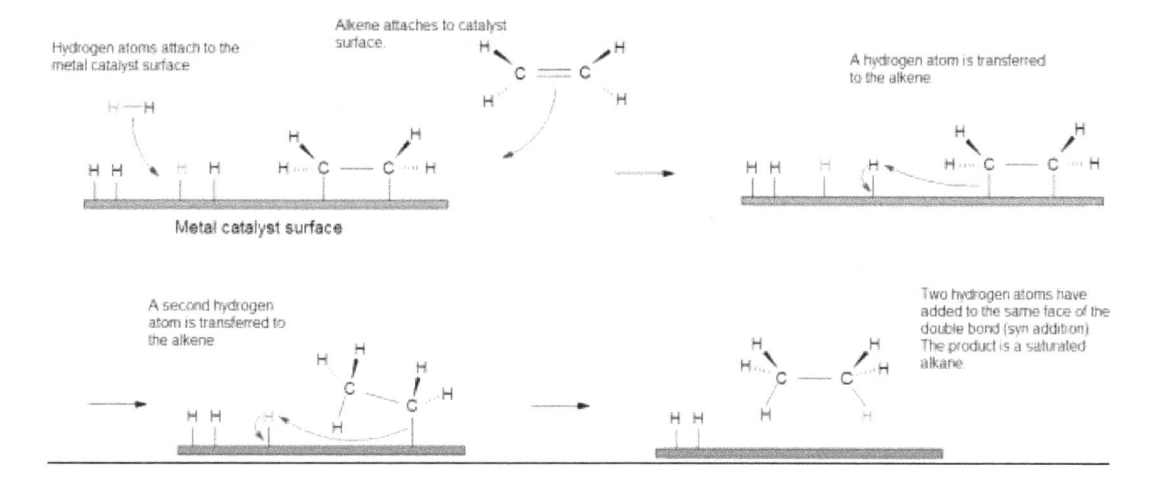

- Reaction summary: H₂ gas adheres on the transition metal surface and makes sigma H-metal bonds. The alkene adheres onto the metal and makes sigma C-metal bond. Addition of hydrogen atoms takes place from the same side.

$$\text{Alkene} \xrightarrow[\text{Pd/Pt}]{\text{H}_2} \text{Alkane}$$

  o Reaction starts with an alkene
    - Transformed to an alkane by the end of the reaction
  o Regioselectivity: Non-Markovnikov
  o Stereoselectivity: Syn-stereoselectivity
    - Hydrogens add to the same face
  o No carbocation rearrangement in this reaction

CHAPTER 7: ALKYNES AND REACTIONS OF ALKYNES

Alkynes and their Properties

Alkynes are unsaturated hydrocarbons containing at least one triple bond.

- Nonpolar
- Dissolve in organic solvents
    - Slight solubility in polar solvents
    - Insoluble in water
- Slightly higher boiling point than alkanes and alkenes
- Acidity of terminal alkynes is higher than alkanes and alkenes

IUPAC Nomenclature

Naming Alkynes

- Suffix –yne specifies an alkyne (e.g., hexy<u>ne</u>, penty<u>ne</u>)
- Identify the parent chain (longest carbon chain) and number it (always number sequentially)
    - Numbering must also be done in the direction that gives the carbons of the triple bond the lowest number possible
        - Example: $H-\underset{1}{C}\equiv\underset{2}{C}-\underset{3}{CH_2}-\underset{4}{CH_3}$
    - Two carbons define the location of the triple bond
        - But only the first carbon (lowest number carbon) is used in naming

- - Number of carbons in the parent chain gives you the parent name, then add the suffix –yne, and you add the number of the first carbon with a hyphen in front of the parent name
    - So for the alkyne above, there are 4 carbons so the parent name is but- and you would add the suffix –yne to get "butyne" and then you add the number of the first carbon with a hyphen in front of the prefix to get "1-butyne"
- Each substituent has a name and a number (use a hyphen to connect the name and number)
  - Number of the substituent is determined by which carbon it is on
    - Example: H_3C—C(H_3C)—C≡CH
    - Methyl group (CH_3-) is on C_3 so the substituent would be named 3-methyl
    - You combine the name and number of the substituent with the parent name so the name of the compound would be "3-methyl-1-butyne"
  - If there are two or more of the same substituent, add a comma to separate the substituent numbers and add a prefix to indicate how many of the substituents you have
    - Two of the same substituent (di-)
    - Three of the same substituent (tri-), and so on and so forth

- If there are two or more different substituents:
    - List them in alphabetical order
- Unlike alkanes where numbering the parent chain must be done so that substituents get the smallest possible numbers, alkynes must always be numbered so the carbons in the triple bonds get the smallest possible numbers
- There may be cases where there is both a double bond and triple bond present in the compound that you are trying to name
    - Start the numbering of the compound from the end closest to the first multiple bond
    - If both the double bond and triple bond are located similar distances from either end of the compound, the double bond gets higher priority (i.e. start numbering from the end closest to the double bond)

Preparation of Alkynes

$$H-C\equiv C-H \;+\; Na^{+}\; {:}\overset{\ominus}{N}\!-\!H \;\;\rightleftharpoons\;\; H-C\equiv C{:}^{\ominus}$$

Creating an Alkyne Anion: Sodium Amide   Acetylide Anion

- Acetylide is a carbanion that is also an alkyne anion
- Alkyne anions are good nucleophiles and strong bases
    - They participate in nucleophilic substitution reactions with alkyl halides to form C-C bonds to alkyl groups
        - Since alkyne anions are also strong bases, alkylation is practical only with methyl and primary (1°) halides

- With 2° and 3° halides, the major reactions are elimination reactions

Elimination Reaction: HC≡C⁻ Na⁺ + Bromocyclohexane → HC≡CH + Cyclohexene + Na⁺Br⁻
(Sodium acetylide)
(Acetylene)

- Alkylation of alkyne anions is a convenient method for the synthesis of terminal alkynes

Synthesis of a Terminal Alkyne: HC≡C⁻ Na⁺ + 1-Bromobutane → 1-Hexyne + Na⁺Br⁻
(Sodium acetylide)

- A terminal alkyne can be converted to an internal alkyne if alkylation is repeated

Conversion of a Terminal Alkyne to an Internal Alkyne:

CH$_3$CH$_2$C≡C⁻ Na⁺ + CH$_3$CH$_2$-Br → CH$_3$CH$_2$C≡CCH$_2$CH$_3$ + Na⁺Br⁻
(Sodium butynide) (Bromoethane) (3-Hexyne)

Preparation of Alkynes from Alkenes

- Reaction of a vicinal dibromoalkane with two moles of a base results in two successive dehydrohalogenation reactions (removal of H and X from adjacent carbons) and formation of an alkyne

  ○ Most commonly used base is sodium amide, NaNH$_2$

  ○ **Step 1:** CH$_3$CH=CHCH$_3$ + Br$_2$ $\xrightarrow{CH_2Cl_2}$ CH$_3$CH(Br)-CH(Br)CH$_3$ + 2 NaNH$_2$ (Sodium amide)
  (2-Butene)

  ○ **Step 2:** CH$_3$CH(Br)-CH(Br)CH$_3$ + 2 NaNH$_2$ $\xrightarrow[-33°C]{NH_3(l)}$ CH$_3$C≡CCH$_3$ + 2 NaBr + 2 NH$_3$
  (Sodium amide) (2-Butyne)

- To synthesize a terminal alkyne from a terminal alkene, 3 moles of base are required

  - **Step 1:** $CH_3(CH_2)_3CH=CH_2$ (1-Hexene) $\xrightarrow{Br_2}$ $CH_3(CH_2)_3\overset{Br}{C}H-\overset{Br}{C}H_2$ (1,2-Dibromohexane)

  - **Step 2:** $CH_3(CH_2)_3\overset{Br}{C}H-\overset{Br}{C}H_2$ (1,2-Dibromohexane) $\xrightarrow[2\,HBr]{3\,NaNH_2}$ $CH_3(CH_2)_3C\equiv C^-Na^+$ (Sodium salt of 1-hexyne)

  - **Step 3:** $CH_3(CH_2)_3C\equiv C^-Na^+$ (Sodium salt of 1-hexyne) $\xrightarrow{H_2O}$ $CH_3(CH_2)_3C\equiv CH$ (1-Hexyne)

Reaction: Addition of HX to an Alkyne

- X is a stand-in for a Group 7 element (e.g., Cl, Br)
- Mechanism steps (using HBr as an example)
  - **Step 1:** Add a proton
    - This step requires 1 mole of HBr

    $H_3C-C\equiv C-H$ + $H-Br$ (1 Mole) $\rightleftharpoons$ $[H_3C-\overset{+}{C}=CH_2]$ $:Br:^-$

    - Product of this step is a unstable vinylic carbocation
    - There are two possibilities in terms of which carbon the positive charge can end up on
      - A 2° vinylic carbocation is preferred over a 1° vinylic carbocation

- 2° vinylic carbocation is connected to two carbons
- 1° vinylic carbocation is connected to one carbon
- **Step 2:** Attack of the nucleophile

- **Step 3:** Add a proton
  - This step requires another mole of HBr

  - Note that the positive charge ends up on the more substituted carbon
    - 2° carbocation is more stable than a 1° carbocation

- Positive charge is stabilized through resonance
  - **Step 4:** Attack of the nucleophile

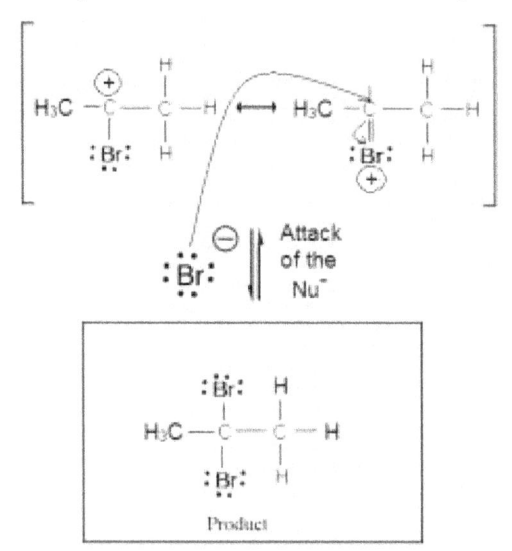

$$\left[H_3C-\overset{+}{\underset{:\ddot{B}r:}{C}}-\underset{H}{\overset{H}{C}}-H \longleftrightarrow H_3C-\underset{:\ddot{B}r:}{C}-\underset{H}{\overset{H}{\underset{+}{C}}}-H \right]$$

:Br:⊖ Attack of the Nu⁻

$$H_3C-\underset{:\ddot{B}r:}{\overset{:\ddot{B}r:}{C}}-\underset{H}{\overset{H}{C}}-H$$

Product

- Final product with 2 moles of HBr is a geminal dihalide
- Reaction Summary: addition of a proton to the alkyne forms an unstable vinylic carbocation. Addition of another mole of HX forms a 2° carbocation with the positive charge on the carbon bearing the halogen which is stabilized by resonance. The final product with 2 moles of HX is a germinal dihalide.

$$\text{Alkyne} \xrightarrow{\text{2 Moles HX}} \text{Geminal Dihalide}$$

  - Reaction starts with an alkyne
    - Transformed to a germinal dihalide by the end of the reaction

- Markovnikov regioselectivity can be used to determine which carbon the hydrogens are adding during the reaction
    - Hydrogen adds preferentially to the less substituted carbon (carbon atom bearing the greater number of hydrogens)

Reaction: Addition of X₂ to an Alkyne

- X is a stand-in for a Group 7 element (e.g., Cl, Br)
- Mechanism steps (example using Br₂)
    - **Step1:** Reaction with 1 mole of Br₂

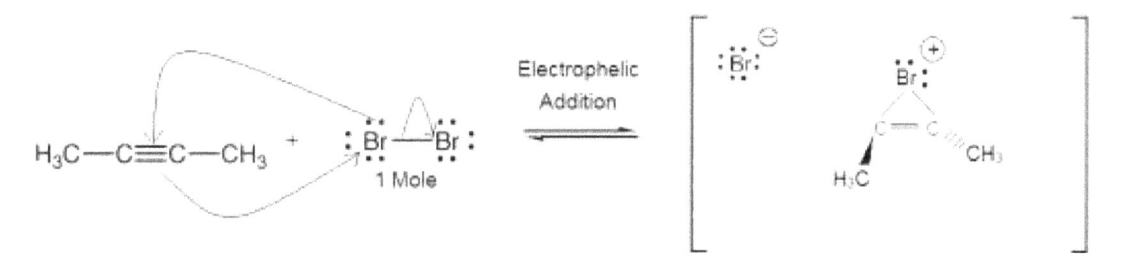

        - The halide ion (the nucleophile) attacks from the **opposite** side of the bromonium ion and opens the three-membered ring

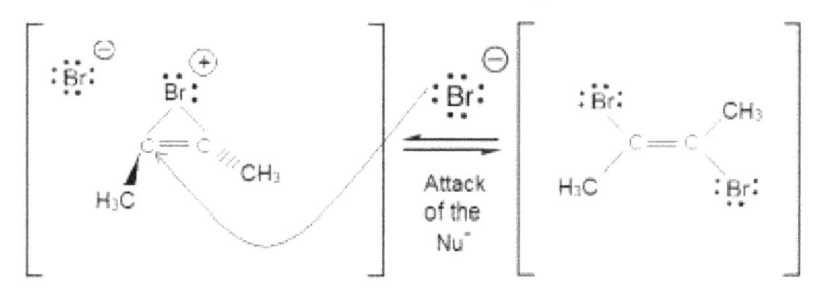

- Product of the reaction between an alkyne and 1 mole of Br₂ produces a dibromoalkene
  ○ **Step2:** Reaction with another 1 mole of Br₂

$$\underset{H_3C}{\overset{:\ddot{Br}:}{}}C=C\underset{:\ddot{Br}:}{\overset{CH_3}{}} + :\ddot{Br}-\ddot{Br}: \rightleftharpoons H_3C-\underset{Br}{\overset{Br}{C}}-\underset{Br}{\overset{Br}{C}}-CH_3$$
                                   1 Mole

- Product of the reaction between the dibromoalkane and 1 mole of Br₂ produces a tetrahaloalkane
- Reaction Summary

$$\text{Alkyne} \xrightarrow{\text{1 mole } X_2} \text{Dihaloalkane}$$

$$\text{Alkyne} \xrightarrow{\text{2 mole } X_2} \text{Tetrahaloalakane}$$

  ○ Stereoselectivity: Anti-product
  ○ No carbocation rearrangement in this reaction

Reduction of Alkynes

Reduction of Alkynes with H₂ in the Presence of a Metal Catalyst

- Reaction of alkynes with H₂ in the presence of a metal catalyst (commonly, Pd or Pt) converts the alkyne to an alkane

Reduction of Alkyne with H₂ and a Metal Catalyst:

$$H_3C-C\equiv C-CH_3 \xrightarrow{H_2}_{Pd\ or\ Pt} H-\underset{H}{\overset{CH_3}{\underset{|}{\overset{|}{C}}}}-\underset{H}{\overset{CH_3}{\underset{|}{\overset{|}{C}}}}-H$$

General Reduction of Alkyne with H₂ and a Metal Catalyst: Alkyne $\xrightarrow{H_2}_{Pd\ or\ Pt}$ Alkane

- This is not a selective reduction
    - It results in the **complete** reduction of the triple bond

Reduction of Alkynes by Lindlar's Catalyst

- Lindlar's catalyst is what is referred to as a "poisoned" metal catalyst
    - It lacks the normal activity that we associate with palladium (Pd) catalysts for reducing double bonds (i.e. Lindlar's catalyst can't reduce a double bond)
        - Useful for when you want to create an alkene from an alkyne

Reduction of Alkyne with H₂ and Lindlar's Catalyst:

$$H_3C-C\equiv C-CH_3 \xrightarrow{H_2}_{Lindlar's\ Catalyst} \underset{H}{\overset{H_3C}{{\diagdown}}}C=C\underset{H}{\overset{CH_3}{{\diagup}}}$$

General Reduction of Alkyne with H₂ and Lindlar's Catalyst: Alkyne $\xrightarrow{H_2}_{Lindlar's\ Catalyst}$ Alkane

- This reduction has *syn* stereoselectivity
    - Hydrogens add to the same side

Reduction of Alkynes by Sodium in Liquid Ammonia

- Alkynes can be reduced to *trans* alkenes using Na in NH$_{3(l)}$
- Mechanism steps
    - **Step 1:** One-electron reduction

    $$H_3C-C\equiv C-CH_3 + \cdot Na \xrightleftharpoons{\text{One-Electron Reduction}} \left[H_3C-\dot{C}=\ddot{C}-CH_3 \right]^{\ominus} \, ^{\oplus}Na$$

        - Note that single-barbed arrows are being used
            - They indicate the movement of only one electron
        - Sodium transfers one electron to the alkyne which produces a radical anion
    - **Step 2:** Add a proton

    - **Step 3:** One-electron reduction

- **Step 4:** Add a proton

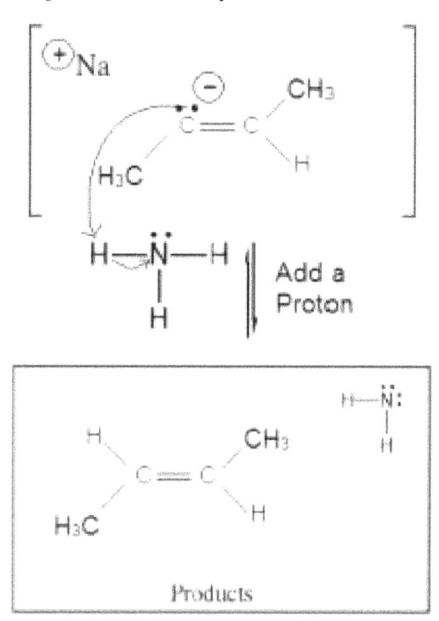

[diagram: sodium cation with vinyl carbanion (H₃C and CH₃ on trans positions) attacking H–N(H)–H ammonia]

Add a Proton

[diagram of product: trans-alkene with H₃C and H on one carbon, CH₃ and H on the other; plus H–N(H)–H]

Products

- Reaction Summary: Na transfers an electron to the alkyne producing a radical anion. The radical anion removes a proton from ammonia and a second atom of Na transfers another electron to the alkyne establishing the *trans* stereoselectivity. The carbanion removes a proton from ammonia to give a *trans*-alkene

$$\text{Alkyne} \xrightarrow{Na/NH_{3(l)}} \text{Alkene}$$

  - Reaction starts with an alkyne
    - It is reduced to a *trans*-alkene by the end of the reaction
    - Reaction conditions do not reduce alkenes so the reaction does not proceed further than an alkene

- Stereoselectivity: always produces a *trans* alkene with anti-addition
  - Hydrogens add to the opposite side
- No carbocation rearrangement in this reaction

Reaction: Hydroboration – Oxidation of Alkynes

- Mechanism steps (using a terminal alkyne as an example)
  - **Step 1:** Simultaneous bond formation
    - This step requires (sia)$_2$BH:
    - In the figure above, you are looking at the transition state and not the intermediate
      - Dashed bond lines (not to be confused with dashed wedges) are showing bonds that are forming and bonds that are breaking
      - Boron adds to the carbon with less steric hindrance

- Keep in mind that "R" is an abbreviation for any group or chemical chain in which a carbon or hydrogen atom is attached to the rest of the molecule

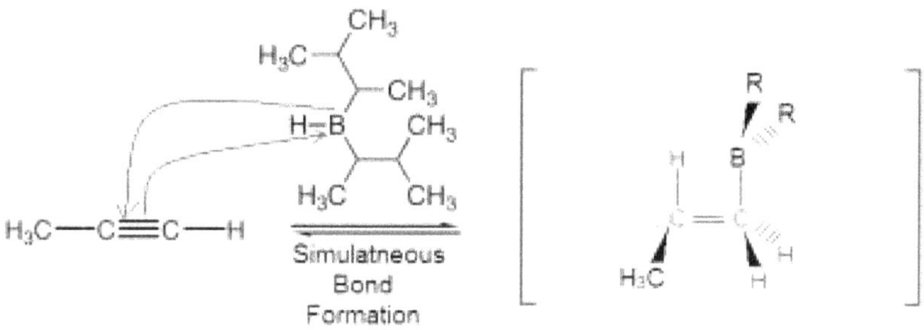

- In the figure above, you are looking at the intermediate

  o **Step 2:** Chemist opens the flask and adds H_2O_2/NaOH

    - Result of this step: bond with boron is replaced with a hydroxyl group (-OH)
    - Creates an enol
      - Enol – compound containing an OH group on one carbon of a C-C double bond

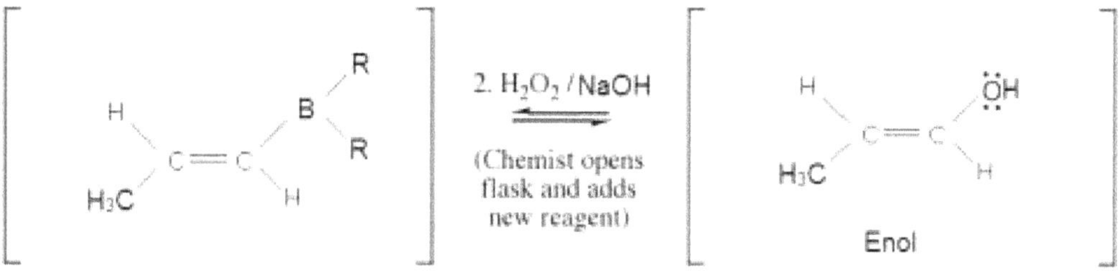

  o **Step 3:** Keto-enol tautomerization

- Enol is in equilibrium with a keto form through the displacement of a hydrogen from oxygen to carbon and through the migration of the double bond from C=C to C=O
    - Keto form predominates at equilibrium
    - Keto and enol forms are tautomers

[Enol] ⇌ (Keto-enol tautomerization) Products

- Reaction Summary: hydroboration of a terminal alkyne takes place using a sterically hindered (sia)$_2$BH to give a syn-product (an enol). Tautomerization of the enol gives an aldehyde.

Terminal Alkyne —1) (sia)$_2$BH; 2) H$_2$O$_2$/NaOH→ Aldehyde

Internal Alkyne —1) BH$_3$; 2) H$_2$O$_2$/NaOH→ Ketone

  - Reaction starts with an alkyne
    - If the starting material is a terminal alkyne, it is transformed to an aldehyde by the end of the reaction

- Terminal alkyne – alkyne with at least one hydrogen atom bonded to the triple bond
    - If the starting material is an internal alkyne, it is transformed to an aldehyde by the end of the reaction
        - Internal alkyne – alkyne with no hydrogen atom bonded to the triple bond
  - Regioselectivity: Non-Markovnikov
  - Stereoselectivity: Syn-product
    - Hydroxyl group (-OH) and the hydrogen add to the same side
  - No carbocation rearrangement in this reaction

Reaction: Electrophilic Addition to Alkynes

- In this reaction, an alkyne is hydrated to form an enol that tautomerises to form a ketone

$$\text{Internal Alkyne} \xrightarrow[H_2SO_4, H_2O]{HgSO_4} \text{Ketone}$$

- Mercury salt acts as a catalyst
  - Reaction without mercury is slow
- Regioselectivity: Markovnikov
- This reaction is very similar to the hydroboration reaction
  - However, note the different regioselectivity between the two reactions

CHAPTER 8: HALOALKANES AND RADICAL REACTIONS

Haloalkanes (aka Alkyl Halide)

- Haloalkane (alkyl halide) - compound that contains a halogen atom (F, Cl, Br, etc.) covalently bonded to an sp^3 hybridized carbon
    - Typically represented by the symbol: RX
- Haloalkene (vinylic halide) – compound containing a halogen atom bonded to an sp^2 hybridized carbon
- Haloarene (aryl halide) – compound containing a halogen atom bonded to a benzene ring
    - Typically represented by the symbol: ArX
        - Ar = aromatic

Van der Waals Forces

- Haloalkenes are associated in the liquid state by van der Waals forces
    - Van der Waals forces pull molecules together
    - When molecules are brought close together, van der Waals attractive forces are overcome by repulsive forces between electron clouds of adjacent atoms or molecules
- Energy minimum - where the attractive and repulsive forces are equal
- Van der Waals radius - distance from the nucleus to the electron cloud surface

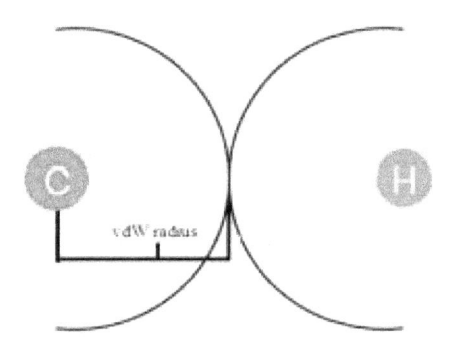

- When orbitals of two atoms are as close as possible but do not overlap, no bonds can be formed
    - This is shown in the picture above
- When atoms are close enough that their orbitals overlap, bonds can be formed
    - A covalent bond distance is about 1 angstrom (1 X10^{-10} meters) 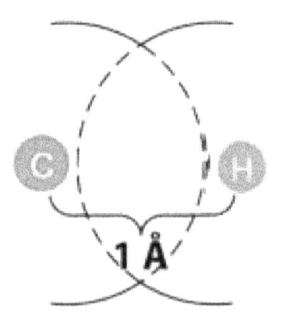
    - A hydrogen bond distance is about 1.8 angstrom
- Nonbonded atoms in a molecule cannot approach each other closer than the sum of their van der Waals radii without causing nonbonded interaction strain

Boiling Points and Polarizability

- Haloalkanes typically have higher boiling points than alkanes (as long as they are of comparable size and shape)
    - Difference is due to the greater polarizability of the three unshared pairs of electrons on an halogen vs. the low polarizability of shared electron pairs of covalent bonds
        - Polarizability - ability of the electron cloud to distort or change in response to another molecule or ion
            - Larger volume occupied by the electron equates to a more polarized molecule
        - Polarizability ranking (weakest to strongest): F < Cl < Br < I
- Branched constitutional isomers have lower boiling points
    - Branching creates a more compact shape, decreased area of contact, decreased stacking, and decreased van der Waals interactions, which lower boiling points

Density

- Densities of liquid haloalkanes are greater than those of hydrocarbons of comparable molecular weight
- Halogens have a greater density than a methyl or methylene group
- Density ranking (least to most dense): CH_4 < CH_3Cl < CH_2Cl_2 < $CHCl_2$ < CCl_3

Bond Length and Strengths

- Bond length ranking (shorter to longer): C-H < C-F < C-Cl < C-Br < C-I
- Bond strength ranking (weakest to strongest): C-I < C-Br < C-Cl < C-H < C-F

Nomenclature

- Identify the parent chain (longest carbon chain) and number it (always number sequentially)
    - Numbering must also be done to give the substituent encountered first the lowest number, whether it is a halogen or an alkyl group
- Halogen substituents are indicated by prefixes: fluoro-, chloro-, bromo-, and iodo-
    - Must be listed alphabetically while naming
    - Must also indicate which carbon of the parent chain it is on by placing the carbon number preceding the name of the halogen with a hyphen
        - Example: 3-Chloropropene
- Priority order: double bonds > triple bonds > halogen substituent
    - Double bond must be given the lowest set of numbers possible

Radical Chain Mechanism

- Radical – chemical species that has one or more unpaired electrons
    - Radicals are formed by hemolytic bond cleavage

- Order of stability of alkyl radicals: 3° > 2° > 1° > methyl

Steps of Chain Reaction

Chain length refers to the number of times the cycle of chain propagation steps repeats in a chain reaction.

- Chain initiation
    - Characterized by formation of reactive intermediates (radicals, anions, or cations)
- Chain propagation
    - Characterized by the reaction of a reactive intermediate and a molecule to form a new radical or reactive intermediate and a new molecule
- Chain termination
    - Characterized by the destruction of reactive intermediates

Reaction: Radical Halogenation of Alkanes

- Halogen reactivity: F_2 > Cl_2 > Br_2 > I_2
    - Only chlorination and bromination are useful in a laboratory setting
    - Bromination is more selective than chlorination
- Mechanism steps:
    - **Step 1:** Initiation
        - Heat or UV light causes homolytic bond cleavage

- This type of bond breaking results in the bonding electron pair being split evenly between the products

$$:\ddot{B}r-\ddot{B}r: \xrightarrow[\text{Homolytic Bond Cleavage}]{h\nu \text{ or heat}} [\cdot Br] + [\cdot Br]$$

- Step 2: Propagation
  - End result is that a haloalkane is produced
    - Also, another Br radical is produced to propagate the reaction

- Step 3: Termination
  - Various reactions between the possible pairs of radicals occur

- Form X₂, a hydrocarbon, and the product (a haloalkane)

$$:\!\ddot{B}r\cdot + \cdot\ddot{B}r\!: \rightleftharpoons \;:\!\ddot{B}r\!-\!\ddot{B}r\!:$$

$$H_3C-CH_2\cdot + \cdot CH_2-CH_3 \rightleftharpoons CH_3-CH_2-CH_2-CH_3$$

$$H_3C-CH_2\cdot + \cdot\ddot{B}r\!: \rightleftharpoons CH_3-CH_2-Br$$

- Reaction Summary: heat or UV light causes hemolytic cleavage of the weak halogen bond and generates two radicals. Bromine radical extracts a hydrogen to form H-Br and a methyl radical. The methyl radical extracts a bromine atom to form another bromine radical and the haloalkane product. Various reactions between radicals occur and they remove radicals from the reaction cycle.

$$\text{Alkane} \xrightarrow[\text{Br}_2 \text{ or Cl}_2]{h\nu \text{ or heat}} \text{Haloalkane}$$

  ○ Reaction starts with an alkane
    ▪ It is transformed to a haloalkane by the end of the reaction
    ▪ Reaction conditions do not reduce alkenes so the reaction does not proceed further than an alkene
    ▪ Reaction proceeds through a radical chain mechanism

- Involves radical intermediates
    - Termination steps have low probability
        - Radical species are present in low concentrations

Reaction: Allylic Bromination of Alkenes

- Allylic Carbon – C atom adjacent to a C-C bond
- Allylic Hydrogen – H atom on an allylic carbon
- Mechanism steps:
    - **Step 1:** Initiation
        - Heat or UV light causes homolytic bond cleavage

    - **Step 2:** Propagation
        - End result is that a bromoalkene is produced
            - Also, another Br radical is produced to propagate the reaction

- **Step 3:** Termination
  - Various reactions between the possible pairs of radicals occur

- Reaction Summary:

$$\text{Alkene} \xrightarrow[\text{NBS}]{\text{hv or heat}} \text{Bromoalkene}$$

- Reaction starts with an alkene
    - It is transformed to a bromoalkene by the end of the reaction
    - Reaction proceeds through a radical chain mechanism
        - Involves radical intermediates
    - Termination steps have low probability
        - Radical species are present in low concentrations

Reaction: Radical Addition of HBr to Alkenes

- Addition of HBr to alkenes gives either Markovnikov addition or non-Markovnikov addition (depends on reaction conditions)
    - When radicals are absent, Markovnikov addition occurs
    - When peroxides or other sources of radicals are present, non-Markovnikov addition occurs
- Addition of HCl and HI gives only Markovnikov products
- Mechanism steps:
    - **Step 1:** Initiation

$$R-\ddot{O}-\ddot{O}-R \xrightarrow{heat} R-\ddot{O}\cdot + \cdot\ddot{O}-R$$

Peroxide

$$H-\ddot{Br}: + [\cdot\ddot{O}-R] \rightleftharpoons [\cdot Br] + H-\ddot{O}-R$$

- **Step 2:** Propagation
    - End result is that a bromoalkane is produced
        - Also, another Br radical is produced to propagate the reaction

- **Step 3:** Termination
    - Various reactions between the possible pairs of radicals occur
    - Follows the same pattern discussed in the previous two reactions

- Reaction Summary:

$$\text{Alkane} \xrightarrow[\text{Br}_2]{\text{hv or heat}} \text{Bromoalkane}$$

    - Reaction starts with an alkane
        - It is transformed to a bromoalkane by the end of the reaction

- - - Reaction proceeds through a radical chain mechanism
      - Involves radical intermediates
    - Termination steps have low probability
      - Radical species are present in low concentrations
  - Regioselectivity:
    - When radicals are absent, Markovnikov addition occurs
    - When peroxides or other sources of radicals are present, non-Markovnikov addition occurs
  - Carbocation rearrangement is possible in this reaction

Chapter 9: Nucleophilic Substitution and β-Elimination

Nucleophilic Substitution

Nucleophilic substitution reactions are any reactions in which one nucleophile substitutes for another at a tetravalent carbon.

- Nucleophile – molecule or ion that donates a pair of electrons to another atom or ion to form a new covalent bond
    - Nucleophiles are also Lewis bases
- There are two limiting mechanisms for nucleophilic substitutions
    - Fundamental difference between the two mechanisms is the timing of bond-breaking and bond-forming steps

S$_N$2 Reactions

- S$_N$2 reaction – reaction during which bond-breaking and bond-forming steps occur simultaneously (simultaneous attack of the nucleophile and departure of the leaving group)
    - S = substitution
    - N = nucleophilic
    - 2 = bimolecular (both reactants are involved in the rate-determining step)

Transition state with simultaneous bond breaking and bond forming

- S$_N$2 reactions result in inversion at the chiral center

Kinetics of S$_N$2 Reactions

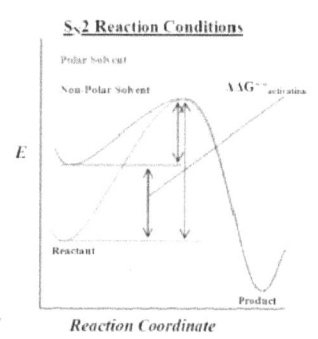

S$_N$2 Reaction Energy Diagram:

- Reaction occurs in one step
- Reaction leading to the transition state involves both the haloalkane and the nucleophile
    - Results in a 2nd order reaction

S$_N$1 Reactions

- S$_N$1 reaction – reaction during which the bond-breaking between carbon and the leaving group is entirely completed before bond-forming with the nucleophile begins
    - S = substitution

- N = nucleophilic
- 1 = unimolecular (only one reactant is involved in the rate-determining step)
- In an S_N1 reaction, the R and S enantiomers are formed in equal amounts
  - The product is a racemic mixture
- Rearrangements are common in S_N1 reactions
  - Make sure to check to see if the initial carbocation can rearrange to a more stable one

Kinetics of SN1 Reactions

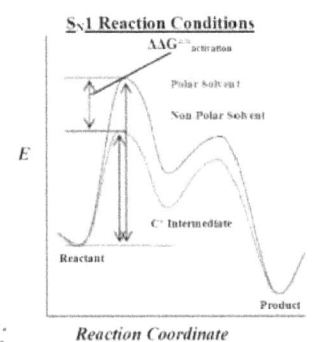

S_N1 Reaction Energy Diagram:

- Reaction occurs in two steps
- Reaction leading to formation of the transition state for the carbocation intermediate involves only the haloalkane and not the nucleophile
- Result in a 1st order reaction

Leaving Groups

- More stable an anion, the better its leaving ability
- Most stable anions are conjugate bases of strong acids

- Ranking of reactivity as a leaving group (most reactive to least reactive): I- > Br- > Cl- > H2O >> F- > CH3COO- > HO- > CH3O- > NH2-

Solvents

- Protic solvent - solvent that is a hydrogen bond donor
    - Most common protic solvents contain -OH groups
- Aprotic solvent - solvent that cannot serve as a hydrogen bond donor
    - Nowhere in the molecule is there a hydrogen bonded to an atom of high electronegativity
- Solvents are classified as polar and nonpolar
    - Most common measure of solvent polarity is the dielectric constant
        - Dielectric constant - measure of a solvent's ability to insulate opposite charges from one another
            - Greater value of the dielectric constant of a solvent equates to a smaller interaction between ions of opposite charge dissolved in that solvent
            - Polar solvents have a dielectric constant > 15
            - Nonpolar solvents have a dielectric constant < 15

Solvent – S$_N$2

- Most common type of S_N2 reaction involves a negative nucleophile and a negative leaving group
    - The weaker the solvation of a nucleophile, the less the energy required to remove it from its solvation shell and the greater the rate of S_N2

Solvent – S_N1

- S_N1 reactions involve creation and separation of unlike charges in the transition state of the rate-determining step
- Rate depends on the ability of the solvent to keep these charges separated and to solvate both the anion and the cation
- Polar protic solvents are the most effective solvents for S_N1 reactions

Nucleophilicity and Basicity

Since all nucleophiles are also bases, the correlation between nucleophilicity and basicity are studied.

- Nucleophilicity - kinetic property measured by the rate at which a nucleophile causes a nucleophilic substitution under a standardized set of experimental conditions
- Basicity - equilibrium property measured by the position of equilibrium in an acid-base reaction
- Polar protic solvents
    - Anions are highly solvated by hydrogen bonding with the solvent
    - The more concentrated the negative charge of the anion, the more tightly it is held in a solvent shell

- - The nucleophile must be at least partially removed from its solvent shell in order to participate in S_N2 reactions
  - Nucleophilicity ranking: I⁻ > Br⁻ > Cl⁻ > F⁻
- Polar aprotic solvents are very effective in solvating cations
  - But they are not nearly so effective in solvating anions
    - This means they participate readily in S_N2 reactions
    - Nucleophilicity parallels basicity: F⁻ > Cl⁻ > Br⁻ > I⁻
- In general, in a series of reagents with the same nucleophilic atom: anionic reagents are stronger nucleophiles than neutral reagents
  - This trend parallels the basicity of the nucleophile
- In general, when comparing groups of reagents in which the nucleophilic atom is the same: the stronger the base, the greater the nucleophilicity

Summary of S_N2 and S_N1

Type of Alkyl Halide	S_N2	S_N1
Methyl (CH₃X)	S_N2 is favored.	S_N1 does not occur.
Primary (RCH₂X)	S_N2 is favored.	S_N1 rarely occurs.
Secondary (R₂CHX)	S_N2 is favored in aprotic solvents with good nucleophiles.	S_N1 is favored in protic solvents with poor nucleophiles. Look out for carbocation rearrangement.
Tertiary (R₃CX)	S_N2 does not occur because of steric hindrance around the reaction center.	S_N1 is favored.
Substitution at a Stereocenter	Inversion of configuration. The nucleophile attacks the stereocenter from the side opposite the leaving group.	Racemization is favored. Carbocation intermediate is planar, and attack of the nucleophile occurs with equal probability from either side.

β-Elimination

β-Elimination is a type of reaction in which a small molecule (e.g., HCl, HBr, HI, or HOH) is split out or eliminated from adjacent carbons.

- Zaitsev Rule
    - Major product of a β-elimination is the more stable (more substituted) alkene
    - Example:

2-Bromo-2-methylbutane + CH₃CH₂O⁻Na⁺ / CH₃CH₂OH → 2-Methyl-2-butene (major product) + 2-Methyl-1-butene

- There are two limiting mechanisms for β- elimination reactions (E1 and E2)

E2 Mechanism

- Breaking of the R-LG and C-H bonds occurs simultaneously
    - Both R-LG and the base involved in breaking of the C-H bond are involved in the rate-determining step
- Kinetics of E2
    - Reaction occurs in one step
    - Reaction is 2nd order
- Regioselectivity
    - With a strong base, the major product is the more stable (more substituted) alkene
    - With a strong and sterically hindered base such as tert-butoxide, the major product is often the less stable (less substituted) alkene

E1 Mechanism

- Breaking of the R-LG bond to give a carbocation is fully completed before reaction with the base to break the C-H bond
    - Only breaking of the R-LG bond is involved in the rate-determining step

- Kinetics of E1
    - Reaction occurs in two steps
    - Rate-determining step is carbocation formation
    - Reaction is 1st order
- Regioselectivity
    - E1 always follows the Zaitsev rule
        - Major product is the more stable (more substituted) alkene

Summary of E2 vs. E1

Type of Alkyl Halide	E2	E1
Primary (RCH_2X)	E2 is favored.	E1 does not occur.
Secondary (R_2CHX)	Main reaction with strong bases such as OH and OR.	Main reaction with weak bases such as H_2O, ROH.
Tertiary (R_3CX)	Main reaction with strong bases such as OH and OR.	Main reaction with weak bases such as H_2O, ROH.

S_N vs. E

- Because many nucleophiles are also strong bases (e.g., -OH and -OR) S_N and E reactions often compete
- Ratio of S_N/E products depends on the relative rates of the two reactions

Type of Alkyl Halide	Favored Reaction(s)	How to Decide Which Reaction is Occurring
Methyl (CH_3X)	Only S_N2	
Primary (RCH_2X)	S_N2 or E2	Strong, bulky base such as (t-BuOK) → E2 No strong, bulky base → S_N2
Secondary (R_2CHX)	S_N2, E2, and S_N1/E1 (Occur Together)	Strong base → E2 Polar protic solvent and no strong base → S_N1/E1 Strong nucleophile and no polar protic solvent or strong base → S_N2
Tertiary (R_3CX)	E2 or S_N1/E1 (Occur Together)	Strong base → E2 No strong base → S_N1/E1

CHAPTER 10: ALCOHOLS AND THEIR REACTIONS

Alcohols

Structure

- Functional group of an alcohol is an -OH group bonded to an sp³ hybridized carbon
    - Bond angles = ~109.5 about the hydroxyl oxygen atom
- Oxygen is sp³ hybridized
    - Two sp³ hybrid orbitals form sigma bonds to a carbon and hydrogen
    - The remaining two sp³ hybrid orbitals each contain an unshared pair of electrons

Nomenclature

- Parent chain is the longest chain that contains the OH group
- Priority order: hydroxyl group > double bonds > triple bonds > halogen substituent
    - Number the parent chain to give the OH group the lowest possible number
- Change the suffix –e to ol

Examples of Alcohols: 1-Propanol (1°), 2-Propanol (2°), 1-Butanol (1°)

- Compounds containing more than one OH group are named diols, triols, etc.

Physical Properties

- Alcohols are polar
  - Interact with themselves and with other polar compounds by dipole-dipole interactions
    - Dipole-dipole interaction – attraction between positive end of one dipole with the negative end of another
- Hydrogen bonding occurs when the positive end hydrogen bonding of one dipole is an H bonded to F, O, or N (atoms of high electronegativity) and the other end is F, O, or N
  - Hydrogen bonds are weaker than covalent bonds but still contribute to physical properties
- Molecules with higher hydrogen bonding interactions typically have a higher boiling point
- Relative to alkanes (of comparable size and molecular weight)
  - Alcohols have higher boiling points and are more soluble in water
    - Additional –OH groups increase solubility and boiling points

Reaction: S_N2 Reaction of 1° Alcohol with HX

- Mechanism steps
  - **Step 1:** Add a proton

[Mechanism diagram: H₃C-O-H + H-Br → H₃C-O(+)H-H with Br(−), labeled "Add a Proton"]

- **Step 2:** S_N2 (Simultaneous Attack of the Nucleophile and Departure of the Leaving group)

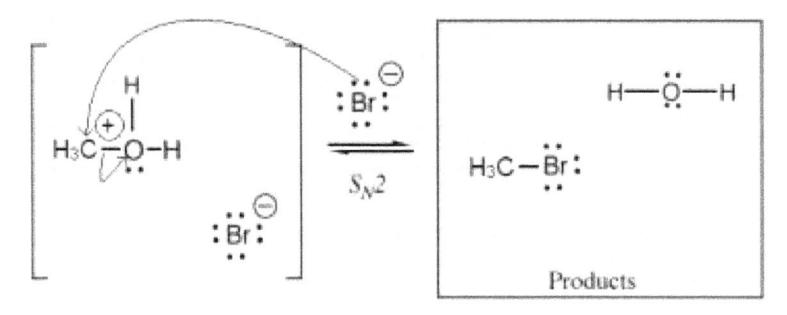

[Mechanism diagram: protonated methanol with Br(−) attacking → H₃C-Br + H-O-H (Products)]

- Reaction Summary: first step of the reaction is the protonation of the OH group to convert it to a good leaving group. This is the fast step. The second step is simultaneous attack of the nucleophile and departure of the leaving group. This is the rate determining step. Primary alcohols produce a haloalkane with HX by S_N2 mechanism.

Primary Alcohol —HX→ Haloalkane

  - Reaction starts with a primary alcohol
    - Transformed to an haloalkane by the end of the reaction

Reaction: S_N1 Reaction of 2° and 3° Alcohol with HX

- Mechanism steps
    - **Step 1:** Add a proton

    - **Step 2:** S$_N$1 – Departure of the Leaving Group

    - **Step 3:** S$_N$1 – Attack of the Nucleophile

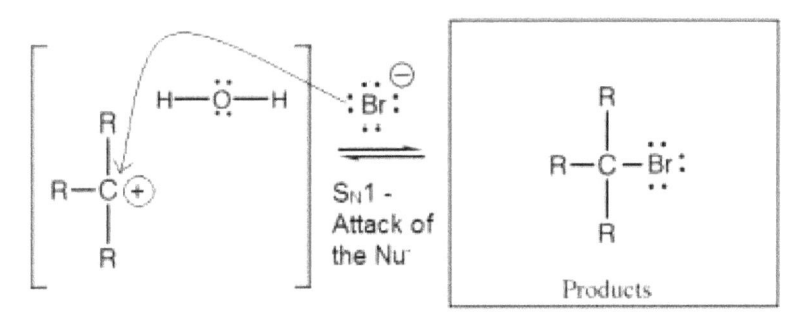

- Reaction Summary:

    2° or 3° Alcohol $\xrightarrow{HX}$ Haloalkane

    - Reaction starts with a secondary or alcohol

- Transformed to an haloalkane by the end of the reaction
  - When this reaction occurs with a secondary alcohol, carbocation rearrangement is possible due to hydrogen shift

Reaction: S_N2 Reaction of 1° and 2° Alcohol with PBr₃

- This is an alternative method for the synthesis of 1° and 2° bromoalkanes
  - Results in less rearrangement than reaction with HX
- Mechanism steps
  - **Step 1:** Attack of the nucleophile

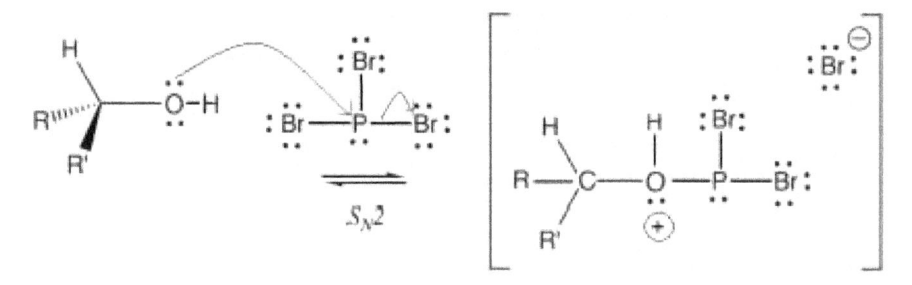

  - **Step 2:** S_N2 (Simultaneous Attack of the Nucleophile and Departure of the Leaving group)

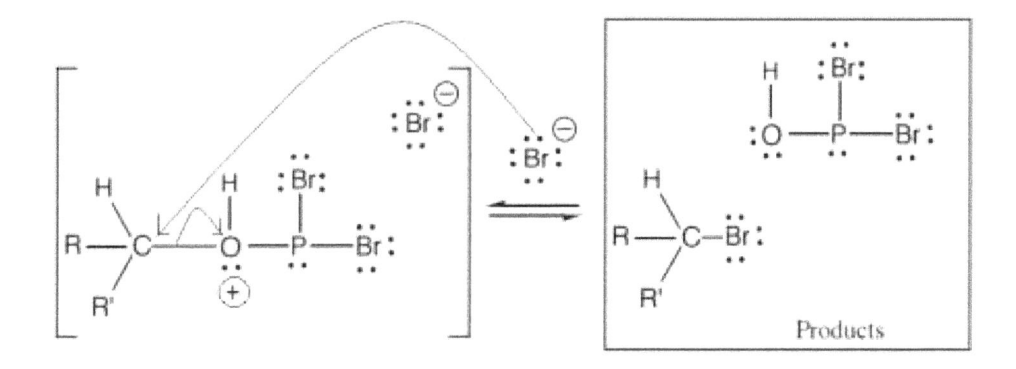

- Reaction Summary:

  1° or 2° Alcohol $\xrightarrow{PBr_3}$ Haloalkane

    - Reaction starts with a primary or secondary alcohol
        - Transformed to an haloalkane by the end of the reaction
    - Steroselectivity: Reaction results in inversion at the chiral center

Reaction of Alcohols with Thionyl Chloride (SOCL$_2$)

- Mechanism steps
    - **Step 1:** Attack of the nucleophile

- **Step 2:** Remove a proton

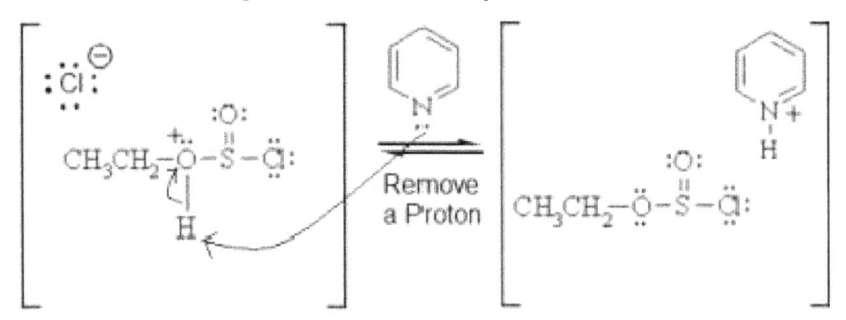

- **Step 3:** S$_N$2 (Simultaneous Attack of the Nucleophile and Departure of the Leaving group)

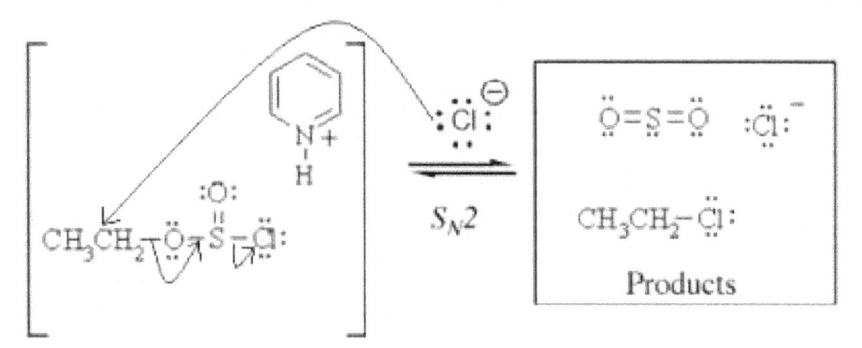

- Reaction Summary:

  $$\text{Alcohol} \xrightarrow[\text{Pyridine}]{\text{SOCl}_2} \text{Alkyl Chloride}$$

  - Reaction starts with a alcohol
    - Transformed to an alkyl chloride by the end of the reaction
  - Steroselectivity: Reaction results in inversion at the chiral center

Reaction: Dehydration of 2° and 3° Alcohol

- Mechanism steps
    - **Step 1:** Add a proton
        - First, H_2SO_4 reacts with H_2O to produce H_3O^+ and HSO_4^-

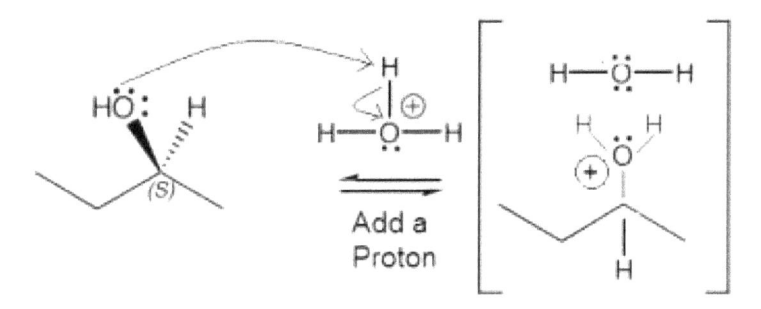

    - **Step 2:** E1 – Departure of the leaving group

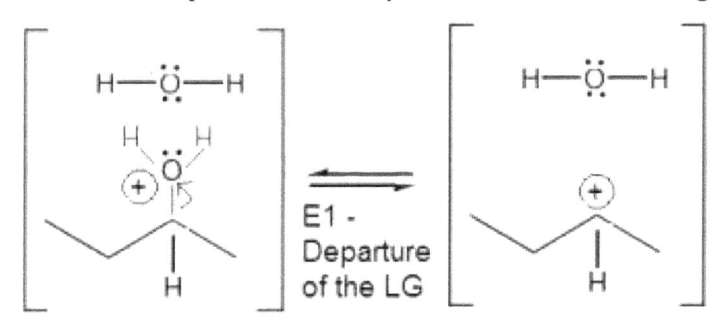

    - **Step 3:** Remove a proton

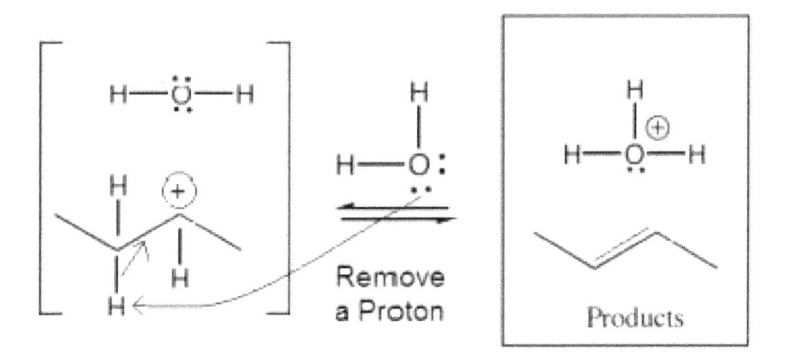

- Reaction Summary:

    2° or 3° Alcohol —— HX ——> Alkene

    - Reaction starts with a secondary or tertiary alcohol
        - Transformed to an alkene by the end of the reaction
    - Regioselectivity: Zaitsev product
        - Alkene with the greater number of substituents on the double bond predominates
    - Steroselectivity: E-product
        - Higher priority groups are on the opposite side

Reaction: Chromic Acid Oxidation of Alcohols

- Mechanism steps
    - **Step 1:** Several steps
        - Typically, you aren't going to be required to know the exact steps that take place, but you are probably going to be asked to remember the product of the first step

- **Step 2:** Remove a proton

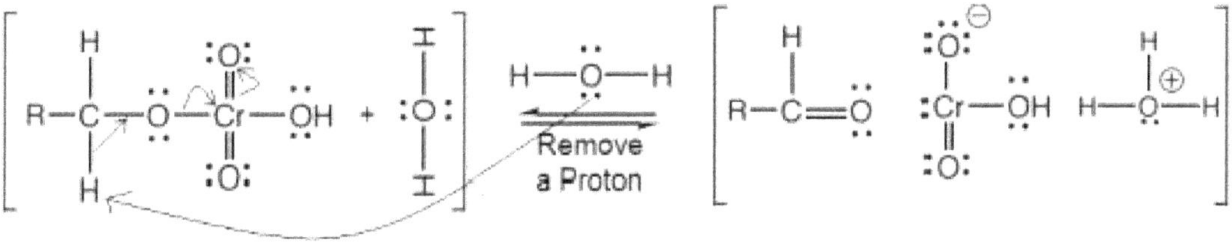

- **Step 3:** Add a proton

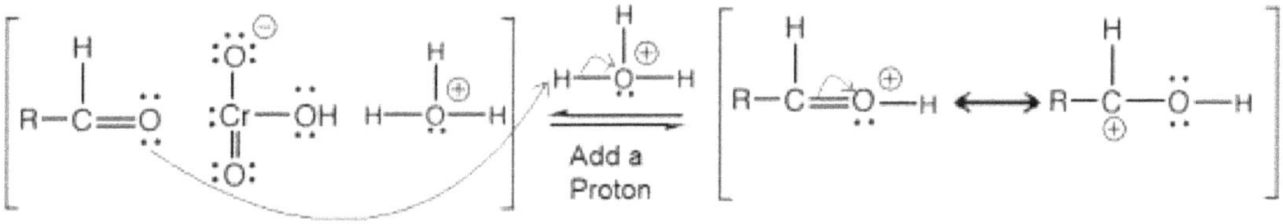

- **Step 4:** Attack of the nucleophile

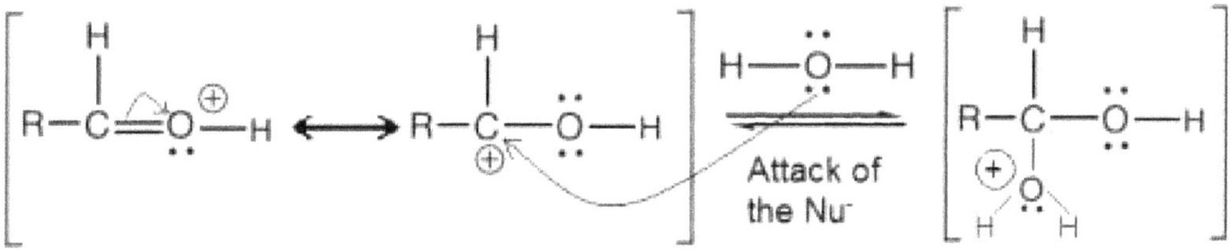

- **Step 5:** Remove a proton

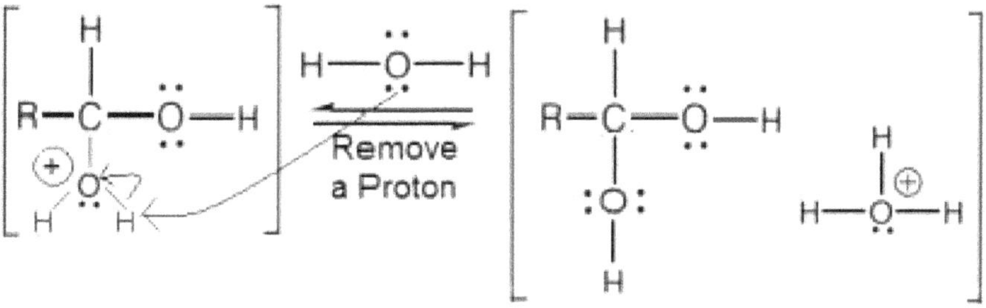

- **Step 6:** Several Steps

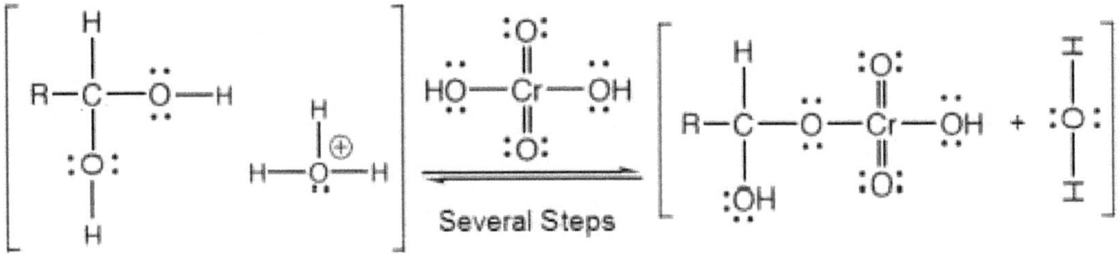

Step 7: Remove a proton

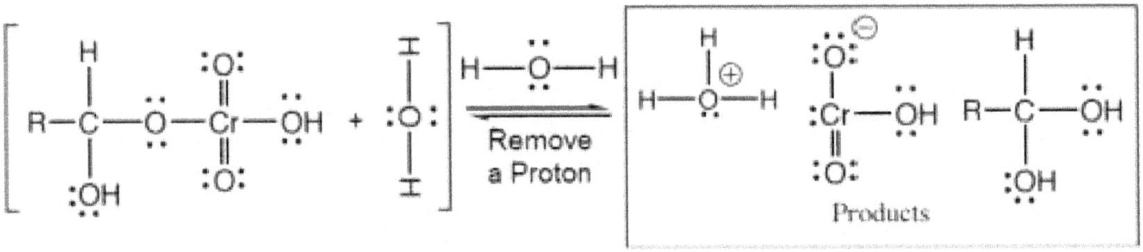

- **Reaction Summary:**

Primary Alcohol —H₂CrO₄→ Aldehyde —H₂CrO₄→ Carboxylic Acid

2° Alcohol —H₂CrO₄→ Ketone

- Reaction that starts with a primary alcohol, results in the formation of a aldehyde or carboxylic acid depending on the reaction conditions
- Reaction that starts with a secondary alcohol, results in the formation of a ketone
- Tertiary alcohols are not oxidized by chromic acid (H₂CrO₄)

PCC Oxidation of Alcohols

- Pyridinum chlorochromate (PCC) is selective for the oxidation of 1° alcohols to aldehydes
    - It doesn't oxidize aldehydes further to carboxylic acids
- PCC oxidizes a 2° alcohol to a ketone

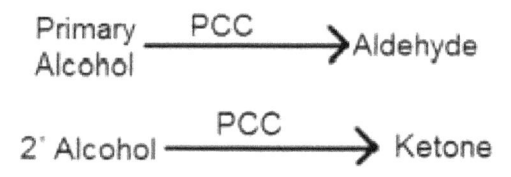

$$\text{Primary Alcohol} \xrightarrow{\text{PCC}} \text{Aldehyde}$$

$$\text{2° Alcohol} \xrightarrow{\text{PCC}} \text{Ketone}$$

CHAPTER 11: ETHERS AND EPOXIDES

Nomenclature

- Parent chain is the longest carbon chain in a molecule
- Name the OR group as an alkoxy substituent

	Suffix	Prefix
-OH	-ol	Hydroxy-
-C=C-	-ene	
-C≡C-	-yne	
X, R, OR		Halo, alkyl, alkoxy

Cyclic Ethers

- Prefix ox- is used to represent an oxygen that is part of a ring structure
- Suffixes –irane, -ethane, -olane, and –ane are used to indicate whether three, four, five, and six atoms are in a saturated ring

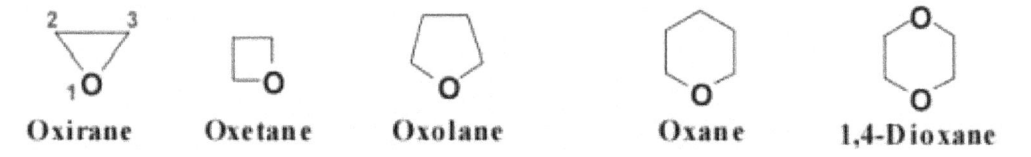

Oxirane   Oxetane   Oxolane   Oxane   1,4-Dioxane

Physical Properties of Ethers

- Ethers are polar compounds
    - Despite being polar compounds, only weak dipole-dipole attractive forces exist between their molecules in the pure liquid state
- Boiling points of ethers are lower than alcohols (as long as they are of comparable molecular weights)

- Boiling points of ethers are close to those of hydrocarbons (as long as they are of comparable molecular weights)
- Ethers are hydrogen bond acceptors

Preparation of Ethers
Williamson Ether Synthesis

- Synthesis of ethers by the S_N2 displacement of halide, tosylate, or mesylate by alkoxide ion

General Williamson Ether Synthesis Reaction:

$$R-O^{\ominus} + R'-X \xrightarrow{(S_N2)} R-O-R' + X^-$$

- Reaction works best (i.e. yields are highest) with methyl and 1° halides
  - Yields are lower with 2° halides
    - Yields are lower because of competing β-elimination reaction that occurs simultaneously
  - Reaction fails with 3° halides
    - Only β-elimination reaction occurs, not S_N2

Acid-catalyzed Dehydration of Alcohols

- This is a specific example of an S_N2 reaction, where a poor leaving group (OH⁻) is converted to a better one (H_2O)

$$R-OH + H-OR' \xrightarrow[\text{Heat}]{H_2SO_4} R-OR'$$

Acid-catalyzed Addition of Alcohols to Alkenes

$$\underset{R}{\overset{R}{C}}=CH_2 + H-OR' \xrightarrow[\text{Heat}]{H_2SO_4} \underset{R}{\overset{R}{C}}\underset{CH_2H}{\overset{OR'}{C}}$$

- Highest yields when using an alkene that can form a stable carbocation
    - Or, using a 1° alcohol that is not likely to undergo acid-catalyzed dehydration

Synthesis of Epoxides

Epoxides are cyclic ethers in which one of the atoms of a 3-membered ring is oxygen.

Example of an Epoxide (Oxirane):

- Simple epoxides are named as derivatives of oxirane
- Prefix epoxy- is used to represent when the epoxide is part of another ring system

Air Oxidation of Ethylene

$$2\ H_2C=CH_2 \xrightarrow[Ag]{O_2} 2\ H_2C-CH_2 \text{ (epoxide)}$$

- Typically seen manufactured using this method for use in industry

Epoxide Formation with Peroxycarboxylic Acid

[Reaction scheme: alkene with R,R,CH2 + RCO3H / CH2Cl2 → epoxide]

- In this reaction, an alkene reacts with peroxycarboxylic acid in a single step (electrophilic addition) to produce an epoxide
- Stereoselectivity: Diastereoselective
    - Stereoisomer you get depends on the configuration of the alkene you start with
        - A *cis*-2-butene gives only *cis*-2,3-dimethyloxirane
        - A *trans*-2-butene gives only *trans*-2,3-dimethyloxirane

Preparation of Epoxide from a Halohydrin

$$CH_3CH=CH_2 \xrightarrow{Cl_2, H_2O} CH_3\underset{Cl}{CH}-CH_2\text{(OH)} \xrightarrow[S_N2]{NaOH, H_2O} CH_3\overset{O}{\overset{\frown}{CH-CH_2}}$$

- Stereoselectivity: Diastereoselective
    - Stereoisomer you get depends on the configuration of the alkene you start with

[Reaction: cis-2-Butene → (1. Cl2, H2O; 2. NaOH, H2O) → cis-2,3-Dimethyloxirane]

Ring Opening of Epoxides

3-membered rings have strains associated with them, because of this; they readily undergo a variety of ring-opening reactions.

Acid Catalyzed Hydrolysis of Epoxides

- Mechanism steps
    - **Step 1:** Add a proton

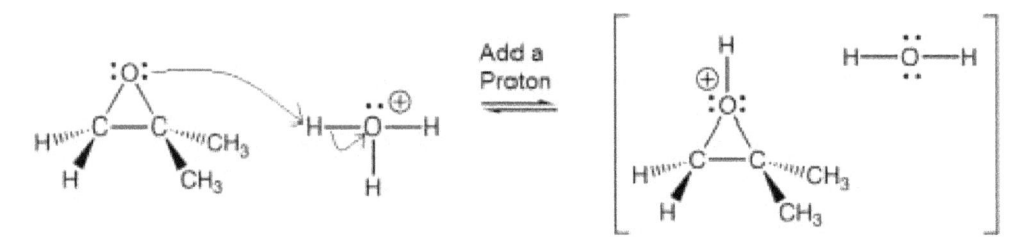

    - **Step 2:** Attack of the nucleophile

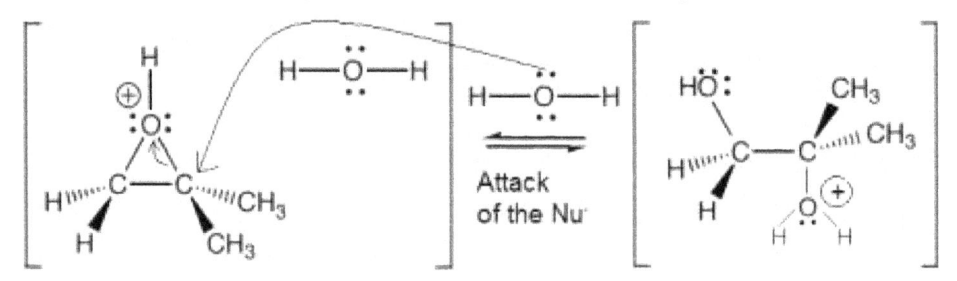

    - **Step 3:** Remove a proton

- Reaction Summary: in acid, the epoxide oxygen is protonated to make a bridged oxonium ion. The nucleophile (H₂O) attacks the carbon which is more carbocation-like from the opposite side. Removing a proton gives a diol.

$$Epoxide \xrightarrow[H_2O]{H_2SO_4} Diol$$

- Regioselectivity: nucleophile attacks the most substituted Carbon
- Stereoselectivity: Anti-product
    - -OH groups are on opposite sides

Reaction: Base Catalyzed Hydrolysis of Epoxides

- Mechanism steps
    - **Step 1:** S_N2 (Simultaneous Attack of the Nucleophile and Departure of the Leaving Group)

    - **Step 2:** Remove a proton

- Reaction Summary:

$$\text{Epoxide} \xrightarrow[\text{H}_2\text{O}]{\text{OH}^-} \text{Diol}$$

- Regioselectivity: nucleophile attacks the least substituted Carbon
- Stereoselectivity: Anti-product
    - -OH groups are on opposite sides